THE DEATH OF A POET

THE DEATH OF A POET

The Last Days of Marina Tsvetaeva

Irma Kudrova

Introduction by Ellendea Proffer
Translated from the Russian by Mary Ann Szporluk

 State Library OF Ohio

OVERLOOK DUCKWORTH
Woodstock • New York • London

First published in the United States in 2004 by
The Overlook Press, Peter Mayer Publishers, Inc.
Woodstock & New York

WOODSTOCK:
One Overlook Drive
Woodstock, NY 12498
www.overlookpress.com
[for individual orders, bulk and special sales, contact our Woodstock office]

NEW YORK:
141 Wooster Street
New York, NY 10012

LONDON:
Gerald Duckworth & Co. Ltd.
Greenhill House
90-93 Cowcross Street
London EC1M 6BF

⊗ The paper used in this book meets the requirements for paper
permanence as described in the ANSI Z39.48-1992 standard.

Library of Congress Cataloging-in-Publication Data

Kudrova, I. V.
[Gibel' Mariny TSvetaevoi. English]
The death of a poet : the last days of Marina Tsvetaeva / Irma Kudrova ;
translated by Mary Ann Szporluk.—1st ed.
p. cm.
Includes bibliographical references and index.
1. ëivetaeva, Marina, 1892-1941—Last years.
2. Poets, Russian—20th century—Biography. I. Title.
PG3476.T75Z4513 2004   891.71'42—dc22 [B]   2003063980

Book design and type formatting by Bernard Schleifer
Printed in the United States of America
ISBN 1-58567-522-9
FIRST EDITION
1 3 5 7 9 8 6 4 2

CONTENTS

SATURN'S CHILDREN

It is a commonplace of forensic science that the dead can be made to speak, long after their tongues grow still. Much to the surprise of those who thought mass graves meant mass erasure, the same is true of dead regimes. Historians have long noted the tendency of illegitimate regimes to keep records, as if the appearance of legality were the same as legality itself. Irma Kudrova's book, which makes use of many documents of the Russian terror, is many things: an examination of the people and the circumstances surrounding the suicide of the great poet Marina Tsvetaeva, using testimony from new witnesses and material from closed archives; a case study in terror; and a strangely intimate portrait of one group of people united by the nets of interrogation and by the fact that many of them had worked as spies for the Soviet Union while living in Europe.

Born in 1892 to an intellectual Muscovite family, Marina Tsvetaeva was famous as a poet from an early age. Her poetry was intensely original in every sense, as the other major poets of the time acknowledged. She was romantic and self-willed, and it is not surprising that she married a man who turned out to be fateful for her.

Sergei Efron came from a family of radical political activists. He was a cadet in the Officers' Academy and seemed to Tsvetaeva to be a man of action, noble and pure. Despite his family's background, Efron went off to fight against the Bolsheviks during the civil war, and ended up emigrating when the White Army dispersed. Tsvetaeva was stranded in Moscow for a time, with her two daughters, and no news of her husband. She swore that if he survived she would follow him "like a dog." In the horrendous conditions of post-civil war Moscow, Tsvetaeva almost starved, so she put her youngest daughter in an orphanage, where she would be better fed, but the child soon died of malnutrition.

She and her daughter left Russia in 1922 to rejoin Efron, and would spend the next seventeen years in Europe, finally settling in France. Tsvetaeva knew French and German and was at home in those cultures, and this period in Europe, although very difficult materially, was at first good for her work, and in 1925 her son Georgy ("Mur") was born.

Isolation is a danger for any émigré writer, as one gradually senses the loss of audience, and for Tsvetaeva, who was evolving as a poet, this isolation was especially painful. By 1927 she was writing Pasternak that "I don't have one human being who would, even for an hour, prefer poetry to everything else." By 1932 the political currents of the Russian emigration were affecting her more and more, as she wrote in another letter: "I'm set apart from the Russians by the nature of my poems, which no one understands, by unorthodox thinking, taken by some for Bolshevism, by others for monarchism or anarchism . . . in effect, set apart by my entire self."

In the 1930s, when economic depression was widespread in Western Europe and America, some Russian émigrés began to long for Russia, where things appeared to be better and at least the nation was involved in the great work of building socialism: others hardened their anti-communist attitudes, citing letters and evidence from those who had traveled to the Soviet Union. As time went on, this polarization was sharpened by the rise of the Nazis. In the drastic simplification in fashion everywhere, one was either pro-Soviet or pro-Nazi. Democracy as a system seemed weak and ineffectual.

What was clear to Tsvetaeva was that she was an outsider in her family; even her young son was drawn into the battle between his parents. "Mur lives torn between my humanism and the virtual fanaticism of his father," she wrote in a letter of 1935. Efron did not see a role for himself in France, which had its own bitter political polarization, and unbeknown to his wife, he had begun to work for the Soviet secret police. Their daughter Ariadna ("Alya") began to work for a journal in Paris which had ties to the Soviet Union.

Efron kept asking her to go back to Russia with him, but she steadily refused. She was dismayed when her daughter left for Moscow in March 1937, the first Efron to return.

In 1936-37 a series of major events shook the faith of even pro-Soviet westerners, as Stalin engineered the show trials of the old Bolsheviks. Sophisticated analysts in France found it unbelievable that those who had fought for revolution were now spying for foreign powers. People like Efron and his daughter, however, would have never regarded a Soviet newspaper with scepticism. The purge had begun, although few knew it at first, and it played out in Europe as well as in the Soviet Union.

The first shocking event on Western soil was the kidnapping and execution of the leader of the Union of Tsarist Veterans in Paris. The death of General Evgeny Miller, which comes up in this book, was part of a web of events leading to the arrest and execution of seven major generals of the Soviet Union in June 1937, which preceded the purge of the Soviet Army. The next notorious assassination took place in Switzerland. The Soviet spy Ignace Reiss was an NKVD Resident who decided to defect when he understood that the secret police themselves were being purged back in Moscow. Efron was a fairly low level Soviet operative, but he helped recruit the team that undertook this operation. The assassins managed to kill Reiss, but some of them were caught, and when they were interrogated by the French authorities, Efron's name came up, which in turn led his superior at the Soviet Embassy to order him to leave the country immediately.

Tsvetaeva was stunned when her husband explained he had to leave for Russia, because he was being blamed for something he hadn't done. The poet's position in the emigration became impossible. The émigré world had known that her husband was friendly with people in the Soviet Embassy, and that he had been involved in the Eurasian movement, which had become infiltrated by Soviet agents. It was hard for outsiders to believe that Efron's wife was ignorant of her own husband's activities. But denial is a powerful force, and Tsvetaeva appears to have truly thought there was a mistake up until her own return to Russia. Marina and her son went back to Moscow in June 1939, which is the point at which this book takes up the story.

In many ways Tsvetaeva's life is emblematic of the pain of the Russian psyche as it collided with the twentieth century. The original impulse for this work was Kudrova's fascination with the fate of one of Russia's greatest poets. Was her suicide purely personal or political in nature? What could be discovered? The most chilling material here concerns the degree to which the people around Tsvetaeva were reporting to the secret police. The parallels with East German cases are instructive. For all the cultural differences between these two nations, under totalitarian regimes the outcome was the same. Tsvetaeva had always been most afraid of "nonhumans" as a source of cruelty in the world, but she never suspected how close they were to her.

Dostoevsky's character Shatalov in *The Devils* had envisioned a world in which everyone would inform on everyone else, and here it is, in the records of interrogation, specifically in reference to "reporting" done voluntarily long before arrest. But what is interesting to a non-Russian reader is that many of the people who are "reporting" every comment to the authorities were not educated under the Soviet system, and had not spent much time in the Soviet Union. Many of the spies had had no experience of the Soviet world until they went back; some had had French educations, and all had lived in free countries. That none of this mattered is suggestive, as is the fact that they apparently never questioned the nature of the show trials or the execution of the heads of the army, matters that were thoroughly discussed in French newspapers and Russian circles in Paris. Efron, the man of action, seems not to have understood the nature of the people interrogating him until it was very late.

These "foreign-Russians" were true believers who had dedicated themselves to a country they had not experienced first hand. They could believe that a "mistake had been made" in their cases but that still, socialism would be built, and it was worth some sacrifice. In this they were very like the party leaders who told themselves that even if they were innocent, if the Party required their sacrifice, it must be for a reason they didn't understand.

Tsvetaeva herself would have understood if she had been arrested herself, but to have her husband and daughter arrested bewildered her. This she could never have imagined: why would the Soviets kill those who were dedicated to the cause? But this was the central point about the terror of the late 1930s: even experienced NKVD officers could not believe what was happening to them as it happened, so how would ordinary people be able to understand it? This was a closed system of thought, and only those who had free minds and a very dark view of humanity could understand what was really happening.

Tsvetaeva's suicide ("I have been searching for a hook . . .") echoes down the corridors of Russian cultural history for many reasons, not least because it is associated with the terror, truly a time of civic suicide in her country. The mythological cliché we use to describe such situations is always that of Saturn, especially as drawn by Goya. Stalin did finally devour the children of the Revolution, the children of the socialist idea, but long before that, as illustrated in painful detail in this book, he destroyed their souls.

—*Ellendea Proffer*

AUTHOR'S PREFACE

This book is based on new material and a reevaluation of known sources. The new sources include notes from my own meetings and conversations with people who were witnesses to Marina Tsvetaeva's last days as well as material from private archives (including those of Russians abroad) and from the State archives.

The diary of Georgy Efron, Tsvetaeva's son, was of great help. It is the most important document directly relating to the years covered herein: 1939-1941. The diary, which he diligently kept in Moscow and in Yelabuga, is now in the Russian State Archive of Literature and Art in Moscow. Unfortunately, I was only given access to individual entries from the diary, and I know only too well that I will therefore someday need to supplement and correct much in the story to which I now call the reader's attention.

My research in another state depository—the KGB archive (I'll call this institution, which has changed names so often, by an old one)—turned out to be much more fruitful. Thanks to the help of Anastasia Ivanovna Tsvetaeva, Sofia Nikolaevna Klepinina-Lvova, and Alexander Emmanuilovich Litauer, I had the opportunity to acquaint myself with the investigations not only of Tsvetaeva's husband and daughter, but also of people in whose midst Marina Tsvetaeva found herself immediately after she returned to her homeland.

The fact that I was able to read not only one or two but several case files aided my research enormously. The chance to juxtapose and compare cases; the recurring concrete details—especially from the confrontations of suspects, during which the stenographer (but not the investigator!) recorded unedited reactions and replies; the sheer amount of unexpected information (in particular, when the prisoner under investigation was first questioned and, as a rule, was asked to talk about himself or herself) all proved to be extremely valuable for a biographer's work.

The thick volumes of interrogation records were intermixed with other materials connected to the trials and rehabilitations. It was terrible to open them. It took place all too recently. Still, it's not the nineteenth century. It's possible that those investigators can still be found; moreover, the methods used to conduct investigations in those years were still being used not so long ago. The yellowish-brown volumes all look alike, with their yellowed pages. At the bottom of each is the prisoner's signature in ink—but how these differ from one another! Blood shows through the words typed there.

This sounds almost hysterical. In fact, I do lack the impassivity that is so invaluable for an investigator. I repeat Tsvetaeva's favorite motto: "*Laissez dire!*"—let them say whatever they want. I didn't take up the pen in search of praise or criticism.

The unbiased reader might ask another question, however: how much of the secret police material must we know in order to reconstruct the last days of a great poet's life? Isn't the author too absorbed in the history of arrests and interrogations? Is her interest in the secret police investigators warranted? Hasn't she exaggerated the atmosphere of general fear, making petty bureaucrats in far-off Yelabuga, for example, deny Tsvetaeva any request after only a cursory glance at her passport?

No, the author has not been carried away by a theme currently in vogue. The fashionability, if you like, of this troubled me at first, and still bothers me. However, on the other side of the scales is duty, as I understand it. Duty to the fate of a poet I love, a person and woman I admire.

After she returned to her homeland, Marina Tsvetaeva shared the fate of many of her remarkable contemporaries. The sticky nets of the secret police hampered her from her first steps. What would be the point of ignoring this, now that it is finally possible to learn the truth?

It was Tsvetaeva's fate to absorb the tragic tension of our age even more powerfully, because she was a poet; that is, someone who is shaken by the elements (of nature and time) more strongly than anyone else. According to the same natural law by which the tallest tree attracts lightning during a storm, Marina Tsvetaeva perished during her country's dark hour.

—IRMA KUDROVA
St. Petersburg, 1995

CHAPTER 1

BOLSHEVO

I'm drained—an emptied cup—
The bottom glows.
How can one go back
To a ravaged home?
                    —"My Country," 1931

1

Marina Tsvetaeva and her son Georgy (Mur) boarded the ship *Maria Ulyanova* on 12 June 1939. It departed Le Havre at 7:15 A.M.

In expectation of rough waters in the North Sea, Tsvetaeva immediately took the medicine she had brought with her and lay down in the cabin. Before the ship sailed, she had spotted a book in a store that she had long sought. It was Saint-Exupéry's *Wind, Sand and Stars (Terres des Hommes)* and she read it while lying on the bunk. The steady throb of the ship's engine was like a beating heart.

For the entire first day the fourteen-year-old Mur firmly resisted the rocking and spent all his time on deck or in the music room. Besides Tsvetaeva and her son, there was only one Russian on the boat—an elderly man. The rest were very young Spaniards—refugees from the Spanish Civil War. Even before boarding the ship, they were playing games on the shore, fooling around, and singing. Such behavior continued for the whole trip. Every evening there were dances, and for some reason the young people dressed all in green.

The excited and joyful Mur would run to his mother for a moment, stand on one leg, say a few words, and then run back.

After they passed through the North Sea, the roughness ended. Now Marina came on deck to see the land they were sailing past. She was struck by Denmark. It "went straight to my heart," she wrote in her diary when she returned to the cabin.

The ship passed by some kind of castle or fortress or perhaps a church—the roof had turned green over the years. The forest also seemed to be from a fairy tale—soft and gray, like smoke, from which the sharp tops of roofs poked out. "Thickset Denmark," Marina wrote.

She crossed the ship from side to side, sending imaginary greetings first to Hans Christian Andersen, then, when passing Sweden, to Selma Lagerlöf. Sweden was different from Denmark: the roofs of the buildings were red and everything seemed a plaything and brand new. She watched beautiful sailboats with faded green and red sails.

For some reason, two days in a row at the same time—from five to six—a distinct peal of bells sounded over the water. The beauty of the sunsets was astounding: crimson foam, a golden sky, and in the sky appeared writing of some sort. Marina tried to make out the characters. She was certain that they were addressed to her, but she couldn't decipher them. The sun fell behind the horizon, swallowed by the sea.

"Mur, look how beautiful it is!" she said.

"Beautiful," Mur replied, appearing beside his mother for a moment and then running off.

The Baltic Sea brought cold. The water was a dark gray-blue color, reminding Marina of the Oka River in the fall—the waters of her childhood. They sailed past the island of Gotland. In Marina's diary entries there is apprehension and sadness. Would her husband come to meet them, she wondered as they neared Kronstadt.

At last the ship was being moored at the wharf. It was time for the exhausting process of examining the passengers' luggage. The customs agents thoroughly combed through all of Tsvetaeva's suitcases and bags. They especially liked Mur's drawings and grabbed them for themselves without permission. "It's good they don't like manuscripts!" Tsvetaeva later wrote. Then Marina and Mur had to hurry to catch the train. As it turned out, they were to travel that very night to Moscow, together with the Spaniards.

At last the examination was over, and the passengers disembarked. They were all taken by bus to a special train. It traveled four kilometers out of the city and came to a stop until eleven o'clock at night.

Mur went off with the Spaniards by bus to look around the city. Tsvetaeva stayed to guard their things. Her husband, Sergei Yakovlevich Efron, would obviously not meet them.

They reached the station in Moscow by the next morning. When she was anxiously imagining this day while still in France, whom had Tsvetaeva hoped to see there? Her husband, daughter, sister? Perhaps Boris Pasternak as well? Wouldn't he have been told she was coming?

Only her daughter Ariadna (Alya) was on the platform, however. Now twenty-six, she was accompanied by a man of medium height who was a bit on the plump side. He had a charming, bright smile and was somewhat hard of hearing, as soon became clear. He was introduced as Samuil (Mulya) Gurevich, Ariadna's friend and colleague.

The group hired porters and immediately headed for Yaroslavl Station, right next to Leningrad Station. From there they took a train to Bolshevo, where Sergei (Seryozha) was now living.

It is possible to get to Yaroslavl Station by a back way without going into the broad square in front of the station. But wouldn't they have taken a quick look at a small part of the city that Tsvetaeva had so loved and once celebrated in her verse? After so many years of separation and so many ordeals! They probably did go to the square, but the porters were waiting, and an ill Sergei Yakovlevich was waiting in Bolshevo. Besides, could Marina Ivanovna have imagined that she would now become a prisoner in Bolshevo for five months, allowed only a few short and unauthorized trips to the capital?

Today it takes about an hour to go to Bolshevo on the suburban electric train. The train was much slower then. There would have been enough time for mother and daughter, and brother and sister, to talk—to explain the most important matters and ask the most pressing questions. They had kept up a regular correspondence, but it had had to go through official channels and neither side had been deluded about the completeness of the information that got through.

Yes, Seryozha was sick again—the same illness, although he was not confined to bed. He could walk and perhaps would even meet them at the station in Bolshevo.

Marina's sister Anastasia (Asya)? Where was she? Why hadn't she come?

Asya had been arrested. Back in 1937, in the early fall, in Tarusa. A month and a half before Sergei Yakovlevich arrived from France.

But why, what for?

No one knew.

They didn't know? How could that be? What about Andryusha, Asya's son?

He had also been arrested. He had been visiting his mother when they came for her.

Hadn't Seryozha found out what it was all about?

He had tried but he couldn't. He had also hoped to help their old friend Dimitry Petrovich Svyatopolk-Mirsky.[1] Efron was convinced he would be able to help free him, but nothing came of it. (Mirsky was a brilliant critic and philologist, well known among the Russian emigration, and a popular professor at Kings College, London. He returned to Russia in 1933 and was arrested in 1937. Tsvetaeva might have learned about his arrest earlier from their common acquaintance Vera Traill, who returned to Paris from Moscow in the fall of 1937.)[2]

What about Seryozha's sisters, Liliya and Vera?

They were in Moscow. But Vera's husband had been arrested a year earlier. He had still been free when Alya and Seryozha returned.

It's not hard to imagine how Alya had to control herself while discussing these matters. She could have told much more. Her mother also knew the Shukhaevs and Yuz Gordon and Natalya Stolyarova and Nikolai Romanchenko from the Parisian Union for Repatriation.[3] They had all disappeared into the prison system. But it would have been hard to tell Marina about this during the first hours of their reunion. If it hadn't been for Asya's absence at the station, all the sad news might have been put off. Even later, however, Alya was extremely unwilling to talk about it.

Alya was so happy that summer! She was in love and was loved, and nothing unpleasant would stay in her mind. A joyous elation surrounded her like a cloud, no matter where she was. Did her mother know from her letters that Alya had finally met a man whom she called both her husband and intended? Alya called Gurevich husband even many years later, after she returned from the camps and a long and painful exile. "A husband whom God gives only once," she said about her Mulya.

For a long time they had been seeing each other every day while working at Zhurgaz, the publishing house founded by the journalist Mikhail Koltsov.[4] Alya worked on the editorial staff of the weekly *Revue de Moscou*, which was published in French; Gurevich for the journal *Abroad* (*Za rubezhom*). Gurevich often accompanied Alya on her trips to Bolshevo. They would carry a heavy bag from the station with a week's worth of goods for Sergei Yakovlevich. Even though Gurevich was married and hadn't yet left his wife, it seemed certain that he and Alya would be together.

Much in the life of the man whom Alya loved remains obscure and is unlikely to be cleared up completely. There is no doubt that Samuil Davydovich collaborated with the NKVD (People's Commissariat for Internal Affairs, or secret police)—otherwise he simply wouldn't have been able, by the rules of that time, to have held a high position either at Zhurgaz or on the editorial staff of a journal, especialy one connected with foreign matters. Later he worked at TASS (Telegraph Agency of the Soviet Union) and was in close touch with foreign correspondents from Reuters and the Associated Press, which would indicate that he had a fairly high rank in the NKVD.

Gurevich was eight years older than Ariadna Efron and a man of exceptional abilities. Like her, he had grown up outside Russia. He spent his childhood in America, where his father, a professional revolutionary, had emigrated long before the October Revolution. Gurevich came to Russia when he was fifteen. His excellent knowledge of English determined a great deal in his future life. He was said to have studied in school together with Trotsky's son. He was very close to Koltsov, but nonetheless Gurevich's position remained unchanged afer Koltsov was arrested. At about the time he met Ariadna, Gurevich was expelled from the Communist Party for Trotskyite deviation, yet he retained his job even after Ariadna and the other residents of the Bolshevo house were arrested. (These facts raised suspicion among the people close to the situation, many of whom had naïvely believed that there was a comprehensible logic to the operations of the Soviet penal system. Samuil Gurevich seemed to be untouchable. However, it wasn't his fate to die in his own bed: in 1952 he was arrested together with other members of the Jewish Anti-Fascist Committee and shot as an "enemy of the people."

2

Sergei Yakovlevich was ill. In addition to the chronic ailments he had suffered since youth, in Russia he acquired a new one—stenocardia. The first attacks of angina pectoris (*grudnaia zhaba*), as this illness was called then, were so strong that Efron was put in Ekaterinskaya Hospital where he remained for a long time. This occurred at the end of March 1938, five months after his return to the USSR. A change of sanatoriums followed— first to Arkadiya, near Odessa, on the Black Sea, then to Mineralnye Vody. In one of his letters to his sister, Elizaveta Yakovlevna, Efron confessed that in his entire life he had never had such a collection of doctors around him as in these sanitoriums. Did he understand that these sanitoriums belonged to a completely different category? He was being nursed in the most privileged ones, those belonging to the NKVD.

Was his angina just a reaction to great stress? There were more than enough reasons for stress. Everyone said that Sergei Efron had played some role in the murder of the defector Ignace Reiss (Poretsky) in Switzerland in September 1937.[5] That operation had been planned in the innermost circles of the foreign section of the NKVD, and, in that institution's opin-ion, it had been bungled. The murderers left such noticeable tracks that the Swiss police, in cooperation with the French police, were quickly able to catch three of the participants. True, these participants were minor accomplices and the real murderers were able to get away, but nevertheless the police got their hands on a thread that credibly led to Moscow and to that same foreign section. The Bolshevik agency was caught in the act this time, and it was harder for Soviet commentators to talk about "baseless suspicions," as they had when the White General Alexander Kutepov was kidnapped in Paris in January 1930.

The conditions that Efron faced in his homeland were stressful enough on their own, however. During the entire seventeen years he lived abroad he had fervently dreamed about returning, and during that time his impressions of the homeland underwent several transformations. During the last ten years, however, he unconsciously created an image of such holy suffering that all elements of reality were lost. How long did it take for this imagined halo to fade? Did it disappear completely during the brief life he had left?

By late 1937 the country was frozen with fear: the Great Purge was taking place in cities and villages, carried out under the iron will of the People's Commissar, Nikolai Yezhov, a doll-faced dwarf. Postcards with his photo were being sold on every corner then, and when I was in second grade I once bought one at a newspaper kiosk. I liked his little face! My aunt, who had just arrived from a city near Leningrad, saw the postcard among my school notebooks and, with a cry, tore it into shreds before my eyes. I didn't understand very well what had happened, but I remember it clearly. Much later I was told that Aunt Shura had come to ask for advice and help from her brother, my father—her husband, the father of four, had been arrested.

The scale of arrests should have sobered the most romantic head. But a sensible suspicion won't remain long in a stupefied mind. Besides, the very scale of the repressions was not apparent. We descendants know it in figures, facts, and monstrous detail, but at the time there was still plenty of room for rationalization, which is always resourceful. Charges of "bungling" (*golovotiapstvo*) and "wrecking" (*vreditel'stvo*) were constantly heard from loudspeakers and could be used for any purpose. Such slogans were meant to extinguish all doubts—and they did, at least in the thinking of those who had not yet been punished.

Just wait, people reasoned, soon everything will be clear and put right. Despite all his power, Yagoda was arrested, and the Eighteenth Party Congress condemned the "excesses of Yezhov's purges." You can't make an omelet without breaking eggs! The great cause—socialism—cannot be accomplished without mistakes.

In the spring of 1938 the third and largest of the political trials that stunned the civilized world took place in Moscow. In the dock sat members of the Right-Trotskyite bloc, among them Nikolai Ivanovich Bukharin, whom Efron had seen and heard just two years earlier in Paris. Bukharin had been full of energy and high spirits. Excerpts of his lecture in French at the Sorbonne were later printed in the journal *Our Union (Nash soiuz)*, which came out in Paris under the aegis of the Union for Repatriation. At the time Efron sent his colleague Nikolai Klepinin to the Lutetia Hotel, where Bukharin was staying, to make the necessary arrangements.

Bukharin's trial took place in the relatively small October Hall of the House of Soviets, which held approximately three hundred spectators. Was Sergei Efron one of them? In theory he might have been: NKVD employees took up almost two-thirds of the hall. Efron's presence can only be surmised, but his old friend Ilya Ehrenburg definitely was there. Ehrenburg had recently come to Moscow from Spain, and was admitted into the hall as a correspondent of the paper *Izvestiia*. At one point he found himself right next to Bukharin. They had been acquainted for a long time, but Bukharin had changed so much that he didn't recognize him.

One incident at the trial provoked a lot of speculation: one of the defendants, Deputy Foreign Commissar Nikolai Krestinsky, in the hearing of all, retracted the deposition he had made during his preliminary investigation. This incident planted a seed of doubt in sceptics who had long suspected that the trials were staged. The impression was quite strong, but people were cautious about discussing the incident and did so only within the narrowest circles.

It must have been extremely alarming for Efron and his old com-
rades-in-arms from the secret service in France to hear the name S.
Chlenov mentioned at the trial—and in a dangerous context. Chlenov was
a diplomat who represented the USSR in Paris. What would that mean for
those who had dealt with him recently?

Mikhail Feldshtein, a lawyer and childhood friend of Sergei Efron
who later married Sergei's sister Vera, tried to inform Efron about Soviet
reality and open his eyes to the truth.

"But if that's true, one must protest!" exclaimed the starry-eyed
Efron after he had listened to all the horrors.

Feldshtein was arrested in the summer of 1938.

Such terrible and incomprehensible facts might have been true, but
for Efron the most difficult information involved the émigrés who had
returned from France. He knew them all by sight. Now he was hit by a
torrent of shocking news: one after another, they were arrested. Under different circumstances such arrests might have been explained away as mistakes or as gossip. But what was he to think about the arrest of his old
friend Mirsky, a clever man, an intellectual, fellow supporter of the journal *Mileposts* (*Versty*) and a fellow Eurasian? Or Nikolai Grigorievich
Romanchenko? Efron knew him in Prague as the purest of souls. To have
doubts about such men was to doubt himself.

Not only former émigrés were disappearing. What was one to think
about the arrest of the poet Osip Mandelstam? Efron could still remember
from twenty years earlier a very young, curly-haired Osip, who would
break into loud laughter at the slightest whim. In 1916, when Mandelstam
was in love with Marina, he traveled from Petrograd to Moscow and
caroused with her friends from Maximilian Voloshin's avant-garde circle.[6]
Who could have imagined Mandelstam would be arrested (for the second
time) in May 1938?

Efron had been returned to his homeland in secret on a special run
of the ship *Andrei Zhdanov*, as part of a group reputed to have been
involved in the Reiss Affair. Four of the group (and, perhaps, there were
no more) can now be named: Sergei Efron, Nikolai Klepinin, E. V. Larin

and P. I. Pisarev. It is only now evident that their selection was accidental, not to mention strange. Later, during his questioning, Klepinin would insist that neither he nor Efron had anything to do with the direct operation against Reiss: they were carrying out other espionage work. The accidental selection of the group can be explained by the fact that the high-ranking NKVD bureaucrats in Paris who were actually responsible for carrying out the operation had been earlier called back to Moscow. The people who tried to cover up their tracks in Paris were not well informed of the whole story.

Since the group had been brought to the USSR in secret, however, they were all given new names when they arrived. Efron was now Andreev; Klepinin became Lvov; and Larin was Klimov. According to the official version Efron had disappeared in Spain. It's clear why: if he (like the others) was in Moscow, that would support the argument that the Soviet Union had played a role in the Reiss operation and in the kidnapping of General Miller.[7] All four men disappeared from France just as the French police discovered the Soviet trail in both cases.

The repatriated men were strongly advised not to make new friends in the Soviet Union, and their encounters with old friends (from pre-emigration days) were limited. But for all that the group received good care in Moscow. In December they were sent for a month to a sanitorium in Kislovodsk for a rest and to build up their strength. When they returned to Moscow, they were settled in the prestigious New Moscow Hotel. There was no hurry to find new work for them. Immediately upon their arrival vague mention was made of a possible trip to China on a special mission, but the bureaucrat who reported this soon left for somewhere—Paris, it was said. He didn't reappear.

Efron and Klepinin were not summoned to their superior at the Lubyanka until February. We don't know if they were spoken to separately or together. They already knew the man who received them—S. M. Shpigelglas, a deputy to A. A. Slutsky, the head of the foreign section of the NKVD. Efron and Klepinin had met with him in Paris, and the last meeting was rather recent—July 1937—but they didn't know his name then. There was another conversation about work in China, again something vague—perhaps because what was going on in the NKVD was incomprehensible and alarming, even for those with comfortable positions in the circles of power.

In the same month of February, Slutsky's body was laid out in an official hall for last farewells: he had died in the office of another deputy, Frinovsky, with a suspicious suddenness that fooled few of his colleagues. Efron and Klepinin were told to wait for a call from Frinovsky with a decision about their future. They spent two nights in a row in the Lubyanka building in painful anticipation (nights, because they were told that they would be seen around 2:00 A.M.—such was the policy then). Both times the meeting was canceled around three o'clock.

Shpigelglas called Klepinin once more in April, again in the middle of the night. (Sergei Yakovlevich was very ill at the time.) He filled two hours with gossip about trivial things, sometimes interrupting with a question: Was Klepinin capable of undertaking a job that might risk his life? "Where? In China?" Perhaps not in China at all, it wasn't necessary to go abroad. Again the talk didn't end in anything concrete. In July Shpigelglas disappeared. The NKVD was zealously devouring its own children.

In the summer of 1938 Yezhov still seemed to be at the height of his power. But soon Lavrenty Beria was appointed his deputy. When the "little People's Commissar" was finally removed from the stage in December (the details of his end remain a mystery), Soviet citizens, eagerly snatching at any sign of hope, would tell each other, "See, evil is being punished"— especially since Beria began by denouncing his predecessor's practice of charging people with "bungling."

People who had worked for Yezhov and had survived did not feel safe. It's difficult to say whose cadre Sergei Efron belonged to, by the way. Evidently he had been recruited by Yan Berzin's people, and not Yagoda's or Yezhov's. Berzin headed military intelligence in the 1930s, and Efron and his comrades always called themselves intelligence agents (*razvedchiki*).

Berzin was also shot in the summer of 1938.

In 1938 Efron was provided with housing in the suburban village of Bolshevo. He was assigned half of a one-story wooden house with two terraces, a fireplace in the sitting room, and parquet floors. Even though a parquet floor had been put down, water still had to be fetched from a well. There was no sewage system either, and the toilet, in customary Russian fashion, was in the courtyard.

The house, or dacha, stood in a grove of pine trees, some distance away from the village. A spacious uncleared lot—simply a part of the forest—was enclosed by a fence. Two similar houses were near by, but their inhabitants couldn't be seen. The Klepinins moved into their half first; Sergei Yakovlevich arrived later, in October, after returning from the latest sanitorium, sun-burned and in good health. Ariadna moved in with him. It was extremely inconvenient for her to take the train from Bolshevo to her editorial job, but her tender love for her father surpassed everything, and until her mother and brother's arrival Alya only rarely spent the night in Moscow, at her aunt's on Merzlyakovsky Lane.

The three secluded villas in Bolshevo were built at the beginning of the thirties for high-ranking officials of Eksportles, the state timber exporting company. The house in which the Klepinins and Efrons were placed had been intended for the company's director, Boris Izrailevich Kraisky. He managed to live there for almost four years until he was arrested in 1937. After that the villa was considered to be the property of the NKVD. They first settled Passov, the head of the NKVD's seventh division, in it. He was there for only several months. After A. A. Slutsky's strange death, his position was given to Passov. But soon Passov was also taken from Bolshevo to the Lubyanka. Not to his own office but to the inner prison. Thus, the sarcastic Nina Klepinina would call the Bolshevo safe house "the house of pre-trial imprisonment."

Before Tsvetaeva's arrival, Klepinina had assumed the role of household leader. By June 1939 there were already nine people, including seven Klepinins, or Lvovs: Nikolai Andreevich, Nina Nikolaevna, their oldest son Alexei with his wife and newborn son, their other son, Dimitry (Mitya), and their twelve-year-old daughter Sofia (Sofa). Nikolai Andreevich and Alexei worked at VOKS (the All-Union Society for Cultural Relations with Foreign Countries). Klepinina was able to find a job only in the summer of 1939, at Intourist; from time to time she left for work at some hotel.

Shortly before Marina and Mur arrived, Nina Nikolaevna gave all the younger people in the house strict advice: don't go into the Efrons' rooms, don't bother Marina Ivanovna, and don't make noise in the sitting room or on the terraces. Nina Nikolaevna was a great admirer of poetry in general, and Tsvetaeva's in particular. "Tsvetaeva is a great poet," she told the children, "and poets are not like ordinary people. Marina Ivanovna's quiet should be sacred."

From then on Mitya and Sofa, and also the young couple, Alexei and Irina, were also strictly forbidden to pester Sergei Yakovlevich unnecessarily. The warning was necessary because Efron allowed the young people to behave with the utmost familiarity. When his health permitted, he liked to fool around with them, accepted all invitations to play, and organized all sorts of games. Always affable and smiling, he never gave anyone—even his own daughter—cause to suspect what was in his heart. True, Dimitry Sezeman (Nina Nikolaevna's sons were from her first marriage and had kept their father's surname) remembers that once, through the wall, he heard Sergei Yakovlevich sobbing loudly. But Sezeman is often an unreliable reporter.

3

"The atmosphere there was wonderful," Ariadna Efron wrote twenty years later about this time in Bolshevo in one of her letters to Boris Pasternak. One can perhaps trust her sincerity, but her words are hard to believe. The atmosphere in Bolshevo might have been wonderful only for Ariadna, who was in love and loved. Yet Nina Gordon, a close friend of Ariadna's, who traveled with her to Bolshevo several times, also remembers a "light, cheerful day" she spent there. In her memoirs Gordon describes a completely idyllic incident:

> . . . a frosty winter evening in 1932.
> Mulya and I are in Bolshevo at Alya's—still before Marina Ivanovna arrived. The four of us have supper—Alya, Sergei Yakovlevich, Mulya and

I—in Alya's room. The stove's lit, there's a dim glow from the light on the ceiling, a checkered cloth on the table, the curtains are drawn, a fresh fir branch on the wall gives off the smell of Christmas; a delicious meal, quiet, cheerful conversation, the hope that Marina and Mur will arrive soon, Alya's jokes, her loud laughter, her father's kind, gently ironic smile. How happy and lively everyone is. Cozy, peaceful…

Who could have imagined then that this quiet was so fragile and unreliable, or how cruelly and mercilessly this family would be destroyed.[8]

Sergei Yakovlevich must have sensed the fragility of the quiet in Bolshevo. Many of his friends and comrades had been arrested. He had tried to help, but couldn't do anything for them. His unsuccessful attempts should have made it clear to him that he was of no importance here, not to anyone, and that his protection was nothing more than a squeak in a mousetrap. Was he beginning to suspect this? Or did he already know?

In truth, nothing going on around him should have been completely unexpected. Less than a month before his hasty departure from France, Efron had learned a lot from his old friend and associate Vera Traill, who had returned to France from Moscow in September 1937. Traill had been in Moscow for some time, teaching in a school for NKVD agents near Moscow, and she brought back news of the many arrests that had touched their mutual acquaintances. Vera Traill gave birth to a daughter on September 20; she was in one of the Paris clinics, and Sergei Yakovlevich visited her everyday for many days. They had plenty of time for stories, discussions, and conversations. I know about this directly from Traill, with whom I exchanged several letters at the end of 1979. (Of all people, Efron wouldn't have suspected Vera of exaggerating or giving false information.)

Repatriates often traveled to Bolshevo; for the most part they were people who had worked abroad in Soviet intelligence together with Efron. They came with frightening news and questions; some came in dismay and in hope of support. In 1938-1939 Tveritinov, Afanasov, Smirensky, Balter, Yanovsky, and Kondratiev all visited. Vadim Kondratiev was the man whom French and Swiss police sought in 1937 for his role in the Reiss Affair. At the time, for purposes of identification, his pictures appeared in a number of French and Belgian newspapers. Because Kondratiev was a relative and friend of the Klepinins, Nina Nikolaevna was summoned to the French police then and persistently interrogated about what she knew. (By that time Nikolai Klepinin was no longer in Paris.) Kondratiev was taken back to the USSR earlier than the others and once there he soon was sent to the south, evidently to a sanitorium. He turned up in Bolshevo at the end of 1937 and spent some time there as the Klepinins' guest.

Kondratiev died of natural causes—from tuberculosis—and thus escaped arrest in the USSR. Perhaps his quick departure for the south, and later his appointment as the director of a sanitorium in the Crimea, saved him. Such cushy jobs were frequently given to the deserving in the secret police cadres. Thus, when Pisarev returned from Belgium, he was appointed director of the capital's Café National, which was loved by both the Muscovite literary elite and NKVD collaborators. Another repatriate with the same merits, Perfiliev, became director of the renowned restaurant Aragvi. Extremely secret meetings were held in the directors' rooms of the National and Aragvi.

In 1939 Vasily Vasilievich Yanovsky came to Bolshevo. (Tsvetaeva was already there.) He came almost straight from Spain and indignantly told about the vicious practices of Soviet NKVD agents in the ranks of the Republican army. Nina Klepinina began to help him compose a report to the NKVD. A symptomatic detail! To the people in Bolshevo the reprisals against "Trotskyite agents" in Spain seemed a scandalous distortion of the correct Party line.

"A wonderful atmosphere?" Ariadna was not the only placid one, however, in spite of the fact that her last months of freedom were passing. In his memoirs Dimitry Sezeman also calls this time, if not wonderful, then "calm," and even "pleasant." He was seventeen then. His mother treated him more gently than her two other children, for a good reason: Mitya had tuberculosis. For more than a year the illness had been flaring up, easing, then flaring up again, and as a result of his mother's anxious attention the boy was a spoiled child.

Irina, Alexei Sezeman's wife, also didn't remember any alarming details about Bolshevo. But it's natural that her happiness and grief were totally centered around her small son—and on her husband, who resourcefully evaded helping his young wife. We can also assume that no serious or dangerous conversations went on in the house when the daughter-in-law was there. In addition to her youth, she was someone new, not one of them.

Irina was surprised by the strange schedule in the house. Her father-in-law and mother-in-law, and sometimes Sergei Yakovlevich would suddenly head off "for work" in Moscow very late at night in a car that had come for them. When they returned in the morning, they were ashen, tired, and silent. Perhaps these were the evening summons to Shpigelglas or Frinovsky? She remembers very well one night when the older people took her husband with them. Nina came into their room. It was late, they were already in bed, and she told her son in a voice that allowed for no questions or discussions, "Come with us."

Alexei went. This incident evoked many feelings in Irina, but not fear. When her husband returned, did he tell her why they took him? Irina doesn't remember. In other words, it didn't make a very strong impression on her and she wasn't frightened. Even today, despite all the details, Irina Pavlovna does not believe there was any foreboding of the catastrophe that would soon explode.

Only Sofia Nikolaevna Klepinina-Lvova insists that there was. She remembers an air of alarm in the Bolshevo house. The adults knew all too well, Klepinina-Lvova writes in her memoirs, that most likely they would have to share the fate of the many completely innocent people who were being arrested all around them. By acting busy and efficient, the older people were trying to conceal the constant fear from the younger ones. During the day they pretended that everything was running normally, and every night they expected an arrest. Half a century later, Sofia Nikolaevna had a chance to read the appalling records of her mother and father's interrogations inside the Lubyanka.

4

June 19, 1939, the day Marina Tsvetaeva arrived at the house in Bolshevo, was a hot summer day. The sky had been clear for several weeks. There was a light smell of warm pine needles and an unimaginable quiet. Even the dog didn't bark when it ran out to meet them. Bilka, whom the Klepinins had brought from Paris, was a white French bulldog, undersized, with funny pink eyelashes, and deaf and dumb.

The Klepinins' daughter-in-law, young Irina, who had been awaiting the Parisian lady's arrival with impatient curiosity, was disappointed. Marina didn't seem exceptional at all; her face was tired, she had cropped graying hair, and wore a dress of the same shade with short sleeves and a wide belt around her small waist. With hardly a greeting Tsvetaeva went into the Efrons' half and stayed there for a long while. Later, of course, they were introduced and stood next to each other in the common kitchen for a long time, working over the kerosene stoves. But there was no intimate contact. Marina Ivanovna remained closed, silent, and unsmiling, as if deep in her own thoughts.

It's not strange that during the first days she was reunited with her husband Marina ignored everyone. Their separation had been too long. Too much had happened during the eighteen months they had spent in different countries. In addition to everything else, Marina Ivanovna probably felt extremely uncomfortable suddenly having to deal with the conditions of a communal apartment. Not only were the "places of use" (*mesta pol'zovaniia*, that remarkable Soviet euphemism) common, but the sitting room was common as well, so that it was impossible to leave other rooms without being seen.

Tsvetaeva's stay in Bolshevo was divided almost in half by the tragic events that would mark this place forever. Only the first nine weeks passed in relative tranquility. I must dispute Victoria Schweitzer's assertion that Bolshevo was "a very peaceful and happy time: everyone was alive and together."[9] Far from it! There are no traces of emotional well-being or even relative tranquility either in Marina Tsvetaeva's preserved notes or in the tales of surviving contemporaries.

It's hard to imagine Tsvetaeva and Efron's meeting. During the long months of separation she bore the cross of general condemnation and rejection by the Russian émigré population. Her husband had compromised her in the eyes of Russian Paris by his hasty disappearance in October 1937. For several weeks in a row his name was constantly in the Parisian newspapers. It figured, in particular, in the testimony of Renata Steiner, who was arrested shortly after Reiss's murder. Even though Efron's specific role in the operation was far from clear, the papers still accused him.

The memoirs of Mark Slonim and Elena Fedotova report Tsvetaeva's reaction at this time. Fedotova tells how Isidor Bunakov-Fondaminsky rushed to Vanves as soon as the newspapers published stories about Marina's interrogation by the French police.[10] For the first time, Fondaminsky saw Tsvetaeva break down in uncontrollable tears. Still unable to recover from her shock, Marina kept repeating the same thing: Sergei Yakovlevich never, never would have been capable of resorting to murder, not for any reason—that was impossible, it wasn't true. Over time the despair, which lay deep in her heart, hardened like stone.

But who believed her words then? The crowd is quick to believe the worst and does so gladly. Who is interested in nuances, circumstances, details that mitigate or refute—if they relate to someone else? Why investigate thoroughly, make comparisons, think? And ignorant people are by far not the only ones susceptible to the passion of censure and the pleasure of indignation. The recent centenary of Tsvetaeva's birth, celebrated in newspaper and journal articles, has reminded us of this. After more than half a century, Sergei Efron's reputation ought to be reconsidered. But the people for whom this was a matter of vital importance are no longer alive.

Marina Ivanovna was firmly convinced of her husband's innocence. Otherwise she would have avoided this dangerous topic when she talked with her acquaintances and friends. But nothing of the sort! Even on the eve of their departure for Russia, as she took leave of her old friend

Chernova-Kolbasina she brought up the matter: "It's true, isn't it, Olga Eliseevna, that you never believed Sergei was guilty of what they accused him of?"

During these months of separation Tsvetaeva's heart was clearly stung by the pain of the cruel injustice done to Sergei Yakovlevich, who was absolutely innocent in her eyes. If she did, in fact, allow that his trust might have been betrayed and he had been drawn into something shady against his will, then it was only through betrayal and only against his will—nothing else. She had an unshakable faith in her husband's purity of thought and intention.

She must have been troubled by many questions during those difficult months, however; for example, when she was shown the strange telegram of January 1937 at the police station (so that she could identify the handwriting) and when a great number of substantiating details were aired in émigré newspapers. After everything she had gone through, they now met in Bolshevo. What did they say to each other? What was asked? Confessed to? We will never find out for sure. Only a few credible fragments have been preserved. Fragments precisely. They are notes Tsvetaeva wrote in her diary practically in code. She made them a year later.

Tsvetaeva had moved from noisy, carefree Paris with its bright store windows and cafés to the Russian countryside. While still in Paris she had referred to Bolshevo as "the country" in letters to her Czech friend, Anna Tesková.[11] Once in Bolshevo, however, Tsvetaeva saw right away that the place where her husband was living was not country, or a village or town, but something in between.

The Bolshevo house, so solid at first glance, stood off by itself, at such a distance from everything and everyone that a sense of foreboding seemed to have settled in its walls. At another time isolation from everyday cares might have been reason to rejoice. There was open space for walks; dry, sandy soil; tall and slender pine trees. And blessed quiet—only rarely did one hear the noise of a passing train.

It was a beautiful, lush summer. There was a primitive shower outside—one could wash off with cold water if the heat became unbearable.

Any place to take a real bath was far away. Sergei Yakovlevich had hammered an iron bar in between two pine trees and hung rings on it for gymnastics. They were rarely used before Mur came. Efron thought the boy was too plump for a fourteen-year-old and that he needed to take up sports. (These rings will reappear later.)

The family was together at last. The Efrons' two rooms were very small; only the sitting room that they shared with the seven Klepinins was spacious. The furniture was extremely primitive, they did not even have a wardrobe. Their clothing, protected by a sheet, hung directly on nails driven into the wall. That was nothing new for Marina Ivanovna: they had almost always lived this way in post-revolutionary years. There were enough provisions in the house. Efron received a salary, even though in the summer months he rarely traveled into the city because of his continuing illness.

The kitchen was also common, unfortunately. It was harder to put off cleaning the mountain of unwashed dishes. Dishwashing became a big event, taking up a lot of time, since there was no water supply or sewage system in the house. On weekdays the families prepared meals separately and ate separately. They ate together on Sundays. They would cover a table on one of the terraces; there was enough room not only for the permanent inhabitants then but also for guests.

5

Guests came infrequently, most often relatives of the Klepinins and Efrons. Among them were Sergei's sister Elizaveta Yakovlevna, a pretty, gray-haired woman with large radiant eyes, and the eighteen-year-old Konstantin, the son of Sergei's other sister, Vera Yakovlevna. Ariadna came. After her mother and brother arrived, she had stopped living in Bolshevo, but when she visited she usually took over the household chores. She washed clothes, cooked dinner, washed dishes. She smiled and was cheerful, but Tsvetaeva wrote a strange phrase about her in her diary at the time: "Enigmatic Alya. Her false gaiety."

People who knew Marina Ivanovna in the Bolshevo period of her life remembered most of all her extreme reserve, a sullen taciturnity, and unexpected angry outbursts. When she left her room to come to the common table, she was distantly polite. Her eyes were lifeless. It was apparently an effort for her to take part in general conversation or to answer a question. Alexei Sezeman's young wife, Irina Goroshevskaya, called her "a woman with an unthawed heart."

S. N. Klepinina-Lvova mentions another detail, which is hard to trust, because it's so at variance with other evidence. Klepinina insists that Tsvetaeva was extremely unfriendly and even stern and cruel to her son Mur. Brought up by a strict but firmly self-possessed mother, the twelve-year-old Sofa literally froze one day when she saw Marina Ivanovna slap Mur in the face for what she remembers as a trivial reason. Mur cried at the time, after hiding from all the others, and once, Sofa Nikolaevna recalls, "he almost ran out in front of a train."

The outwardly cold Tsvetaeva, who had retreated deep within herself, would sometimes explode. Usually her son would be the one to get it. Goroshevskaya remembered another incident when Marina ran out of her room with a mad shriek after she heard Irina drop a saucepan with the children's kasha next to the Efrons' door. This impenetrable reserve, the clear change in relations with her son, and the unhealthy harshness of her reactions suggest that soon after returning to her homeland, Tsvetaeva experienced a powerful shock in Bolshevo, one for which she was totally unprepared, and after which she could not regain her composure.

It's natural to crave seclusion under such circumstances. In the Bolshevo house she couldn't have any privacy. Others could see every step she made. Everyone bothered her, even her adored son—at times he was unbearably stubborn and capricious. Marina frequently vented her anger at him, as something completely hers (in such a situation it's always harder to restrain oneself).

What was wrong? What did all her tension mean? Just half a year later at the Writers' House in Golitsyno, she was perceived differently, as calmer and more responsive. At the common *table d'hôte* there, she even shone at times, and everyone around grew quiet and began listening to her stories about Bohemia and France or her discourses on literary topics.

What had shocked her in Bolshevo soon after (or even immediately upon) her arrival? Perhaps there's nothing more to suspect here: the arrest of her beloved sister was enough; and the arrest of Misha Feldshtein, whom she had known from distant happy days in Koktebel, in the Crimea; and of Svyatopolk-Mirsky, with whom she had developed a friendship in France; and Mandelstam. They were all people whose fates were closely intertwined with her own. Still one can propose an additional reason: that precisely here, in Bolshevo, Marina Ivanovna at long last *understood* with whom her husband had become involved.

In France it was called the Union for Repatriation and the Soviet Embassy (*polpredstvo*), and, after 1936, "Spain." The French government had prohibited any help to Spain. In Tsvetaeva and Efron's home a veil of secrecy had always covered certain topics: among them, the Soviet mission and Spain. But Marina Ivanovna had no desire to go into the details. Her husband's fanatical devotion to the "fatherland's interests" displeased and distressed her. She thought—and wrote about this to Anna Tesková—that fanaticism and humanism exist on different planes and no one is able to combine them. The spouses quarreled and neither won. Tsvetaeva finally gave up. From the start their marriage had been based on toleration for the paths each chose. More than anything Tsvetaeva worried about Efron's influence on their children. She terribly wanted to protect her son and daughter from the plague of fanaticism.

After Sergei Yakovlevich's sudden escape from France it was no longer possible for her to maintain her independent position. Her husband to all intents and purposes had placed her into the hands of his "protectors" (bosses). From now on she was only able to keep up ties with Sergei Yakovlevich by sending and receiving letters through them. Probably these same people dictated her move from Vanves, first to a small hotel in Issi-les-Moulineaux, and then to Hotel Innova on Boulevard Pasteur in Paris.

Right after Efron left, Marina handed in her application to return to Russia, which he hadn't been able to get her to do for seven years. She didn't have to go to the residence on rue de Grenelle: everything was done through trusted intermediaries. One of them turned out to be Vladimir Pokrovsky, a man she had long known as an acquaintance of her husband. He enjoyed the trust of the embassy and Marina Ivanovna received all important instructions through him. He also brought her money—her husband's salary. She took it, of course. What would she and her son live on now? She could no longer count on earnings from her writing or from readings at literary evenings.

If she hadn't known earlier, then before Tsvetaeva traveled to the USSR those people in the embassy must have explained that her husband was a Soviet agent. I'm making this assumption by analogy: in a letter, sent from Turukhansk addressed to the Minister of Internal Affairs, Kruglov (22 September 1954), Ariadna Efron described how before her own return to the fatherland, she was given an instruction (apparently, an intimidating one) in the Soviet embassy in Paris: "Inasmuch as your father is a Soviet agent. . . ." In Tsvetaeva's case nothing concrete is known, but it's easy to guess that she was told then—as an absolute condition—that she would have to stay in Bolshevo for a certain period of time, limit her outside contacts, and so forth.

The word "razvedchik" (intelligence agent, spy) still carried a shade of sacrifice and self-denial, although the scrupulous ear of our contemporaries can recognize even here the questionable taste of a sacrifice that was not just of oneself. Estranged from politics, Marina Ivanovna had no way of knowing that in May 1937 the intelligence service of the Red Army had been combined with the NKVD, and that from that moment Efron was under a department directly linked to the earlier secret police—the GPU (State Political Directorate) and the Cheka.

No explaining away could change the fact that Efron was now serving in *that very institution* that had swallowed Asya and Asya's son Andrei (Andryusha), and all the rest. Once she found herself in Bolshevo, Tsvetaeva must have understood this monstrous situation.

During the four months she spent in Bolshevo with her husband, almost without a break, from 19 June until 10 October 1939, Marina had time to speak about everything. Did Sergei Yakovlevich give her the details of his involvement in the Reiss Affair? Could they possibly have avoided this topic?

Let's ask ourselves what Efron could have known about Reiss himself, independently of his own participation (or nonparticipation) in the case. We can now speculate on this, owing to another of Ariadna Efron's preserved letters, this one from 17 April 1967, addressed to K. V. Voronkov, the secretary of the Union of Soviet Writers. The letter was Ariadna's attempt to rehabilitate—not her mother now—but her father.

Ariadna was convinced that her father not only deserved to have his name cleared of the White Guard stigma, but he deserved recognition for his service to the Soviet land. While describing Efron's activities as a brave agent carrying out dangerous feats for the honor of the fatherland over a period of ten years, she recalled the Lausanne operation in the following context: "That was the 'Reiss Affair' that was discovered by the Swiss police; Reiss was a prominent agent of the NKVD who became a traitor after he went abroad; it was necessary to destroy him."[12]

The formulation is significant in many respects. In any case, it is evidence that neither Ariadna, nor Sergei Efron, had any real knowledge about Reiss's actual "crime." Efron likely had no idea about the existence or the content of the angry letter Reiss had written to the Central Committee of the Party. The group that had been organized to pursue and murder Reiss had certainly been provided with false information and "noble" motives. We've laid out the task—execute it! Such is the usual practice in secret organizations where everything is held together by blind trust toward the leader of the operation. (The text of Reiss's letter and materials clarifying the circumstances of the murder appeared in the émigré press after Efron had been taken to the USSR, where the émigré papers were never available, of course.)

Renata Steiner, who was seized by the police in Switzerland, confessed in court—and she can be trusted completely—that she had no knowledge at all about the planned use of the automobile she had been instructed to rent in her name from a firm in Lausanne (and in which Reiss was killed). Also, she didn't know anything about the gentleman she was earlier instructed to follow in Paris, and later in Mulhouse. She was convinced (she was so informed) that he speculated in weapons and was supplying them to Franco. But who had told her this? Was it Efron? That appears likely. Incidentally, the man was not a speculator, but Lev Sedov, Trotsky's son.

Another of Efron's associates, Vadim Kondratiev, failed to kill Sedov in Antibes only because of an unexpected event. Kondratiev knew his victim well by sight, but had no idea who he was. Likewise, the participants in the kidnapping of General Miller in September 1937 were told that the general was the head of German-Fascist intelligence in France. Certainly there are many examples of such disinformation.

Thus, it's likely that Efron himself also possessed extremely distorted information. To what extent did he come to realize this in Bolshevo? Perhaps the sobs that Dimitry Sezeman recalled should not be written off as the quirks of Sezeman's memory. It's hard to say if Sergei Yakovlevich was open with his wife now, although she didn't need to know much in order to understand the main thing.

"His trust might have been abused—my trust in him remains unchanged." (*Sa bonne foi a pu être surprise, la mienne en lui reste intacte.*)[13] That is how Tsvetaeva spoke about her husband during her questioning by the French police in the fall of 1937. Sergei Yakovlevich's trust had indeed been cruelly abused. Wasn't this knowledge the most difficult shock for Tsvetaeva during her first weeks in the USSR?

6

Two trustworthy pieces of evidence from Tsvetaeva's own pen partly help to illuminate the first weeks of her return. Unfortunately, only "partly," and now we'll see why. Only one year later, after much red tape, did Tsvetaeva receive her luggage from customs and take out of a leather case the notebook in which she had made her last notes in Paris. The first lines she wrote in it in the USSR were dated 5 September 1940. Tsvetaeva quickly covers the events of a year of isolation:

June 18th, arrival in Russia, the 19th to Bolshevo. To the dacha, meeting with S., who is sick. Discomfort. Go to get kerosene. S. buys apples. Gradually pain in my heart. Ordeal with the telephone. The enigmatic Alya, her false gaiety. I live without documents, no one comes by . . .

Note her unusual style: it's almost code. Events and facts are noted bluntly and elliptically. Therefore individual formulations are even more significant. That S stands Sergei Yakovlevich is clear. But it's evident that the essential point is hidden between the lines, behind the lines, and behind the words. A bit later Tsvetaeva explains: "All this is for *my* memory and no one else: If he reads it, Mur won't understand. But he won't read it, he avoids *that sort of thing.*" This explanation is far from complete. The style is also influenced by what Marina Ivanovna had learned from the searches and arrests. A year later she could well imagine the danger of the written word.

The entry continues: "Tortes and pineapples—that doesn't make it easier. Walks with Milya. My *loneliness.* Dishwater and tears . . ."

The Milya mentioned is Emiliya Litauer, an old and close friend of the Klepinins and Efron. She was now thirty-five. Her father had taken her from Russia as a young girl; she studied at Marburg University in Germany, then finished the Sorbonne with a degree in philosophy. She took part in the Eurasian movement and worked on the newspaper *Eurasia,* where she published a series of reviews on philosophical topics, including articles on Husserl and Heidegger.[14] Litauer joined the French Communist Party and left France for the Soviet Union in 1934. After the Klepinins settled in Bolshevo, she was almost a daily guest, and especially close to Klepinina. People today remember Emiliya standing behind Nina Nikolaevna's chair and echoing everything she said.

Returning to Tsvetaeva's diary:

S.'s illness. Fear of his bad heart. Fragments of his life without me—I don't have time to listen: my hands are busy with chores, I listen, but on edge. A hundred times a day to the cellar. . . . I begin to understand that S. is helpless, completely helpless, in everything. . . . The overtone—the undertone of everything—is terror.

Nota bene! Tsvetaeva was leaving shorthand notes for an account of her first days and weeks in Bolshevo. Precisely for the very first days—before her daughter's arrest. The day of the arrest is discussed later. And here comes the admission: "the overtone—the undertone of everything—is terror." One can conclude much from this. But why does "my loneliness" appear in the entry? It sounds strange: in Bolshevo the family was finally together again. Did Tsvetaeva transfer her feeling of being abandoned from 1940 to 1939? In September 1940, when she wrote the entry, she no longer had either her husband or her daughter near her.

Another piece of evidence has been preserved, this one directly from the early days: an entry in the so-called Bolshevo notebook. Tsvetaeva began this notebook a month after her arrival. She pedantically recorded the date: 21 June 1939. Two words are written on the first page: "nature" and "help" (*priroda pomoshch'*), and it's hard to say if it's in Tsvetaeva's hand. They may well have been Marina's words. But it's not clear why they are here.

The notebook was intended for work on translations of Lermontov's poetry into French. His 1939 jubilee (celebrating the 125th anniversary of his birth) was approaching. Tsvetaeva decided to translate several of Lermontov's poems and to offer them to *Revue de Moscou*, the weekly journal where Ariadna worked. In these days Tsvetaeva took up translation not for the sake of earnings but because she suffered unbearably without creative work; she needed to spend several hours of seclusion in the morning at a table with pen in hand. She had always lived that way—why change now?

On the back of a page containing the translation of the poem "In the midday heat, in a valley in Daghestan" is a prose fragment in Tsvetaeva's handwriting, and in French. It's not clear why. In the Bolshevo house everyone except Irina knew French. It wasn't for her sake.

> Here I feel my own poverty, which is fed with scraps (of love and friendship of all the others). Washing dishes the whole day (19th June–23rd July), 34 long days, from 7 a.m. till 1 a.m. "It's all right, it's not for long!" But all the same it's 34 days of *my* life, *my* thoughts . . . Only I, I alone, pour out

the dirty water from the dishes into the garden so that the washbasin under the sink doesn't stain the floor when it spills over. Alone, without any help . . . Yes, simply alone.

Everyone around here is preoccupied with social problems (or seems to be preoccupied): ideas, ideals, etc.—they talk on and on, but no one sees anything wrong about the fact that the skin on my hands is peeling off— overworked from work which no one values.

On the back of the page is the date: 22 July 1939. Further on in the notebook is the text of "A Cossack Lullaby."

Exhaustion, unpleasantness, irritation, complaints—everything merged in this apparently hastily written entry. It was not an attempt to interpret what she had experienced for a month, but only a passing deflection of bitterness. And though the entry was made in a "secret" (from the eyes of mysterious others) French language, there is not half a word in it about what was *outside* the Bolshevo house. The dominant note is alienation from everything inside the house walls. It seems that the dishes and the dirty water in the basin were only an opportunity for Tsvetaeva to admit to herself that she was again among people alien to her.

When Alya first discovered the Bolshevo notebook two decades later, after returning from exile, this entry angered her. In her memory things weren't that way at all. Alya had been in charge of the housekeeping; she, not her mother, had washed the dishes. Veronika Losskaya has cited Ariadna's denial in her book, *Marina Tsvetaeva in Life*.[15] It makes no sense, however, to doubt Tsvetaeva's sincerity before herself. From time to time (I witnessed this) Ariadna's chronic anger at her mother would burst out. Daily work came easily to her and never amounted to suffering. For Marina Ivanovna it did. So much so that she refused to call the domination of "everyday life" the "prose of life," insisting that it wasn't prose, it was tragedy, for everyday life robs the living and keeps them from self-fulfillment.

The entry about loneliness had a new nuance, however. Living in a communal house in the country, Tsvetaeva found herself in close daily contact with people whose spiritual makeup was completely unlike her own. In this case it wasn't a matter of poetic talent. In fact, all of Tsvetaeva's personal friends, the ones she had chosen herself—Prince Sergei Volkonsky, Konstantin Balmont, Sonechka Holliday, Anna Ilinichna Andreevna, Ariadna Berg—were clearly "of a different breed." Even Mark Slonim and Elena Izvolskaya—people who were not lacking in civic spirit—had a different spiritual nature from the Klepinins, Emiliya Litauer, and Sergei Yakovlevich.[16] Not higher or lower, but different, and something that is hard to describe in rational terms. What, if not a difference in nature, had kept Tsvetaeva's own friends from joining the Union for Repatriation, or from contacts with whatever kind of "secret services" there were? They simply had a different genealogy, one without revolutionary Zhelyabovs or Kletochnikovs in it.[17]

Mark Slonim and Anna Ilinichna Andreevna anguished over the loss of their native land as passionately and strongly as the "repatriates," but they simply could not return to Moscow as it was then. The reasons were internal. They made the only choice possible for them. Tsvetaeva's family took away her choice.

Let's return to the notebook. The entry contains the significant, almost contemptuous, slip about how absorbed the people in Bolshevo were with political problems. "Ideas," "ideals," "they talk on and on," Tsvetaeva wrote. We hear the voice from her "Hamlet" cycle of poems that unmasks the heroes' sublime phrases. We hear an echo of the pathos found in the poem "Readers of Newspapers" (*Chitateli gazet*). It was not ideas or ideals themselves that irritated Tsvetaeva, but their two-dimensionality, their lack of vitality, their bookishness. She had spotted such intellectuals long ago: quick to invoke high principles, feeling pain for no less than all humanity but not noticing what was going on right next to them. She saw such endless conversations about "ideals" as a symptom, a distinguishing mark behind which likely lay personality defects, or, to put it more carefully, peculiarities. The notebook entry speaks about Tsvetaeva's sense of herself as a foreign body among the others in Bolshevo. But in the meantime she had no other surroundings. In essence, she was living under house arrest.

In her book on Tsvetaeva, the writer Maria Belkina cites a remark Pasternak made to Anatoly Tarasenkov in November 1939 (the latter recorded it in his diary): Tsvetaeva had returned to her homeland and was living there incognito.[18] Why incognito? Why under lock and key? One can't expect an informative answer from anyone now. But it would seem to be for the same reason that Efron had to use the surname "Andreev." For if Efron wasn't in the USSR, that meant his wife shouldn't be there either. Thus, any departures from Bolshevo, if not prohibited, were "not recommended." For Soviet citizens that was equivalent to the strictest prohibition.

For the whole period—from the middle of June to 10 November 1939, we know for certain of only one trip that Tsvetaeva made to Moscow. In a notebook entry in 1940 the date of this trip is marked by counting back from the day of Ariadna's arrest: "The last happy sight of her—4 days ago—at the S.Kh. [All-Union Agricultural] exhibit, a 'kolkhoznitsa' in a red Czech scarf—my gift. She was radiant."

This means it was August twenty-something. On 21 August Tsvetaeva got her passport, probably in Moscow. Wasn't this the reason she had been able to visit the exhibit? All of this means that Marina found herself doomed to daily contact with people not of her choosing. Doesn't this explain the sharpness of the reproach in the Bolshevo notebook?

7

The Klepinins were a remarkable couple on their own. The pair combined a deep and intense religious zeal with an ardent social activism. Nina (Antonina) Nikolaevna, born Nasonova, was the daughter of a well-known scholar and biologist who became a member of the Academy of Sciences before the revolution. She studied at the Bestuzhev courses for women and later studied painting with Kuzma Petrov-Vodkin. She was secretary of the city food board during the February Revolution. Later, in France, Klepinina joined the Eurasian movement. In the thirties she was one of the founders of an Orthodox parish in Paris, which was under the jurisdiction of the Moscow patriarchate.

At the time of the Civil War, Nikolai Andreevich Klepinin was a lieutenant in Denikin's army; he then stayed on in Constantinople, and in 1926 participated in the First Monarchist Congress abroad. Within a short time he was a member of the Central Committee of the Eurasian organization. He made a trip to America and studied at Boston University. Soon after he returned to France, he worked at the publishing house YMKA Press and became secretary of the Russian Theological Institute in Paris. He was a journalist, a contributor to the weekly journal *Zavtra*, the author of several articles in the philosophical journal *Put'* and two books. Nikolai was a cousin of the priest Dimitry Klepinin, famous for having been an aide during the Second World War to the renowned Mother Maria, who saved Jews from the Fascists.[19]

In 1933 Efron recruited the Klepinins into the Soviet secret service. Nina Klepinina soon headed a Belgian group of émigré secret collaborators. In February 1936 she went on assignment with her family to Norway in order to confirm where Trotsky was living. She even spoke with Lev Davydovich for about five minutes. Later—in the Lubyanka prison after her arrest—she was forced to write an "explanatory note" about this incident.

Both Klepinins loved poetry; they knew it well and were adept in writing occasional verse. Nina Nikolaevna at times translated from Russian to French—most likely, poetry. The Klepinins had known both Efron and Tsvetaeva for a long time. Nina's son, Alexei Vasilievich, claimed that his mother had known Marina Ivanovna from the Bestuzhev courses —they were in the same general group even then. Later they met in Berlin, and then in France, where they always lived fairly close to one another and where they established their special connection to Sergei Efron in the mid thirties.

The Klepinins treated Marina with respect and even deference. That would be revealed during their interrogations, where they also were questioned about Tsvetaeva.

That summer, on days off, "literary evenings" were held at the Bolshevo house. The young actor Dimitry Nikolaevich Zhuravlev read brilliantly on these occasions. He came to Bolshevo with Liliya Efron, who was his director. Zhuravlev liked reading poetry and prose. His favorite audience was here; it was also a splendid platform from which to try out new programs.

Marina Ivanovna also read her poetry. She seemed animated and uplifted—transformed—when she did. What did she read? Neither the twelve-year-old Sofa nor Alexei Sezeman's young wife knew Tsvetaeva's poetry at the time. Irina Pavlovna vaguely remembers "something about white swans."

Had she really read her *Demesne of the Swans?* In the land of the victorious raven? *The Demesne of the Swans,* poems about the White Army, had been composed during the tragic three-year period from 1918 to 1920. But what other swans could there have been, except those doomed ones, among whom was her Seryozha?

"Where are the swans?" "The swans have gone."
"The ravens too?" "The ravens—have remained."

Dimitry Sezeman remembers that Tsvetaeva also read poems by Pushkin that she had translated into French.

On one such evening after Zhuravlev had read from Lev Tolstoy's *War and Peace,* a quarrel broke out. After listening to the episode of Natasha Rostova's first ball, Tsvetaeva commented, "Tolstoy cleverly managed to crawl into the dressmaker's skin. Probably that was good." The "probably" provoked a lively polemic.

Sezeman, who was extremely ill-disposed toward Tsvetaeva and was a man of categorical judgments—all too often based on subjective biases and antipathies—nonetheless paid Marina Tsvetaeva her due, while describing her readings at these evenings. "There were moments," Sezeman writes,

> when, even to a young boy who was not excessively sympathetic, Marina Ivanovna manifested something that markedly distinguished her from any of us.
>
> She sat on the edge of the ottoman as erectly as sit only former teachers from boarding schools and institutes for young noblewomen. She

seemed to be a study in shades of gray: her short cropped hair, her face, the cigarette smoke, her dress, and even the heavy silver bracelets—everything was gray. The verses themselves confused me, they were so unlike the ones that I liked and that my mother so often had read to me. And I had not the slightest doubt about the correctness of my poetic taste. But the way she read, with such defiance or perhaps even despair, had a truly magical, bewitching effect on me, one that I never felt again. With her whole being, without looking at anyone, she affirmed, as it were, that she was ready to answer with her life for every line of verse, because each line—at any case during these moments—was the sole justification for her life. Tsvetaeva read as if she were on the scaffold, although this is not the ideal place from which to read poetry.[20]

It turns out, however, that Tsvetaeva made a secret trip out of Bolshevo in the summer of 1939. The trip was to Tarusa. The precise date of the trip is not known, but most probably it was at the height of summer. Marina Ivanovna traveled by herself to the favorite places of her childhood, though not for memory's sake. She definitely wanted to learn something specific about the conditions surrounding her sister Asya's arrest. Anastasia Tsvetaeva and her son had been taken from Tarusa to the Lubyanka prison. Once in Tarusa, Marina located her sister's friend, from whose house Asya and Andryusha were taken. She listened to the distressing story. Marina spent two days in places where she had once delighted in every sapling and every turn of the road.

Sofia Klepinina recalls in her memoirs that a particular tension had been building in the Bolshevo household shortly before Marina and Mur arrived. That is quite plausible, for at the beginning of the summer anyone who had any kind of relation with VOKS (the All-Union Society for Cultural Relations with Foreign Countries) would have been alarmed. The organization had been in trouble for a long time—from the moment in 1938 when the Soviet People's Commissar for Foreign Trade, Arkady Rozengolts, was removed from his post and hastily put on trial. The chairman of VOKS, the writer Alexander Arosev, who had very recently traveled to Paris with Bukharin, was also arrested.

The Society's varied activities included taking care of the USSR's foreign guests, both delegations and individuals. During receptions journalists would mingle with foreigners and important Soviet figures from various circles and ranks. Interpreters—and, of course, agents of the NKVD—were always present.

VOKS was a refuge for many Russians who had returned from abroad: it was the best place where they could make use of their almost singular advantage over others—a good knowledge of French. In June 1939, Nina Mosina, editor of VOKS's information bulletin, was arrested. She was a former émigrée, one of those Efron had helped to repatriate. Ariadna was also acquainted with Mosina, as were the elder Klepinin, who worked in the Eastern department at VOKS, and Klepinin's stepson, Alexei Sezeman. The inhabitants of the Bolshevo house still had no inkling of how dangerous the charge against the prisoner was for them. Mosina was accused of enlisting "Trotskyite cadres" to work at VOKS.

Any former émigré could easily be so categorized. The journal where Ariadna worked, *Revue de Moscou*, had maintained very direct contacts with Mosina. During recent months Ariadna and the elder Klepinin had been earnestly making efforts to arrange a job for their friend Emiliya Litauer on the editorial staff.

Tsvetaeva was living in Bolshevo when another piece of news became known: on 27 June yet another worker at VOKS was arrested— Pavel Nikolaevich Tolstoi. He was also a repatriated émigré and was from the group Efron had been well acquainted with in France. Ariadna, Emiliya Litauer, and Alexei Sezeman had kept up their contacts with Pavel Tolstoi: he occasionally hired Litauer and Sezeman to do translations.

Did they hide this news from Marina Ivanovna in order to protect her from unnecessary suffering? It's hard to say, although it would be useful to know how open her husband and his friends were with her now. One thing is indisputable, however; the Klepinins and Efron had to have viewed this news as the approaching steps of the Commendatore.

8

How did the inhabitants of the Bolshevo dacha evaluate events? To what extent had they lost the illusions they had brought from emigration about the land of socialism and the great socialist experiment? How much did they still delude themselves with hope? Today, terrible documents from this time—the interrogations records—are available to help us discuss these questions.

Within three or four months, *six* of those people whom Marina Tsvetaeva saw and listened to that summer beneath the dacha's pine trees (or on the house's terrace—or by the fireplace in the living room) would give their depositions in the offices of the NKVD.

One must always bear in mind the reality of forced confessions and the possibility of fabrication, which is not even possible to call slander in view of the conditions in which Soviet prisoners found themselves. But all the same, by comparing the testimonies of the six, where they agree and where they differ, by correlating them with what can be discovered about these people's characters from written and oral sources, it is still possible to separate the invented from the real. Thus, we now have an opportunity to address questions that until rather recently remained unanswered.

Like many others, the inhabitants of the Bolshevo house and their guests maintained certain illusions. Many were beginning to suspect, but still could not believe, that the state was directing the nightmarish events. That was difficult to believe precisely because of the complexity and global scope of these events. How else can one explain the persistent lack of understanding on the part of Western journalists, writers, and scholars who traveled to the USSR or followed developments from the West? The illusions had deep roots.

The émigrés who had recently returned no longer saw the situation through rose-colored glasses, however. In Bolshevo they discussed the country's low standard of life, the meager wages for hellish work, the fact that exploitation had not disappeared in the least, and that Stalin's constitution was a fiction that everyone disregarded. They spoke about ignorance and how uncultured were the editors of Soviet journals and newspapers. They discussed the absurdities of the censorship regulations and also spoke about the outbreak of arrests. Everyone was afraid of everyone else, there was no one you could depend on for support, it was impossible to trust anyone. And the NKVD kept on arresting its own.

Nikolai Klepinin was drinking more; he now could lose control of himself after one glass. Whenever he did, this gentle, clever man uttered the most careless opinions, cursing the highest authorities and circles in the land.

Did Nina Klepinina remember the conversation she had had with her parents in the mid 1930s when they came to Paris on a brief visit? How horrified they were when they heard she intended to return to the homeland with her family! They had tried to warn her about the wave of arrests that had begun, and in response their daughter cheerfully and stubbornly rejected all their warnings. "At least think about your children!" her mother had told her. But Nina brushed that aside.

After she did return and rather quickly understood her mistake, Nina Nikolaevna remained true to herself: even in the USSR she tried to avoid living according to someone else's orders. Like the other repatriated employees of the Soviet secret service, she was forbidden to travel out of Moscow without the permission of the higher authorities. She did travel, however—several times, it seems—to Leningrad to see her brother and friends. Correspondence with people abroad was prohibited, but she did write, taking advantage of any opportunity. It was forbidden to talk with the uninitiated about one's connection to the NKVD (that was called "decoding oneself") but the Klepinins didn't pay much attention to this prohibition either. They had spent their entire youth in a free country—it was foreign and they were poor, but France was free. They couldn't understand the psychology of people in the USSR, who had knuckled under for more than twenty years, and were giving up their external and internal freedom out of fear for themselves and their families.

At home and in their own crowd the Klepinins refused to adapt; they didn't behave cautiously. They would say anything that came into their head. In those years they did not have to fear "ears" in the walls and ceiling—those bug-microphones that twenty-five years later would drive Soviet intellectuals into kitchens or bathrooms to drown out conversation with the noise of a radio or running water. In the Bolshevo house people spoke to each other freely. It soon became clear that this was unwise. There is an appalling amount of detail in the prisoners' depositions.

9

Everyone who came to Bolshevo from Moscow brought a pile of recent newspapers and journals. They were read with bitter intensity, even though it's hard to imagine anything less like real life than Soviet newspapers of the late 1930s. But if you can imagine a distant descendant who believed those pages, he would have concluded that in the summer of 1939 the Soviet Union lived in constant anticipation of the next unprecedented holiday or the latest unprecedented feat.

The top priority for the editors of all Soviet papers, seemingly without exception, was to maintain a state of permanent elation in their readers. They wrote about great construction projects or at least great plans for projects. You'd feel dizzy from news about pilots making record-breaking flights or the completion of the Great Fergana Canal. Improvements to the plan for the Palace of Soviets were discussed in the minutest detail. This grandiose building was to be crowned with a one-hundred-meter-high statue of Lenin. The president of the Academy of Architecture gave patriotic speeches about it, and the architect, Iofan, discussed the unique Soviet style of architecture.

On 20 July yet another pompous physical-culture parade was to take place and the press gave a detailed report of the dress rehearsal. It began at Red Square at 3:00 A.M. on 16 July—a full production with an orchestra. A soccer ball as high as a two-story building rolled around Red Square, somehow managing to carry on its top a group of athletes who stared faithfully at the tribunal. But there were unexpected militant tones in *Izvestiia's* enthusiastic commentary: "Inspired by fortune, the daughters and sons of the great Soviet people remind us that not only do they know how to work and to rest, but they are ready to smash any enemy who would dare attack our beloved homeland." That August, on Aviation Day, a powerful spectacle took place in Tushino. A plane hurled bombs upon a distant object, flames burst out, and thick black clouds covered the horizon. Many people did not know that it had been staged.

The long-awaited grandiose All-Union Agricultural Exhibition was about to open.[21] Issue after issue of *Pravda* and *Izvestiia* ran illustrated stories about the pavilions of the different republics. The Uzbek pavilion had an enormous sculpture of Lenin and Stalin cordially conversing on a bench. August 1, the official opening, became the highpoint of the summer's celebrations.

The former Sukharevsky Market, which twenty years earlier swarmed with people and where the young Tsvetaeva had bargained as best she could in order to feed her two daughters, had been renamed Collective Farm Square. The public holiday was celebrated here. Approximately two hundred flags flew over the main pavilions of the exhibition where the reviewing stands were set up. Beria, Vyshinsky, and other leaders watched the organized parade of citizens pass by.

Normal life resumed after the opening. But every day brought cheerful newspaper reports about delegations from all parts of the country that came to the exhibition. August—the time for the harvest—was at hand, yet thousands of envoys from the countryside continued to get off train cars in the capital's various stations. The newspapers called on their readers to rejoice.

The first page of *Izvestiia* printed Alexei Tolstoi's dithyramb to the Soviet fatherland, modestly titled "The Foundation of Happiness." Tolstoi wrote that the "once poverty-stricken Russia" had risen far ahead of the most advanced countries. "At the plow were Comrade Stalin, the Party, and the government of the USSR, deeply tilling the historical virgin soil of Communism, and relying on the wisdom and creative powers of the peoples of the eleven Soviet republics." Tolstoi was rewarded for his contributions to the fatherland's literature with a special personal account in the state bank. Intoxicated by his own enthusiasm, the writer continued: "At this exhibition the collective farmers can put their hands on their hips and safely say, 'How are you doing out there in your abroad, and what do you have to brag about in these years?' It seems they have nothing to brag about there."

Then on 24 August the front page of all the newspapers displayed a large photo: the contented faces of Joseph Stalin and Vyacheslav Molotov beside the Nazi leader Von Ribbentrop. The press and radio brought news of an event that "shook all progressive humanity," as they would have said just one day earlier. The country that anti-Fascists throughout the world had virtually idolized as an impregnable barrier to German aggression had concluded a nonaggression pact with Hitler. Two days later, the military missions of England and France left Moscow.

Within a few days an extraordinary session of the Supreme Soviet ratified the pact and passed a law establishing compulsory military service. The newspapers reported that when Comrade Stalin appeared in the hall "the applause attained the force of a whirlwind." Exactly one week later came the news that the German army had attacked Poland. The Soviet press clearly favored the aggressor now. The reader was supposed to believe that it was the fault of the Poles: they had not been willing to make any concessions, thus forcing the Hitlerites to take military action.

Although it was not yet evident, the Second World War had begun— a war that Marina Tsvetaeva had thought about with such prophetic horror during her last months in Paris. How did the inhabitants of the Bolshevo house react to the pact? It's easy to guess. They may not have been able to boast about their political farsightedness, but they shared a hatred of Fascism with the entire left European intelligentsia. It was difficult for them—for the moment—to think up any justification or even a simple pragmatic explanation for the Soviet government's action. Only some time later, when there was suddenly an urgent need to "liberate" West Ukraine and West Belorussia from the oppression of Polish landlords and other enslavers, did the sense of what had happened become more clear.

A month or so later Georgy Efron would show some of his drawings to his classmates. They provide indirect evidence of the Bolshevo household's reaction to the peace with the Hitler regime. The drawings were blatant and nasty anti-Fascist caricatures. Mur drew them tirelessly, at home and in school, and distributed them to everyone who asked. Many took the drawings home.

The nonaggression pact was concluded on 23 August. On the 27th, a Sunday, early in the morning, Ariadna was arrested in Bolshevo. The group had expected almost anything, but not that.

10

Ariadna had come to Bolshevo the day before with Gurevich. He stayed for the holiday, as in the past. Emiliya Litauer was also a frequent houseguest during this period. After conducting their search, the Lubyanka agents asked the guests for their documents. On the search record they wrote down their names, addresses, and place of employment. For Emiliya this turned out to be fatal. A few hours later—after Ariadna had been taken away—the agents returned in the same NKVD car with a hastily prepared warrant for Litauer's arrest and took her away too. Ariadna would be free again one day, but that morning was Emiliya's last free one.

When Nina Gordon rushed to Bolshevo in the evening of that terrible Sunday (Gurevich told her what had happened after he returned to Moscow), she found a deadly quiet in the Efrons' half of the house.

> The terrace was empty. Marina Ivanovna and Sergei Yakovlevich were sitting in their room. Both she and he were outwardly calm; only their tightly compressed lips and eyes betrayed their hidden pain. I spent a long time there. We said little. We ate. Then Marina Ivanovna got ready to iron. I said, "Let me iron, I like to iron." She looked at me with a long blank gaze and then said, "Thanks, go ahead" and, after a moment of silence, added. "Alya liked to iron too."
>
> I stood and ironed, without speaking, the whole time silently swallowing the lump in my throat, and Sergei Yakovlevich just sat and sat on the bed and steadily stared at the table. I can't forget his large eyes paralyzed with fright.[22]

Within a few days the sick Efron left for Moscow. It's unlikely that he managed to see anyone with any influence. He didn't have "important contacts" there. Everyone brushed aside such requests and questions: there were hundreds of them. According to Klepinin, Sergei Yakovlevich was now in a state of deep despair. He was certain of his own arrest. Nonetheless he wrote a letter to the People's Commissar. He vouched for the political loyalty of his daughter and Emiliya Litauer. His letter had no effect. There was probably no response. But the letter did arrive: Efron was later reminded of its contents when he was a prisoner in the Lubyanka.

The adults hid what had happened from the younger inhabitants of the house. During these days Dimitry wasn't there. He had been taken to a hospital in Moscow: his tuberculosis had gotten worse. Alexei's family was no longer there either. At the end of the summer all three had also gone to the capital.

Sofa and Mur slept on the far terrace. The search had been conducted in only one room of the house, the one that had been pointed out as Alya's. The police were relatively quiet. They left before 9:00 A.M., taking Ariadna with them. The sound sleep of children protected Mur and Sofa from anxiety for the time being. When they got up for breakfast they were told that urgent business had come up and Alya and Gurevich had left for Moscow. A week later another lie was invented. Right up until his father's arrest Mur was unaware of his sister's fate. Thus, all the greater was his shock when everything was explained in October.

In September, with a bit of a late start, Mur began school. Because he attracted immediate attention, it was easy for his fellow students to remember him half a century later when people began to search in Bolshevo for the least bit of news about Tsvetaeva and her family. Mur was a handsome boy, tall and good-natured. But more than anything else his unusual dress singled him out from the others. He wore strange short pants, ankle-high boots with thick soles, and a jacket covered with zippers. His unusual outward appearance was combined with a sociable nature and easygoing manner. Mur did not flaunt his difference from others; he wasn't arrogant, he was talkative and open. His excellent German and his drawings also singled him out.

There is one strange detail in his schoolmates' stories: they reported that Mur readily talked about Spain, hence many had the impression that he had been there. Were those fantasies or perhaps a conscious participation in the version that the secret police had thought up for his father?

To get to school Mur had to go through a forest, and the walk there and back gave him the chance to connect with his fellow students, although he went to school there for only two months. It's clear that at the time no one had the slightest idea of who his parents were, and his schoolmates never came to Mur's home. Nina Nikolaevna had given the children in the house strict orders: don't invite anyone here and don't go to anyone else's home. They accepted that rule easily, without any questions; perhaps they even liked the idea that they were special. The village children also understood quickly and didn't poke their noses into the foreigners' business.

One day, out of boredom, a boy from the neighboring dacha, also a NKVD one, tried to talk to Mur and Mitya, who were chattering in French at the property's edge. The boy was also an émigré and knew French. The haughty boys ignored him, but he, Leonid Shapiro, remembered this incident many years later, the more so because he later saw the house after it was deserted, with signs of a hurried departure.

For a long time there was no news about Alya. None of the parcels that Marina Ivanovna took to the prison for her was accepted until December.

A peculiar empty stillness settled in the Bolshevo dacha. Nikolai Klepinin now lived in Moscow for long periods; he had a permanent room in the Balchug Hotel. Nina Nikolaevna often traveled to the capital to visit her son in the hospital. It grew cold. It rained more frequently and the fall winds came. Marina Ivanovna's and Mur's warm clothing was still in the luggage, which had arrived from Paris at the beginning of August. The luggage was stuck in customs—at first because Tsvetaeva didn't have a Soviet passport, then because the luggage had been addressed to Alya. Visitors no longer came to the dacha of lepers.

S. N. Klepinina-Lvova's vivid memoir-sketch likely refers to this period:

> The living room windows look out at railroad tracks; Marina Ivanovna is standing by one of the windows in one of her characteristic poses—arms crossed over her chest (a cigarette in her right hand), practically grabbing herself by the shoulders, as if shivering: it's quiet in the house, apparently no one is here except the two of us (this happened often, for I don't remember Marina Ivanovna leaving the house, unlike the other adults). It's quiet, dusk, there are no lights on in the room, no fire in the fireplace. Marina Ivanovna is standing by the window, half-turned to it. I see her profile against the glass but she's looking outside. There's a sense of great loneliness, cold, bleakness . . . Her profile . . . is beautiful: delicate, animated, as if in flight . . .[23]

On 17 September the radio broadcast a speech by Molotov, the foreign minister. He notified the Soviet population that Red Army troops had crossed the Polish border in order to "protect the life and property" of their Slavic brothers in West Ukraine and Belorussia. The period of "liberation" had begun.

One day later the papers and radio were describing the celebrations of the liberated population. As was customary, honored artists took an active part in the latest campaign. The famous Moiseyev dance ensemble departed for West Ukraine. Writers such as Maxim Rylsky, Perets Markish, and Yelena Ryvina celebrated the events in their verse. The poems were full of pathos and noise—and such a deathly cold that it's simply impossible to read any of them today.

Meanwhile the war in Europe raged on. The map of military operations moved from the fourth page of the newspaper to the second. The size of the map kept growing. On 4 October in one leading Soviet paper Tsvetaeva might have read news chilling to her soul: the masterpieces of the Louvre were being packed for evacuation.

On 10 October 1939 came the third arrest in the Bolshevo dacha. Sergei Yakovlevich was taken to the Lubyanka. The search report was signed by Marina Tsvetaeva.

This time everything took place in view of the fourteen-year-old Georgy. Klepinina-Lvova has described his terrible state. There's no point in trying to reconstruct Marina Ivanovna's feelings. One can only imagine that her despair had intensified a hundredfold.

11

Where was Boris Leonidovich Pasternak all this time? Had the old friendship and tenderness really disappeared without a trace by 1939? Didn't Tsvetaeva's return awake their desire to see each other right away? Little is known about this. None of the guests at the Bolshevo house have mentioned Pasternak in their reminiscences.

He had to have known about Marina Ivanovna's arrival soon thereafter. From the time of his 1935 trip to Paris for the anti-Fascist International Writers' Congress, Boris Pasternak had maintained warm relations with Ariadna Efron.[24] The twenty-two-year-old Alya helped Pasternak to cope with the severe depression he was struggling to overcome when he came from Russia.

After Ariadna arrived in Moscow in the spring of 1937 they didn't see each other very often. But suddenly in June 1939, either on the eve of the director Vsevolod Meyerhold's arrest (20 June), or soon thereafter, Pasternak came to see Alya at the journal's editorial office. They went somewhere nearby, to a bench along the boulevard, in order to talk without being overheard. (I remember well the connection with the date of Meyerhold's arrest from a conversation I had with Ariadna in the early 1970s. It means that Pasternak learned right away that Marina was coming and that she would be living in Bolshevo.)

Pasternak spent all of June in Moscow. He interrupted work on his translation of *Hamlet* in order to translate quickly (apparently, this was a specific order) several poems by the Hungarian poet Sandor Petöfi. Pasternak's wife and children, among whom was the one-and-a-half-year-old Lenechka, waited in Peredelkino. Pasternak went there at the very beginning of July.

Peredelkino and Bolshevo are in completely different directions from Moscow. Thus, contact between the two poets would have been difficult in July and August. When did they see each other for the first time? We have no precise information about this.

Pasternak told the critic Anatoly Tarasenkov about Tsvetaeva's arrival only at the beginning of November, and Tarasenkov, who constantly moved in literary circles, was astounded to hear the news. Five months after Tsvetaeva returned to her homeland almost no one knew about it. Maria Belkina's book *Interlocking Fates (Skreshchenie sudeb)* cites a diary entry of Tarasenkov's in which, among other things, appears Pasternak's remark, "She was at my place only once."[25] This might mean that Tsvetaeva came to see Boris Leonidovich by herself. When? In Tarasenkov's entry there is nothing about the arrested daughter or the arrested husband. Did Tsvetaeva perhaps see Pasternak in June before he left for Peredelkino?

Another credible account (E. B. Tager's) presents Pasternak as vacillating about whether to go to see Tsvetaeva. He seemed to be talking about seeing her for the first time. Tager also alludes to a draft of a letter Pasternak wrote to his wife in the fall. From the text of this draft it seems that someone from the fraternity of writers advised Pasternak not to see Marina Ivanovna, that it was too dangerous.

It was not without danger, of course. However, Dimitry Zhuravlev traveled to Bolshevo, and he wasn't anyone's relative. Nina Gordon was there, and her husband had already been arrested. Klepinina's old friend, Lidiya Maximovna Segal-Brodskaya, often visited there with her husband. They took the risk.

A secret meeting can be envisioned, of course. It wouldn't have been so difficult for Pasternak to go to Bolshevo during the time he lived in Moscow. He and Marina could have agreed beforehand, say, by telephone, to meet at the local train platform and, without informing anyone from the Bolshevo house, spend a day walking in the surrounding woods. It's possible, but there is no evidence.

One must remember that in recent months there had been continuous arrests of Pasternak's acquaintances, nearby and far away. In the summer of 1937 his friend, the poet Paolo Yashvili, anticipating his arrest, committed suicide in Georgia. In October of the same year in Tbilisi another of his close friends, Titsian Tabidze, was arrested. By the summer of 1939 in just the one Moscow suburb of Peredelkino more than twenty writers had been arrested. Among them was Boris Pilnyak, with whom Tsvetaeva became friends during his visits to Paris in the early thirties, and Isaac Babel, whom she also met in France. In May 1938 Osip Mandelstam was arrested for the second time. For the past three years Pasternak had been trying to intervene for Mandelstam through Bukharin. Stalin's famous phone call to Pasternak's apartment belongs to this period.[26] In 1935 Boris Pasternak helped Anna Akhmatova compose a letter to Stalin in defense of her husband and son. He then took that letter to the Kremlin gates where there was a special box for such messages.

Pasternak's behavior in all of these situations was irreproachable. Hence, two explanations remain: either he didn't know about the arrests at the Bolshevo dacha for a long time, or there were meetings with Tsvetaeva before November that we don't know about (for no witnesses are left). In 1941, in a letter Tsvetaeva sent to her daughter in the Sevzheldorlag camp in the Russian north, there is a sentence about Pasternak: "I was at his dacha once last fall." In other words, she was talking about the fall of 1940. But it seems likely that in those terrible fall months after Sergei Yakovlevich's arrest no one who was truly close to Marina Ivanovna came to visit her.

12

In the meantime NKVD investigators were busy developing more precise outlines of their latest case, which involved the inhabitants and guests of the Bolshevo house. Let us note one unexpected feature of the interrogation records. The prisoners were questioned persistently, in detail, about each other and about the topics of conversation at their dacha. The whole procedure was carried out with very crude and most likely physical pressure. The investigators were not looking for stories of illnesses or the weather: they needed "anti-Soviet remarks."

Ariadna, the first to be arrested, was the first one to "crack." She began to confess within a month after the first interrogation. As was the usual case in such situations, the more she talked the more they demanded from her. After squeezing out quite minor facts, they used this information to blackmail others, whom they then forced to elaborate on the narrative. Gradually the investigators would accumulate a cluster of "confessions" that would serve as serious and formidable evidence to support charges of "anti-Soviet meetings." When that evidence was presented to the person under interrogation, he or she would try to defend themselves. But how? When you get to this part of the interrogation reports, you experience a severe shock.

"I didn't engage in anti-Soviet conversations," appears in Ariadna Efron's testimony, "and I reported any to the NKVD agents with whom I maintained contact."

"Reported?" How could that be true? Was this just a lie on her part—an attempt to defend herself under unbearable conditions? But let us put this phrase together with what Ariadna told the investigator: before she left Paris, when she was the leader of the youth section of the Parisian Union for Repatriation, she was ordered by the Soviet ambassador to meet with Zinaida Stepanova, an agent of the NKVD, and Alya met with her regularly. Under investigation Alya reported that the meetings usually took place in the Café National. Are we to believe that during these meetings Tsvetaeva's daughter "informed" ("gave accounts," "reported"—who knows what it was called?) about what her closest acquaintances said and how they said it?

By the end of 1937 Stepanova was "dismissed from work" (evidently, she herself was arrested). She was immediately replaced by an "Ivan Ivanovich" and then a "Nikolai Kuzmich." When Klepinin was questioned, he claimed that these people were for the most part meant to authorize everyday matters. Then why did Ariadna ask that Zinaida Stepanova be called in for a face-to-face confrontation?

During one of his interrogations Sergei Efron was presented with evidence of his insincerity and concealment of criminal remarks. The investigators cited the testimony of Pavel Nikolaevich Tolstoi, then that of his daughter, and later that of the others, and they demanded that Efron confirm, supplement, and elucidate the record.

What did Efron say in his defense? He was more restrained and courageous during questioning than many of the prisoners. "I reported about this matter orally," he answered. "I gave warnings that I didn't trust the Klepinins." And what did Alexei Sezeman say when arrested? When charged with having had suspicious ties to the Finnish embassy, he reported that he had once made a written report about this to the NKVD. At the time he had had a completely innocent conversation with a Finnish official, but on his own initiative the law-abiding former émigré composed a report on himself. Chekhov might have laughed about this while composing a comic illustration of supervigilance. It was no longer funny in Soviet times.

During her interrogation Emiliya Litauer described how she first had become acquainted with Count Ignatiev while she was still in France, where he was a member of the Soviet trade delegation.[27] Later they met again in the USSR. Emiliya went to Ignatiev's home legitimately, as an old acquaintance. There, she now said, she kept silent, listened to, and was horrified at the count's opinions on events in the country, in particular, the case of Marshal Tukhachevsky and the other Red Commanders who were executed in 1937. Ignatiev firmly disapproved of these arrests, which he said weakened the Soviet Army. "But I wrote a report about that," Litauer defended herself to the investigator.

Klepinin had helped Emiliya compose these "reports." And he took them "to the right place." What was going on? How were such things possible? Heaven forbid me from casting stones of noble indignation upon unfortunate prisoners in the Lubyanka. That's not the point. But still, how were such things possible—and while they were free?

The people in the Bolshevo house were not exceptional monsters. The point—and the sorrow, and the moral and psychological mystery— lies in the fact that these people were unselfish, self-sacrificing, and sincerely concerned about the general good; moreover, they were deeply religious and in their own eyes, as in the eyes of those around them, they were scrupulously honest. If one can understand what happened to them, one can understand much in the history of the Soviet Union in the thirties. It is completely impossible to understand outside the historical context.

In his memoirs Dimitry Sezeman considered his parents' mistakes in exactly that unhistorical way. They were "paid agents"; that's his entire simple verdict, even though his mother was among those so branded. But quick judgments only impede the search for the roots of good and evil, the attempt to explain reasons and consequences. Without this search you cannot make a diagnosis and cure the illness. At any moment it can flare up with new strength.

In the Soviet Union the epidemic of informing was widespread during the second half of the thirties. And it often took on a respectable cover. Who would call this a denunciation? It's not a denunciation, just "information!" The same epidemic raged in Germany. There, as here, favorable conditions were created for the virus to breed. We know for whom it was useful, there's no reason to belabor the point. But another aspect of the question is more puzzling. What peculiarities of personality allow such a virus to penetrate without resistance, to pervert beyond recognition moral values that had been cultivated for years? Why does the same temptation not affect other people? What protects them?

Twenty years earlier, one evening in 1919, in revolutionary Moscow, the twenty-seven-year-old Marina was bent over her diary, pen in hand, unhurriedly reflecting on a theme that someone else might not have found deserving of such serious attention. Turning shades of meaning over in her mind, writing down each barely glimpsed variant, she listened attentively to the sense of the simplest and most common words: "I want" and "I can," "I don't want" and "I cannot." She apparently felt she had stumbled upon something quite important, something touching the very nature of man, the *depths* of that nature, and perhaps even the *heights* of his spiritual world.

> My "I cannot" is some kind of natural limit, not only mine, anyone's . . . "I cannot" is more sacred than "I don't want to." "I cannot" is all the mastered "I don't want to's," all the corrected attempts to want—it's the final result. My "I cannot" is least of all lack of strength. What's more, it is my

main strength. It is something inside me which in spite of all my wanting (my coercion of myself!) still does not want . . .

The roots of "I cannot" go deeper than one can fathom. . . . I am speaking of the primordial "I cannot," of the mortal "I cannot," of that "I cannot" for whose sake you let yourself be torn apart, of the gentle "I cannot."

I declare: it's "I cannot," not "I don't want to," that makes heroes!

Thus, the young Tsvetaeva considered the real sources of our choice to be in the depths of blood and spirit. The composition of blood is determined at birth. Some have nothing to overcome—they always hear the voice of nature distinctly; for others this prompting does not exist.

A person develops breadth of spirit on his own, however. "I *cannot* do this, even if the whole world is doing it and it doesn't seem shameful to anyone." In order to feel this way, we need *nature*, which is impossible to pervert.

One more thing. Is it an accident that moral rust has so often affected "fighters for social justice"? Isn't it because they accepted on faith the primacy of social interest over the personal? Perhaps. If only we didn't know how often informers were people who immediately took care of their personal welfare.

13

The school holidays began at the very beginning of November and Nina Klepinina left with her daughter for Moscow, to 12 Pyatnitskaya Street, where her mother lived. Nikolai Klepinin still came to the Bolshevo house during this time, however. Perhaps, sharing Tsvetaeva's suffering, the spouses were trying not to leave her completely alone. There was no other place for Marina Ivanovna to live: it didn't seem possible for her to live in her sister-in-law's tiny rooms at Merzlyakovsky Lane.

Then, on the night of 6 November, on the eve of the anniversary of the revolution, three more people from the group were arrested. Klepinina

was roused from her bed at Pyatnitskaya Street, and her son Alexei taken
from Sadovo-Kudrinskaya, his wife's apartment. The third arrest that same
night was at the Bolshevo dacha again. Nikolai Klepinin was presented
with the arrest warrant.

From Nina Pavlovna Gordon's memoirs:

> Marina told me in a muted voice how they came to arrest him,
> how terrible it was to look at him, especially terrible because he
> was alone. He was completely alone, but the dog (do you remember that
> boxer with human eyes?) was fawning upon him the whole time and
> jumping up on his knees. He kept cuddling the dog, the only living crea-
> ture remaining near him; apparently he felt human warmth and love
> from it alone.[28]

Alexei's wife left their child with a friend and rushed to Bolshevo
early in the morning on the electric train. She didn't know that Nina
Nikolaevna wasn't there. She made her way to the familiar house through
rain and snow and a piercing wind. Their part of the house was empty. In
her current memory there is a strange displacement: she remembers that
she saw bare, needleless trees.

The house seemed deserted. There was just a strange rattling noise
that kept repeating, like a metronome tapping out the last minutes. Later,
turning around, she understood: the wind was swinging the gymnastics
rings that Sergei Yakovlevich had hung between the pine trees, knocking
them against each other. Irina frantically knocked at the door of the
Klepinins' terrace. But the door on the other side of the house opened and
Tsvetaeva appeared in the doorway.

The wind tousled her graying hair, the raincoat thrown over her
shoulders barely stayed in place.

"They arrested Alyosha last night," Irina said.

Marina Ivanovna crossed herself several times, she looked pale as a
ghost. It was terrible to look at her.

"Leave, child, leave here as soon as you can, God be with you. They
took Nikolai Andreevich away early this morning."

Marina reminded Irina of Pushkin's mad miller. Within two days Tsvetaeva and her son fled Bolshevo for Moscow.

A few days later the young boy from the neighboring house, the one with whom Mur and Mitya didn't want to talk that summer, wandered into the dacha, after wondering why he hadn't heard any voices from there for a long time. The door to the terrace was half open. The boy pushed it and went inside. Confusion reigned in the rooms, books were strewn on the floor. He picked up a few. The books were in French. He couldn't resist the temptation and took back home one volume of Boccaccio and one of Voltaire.

LUBYANKA

1

Early on the morning of 27 August 1939, Ariadna Efron walked down the steps of the Bolshevo house. She would never see her father, mother, or brother again.

"She leaves without saying good-bye!" we read in Marina Tsvetaeva's diary. "I: 'Alya, how can you go without having said good-bye to anyone?' She waves, in tears, over her shoulder! The commandant (an old man, kindly), 'That's better. Long good-byes mean extra tears . . . '"

Many years later Ariadna recalled this day:

> 27 August . . . I saw my family for the last time; at dawn that day we parted forever; the morning was such a clear and sunny one—two pleasant young men in identical suits and with identical blue gendarme eyes took me in a very civilian looking car from Bolshevo to Moscow; my whole family stood in the doorway of the dacha and waved to me; their faces were pale from the sleepless night. I was certain that I would return within three days or so, not later, that everything would be cleared up instantly; but at the same time I couldn't help but cry, looking out the car's back window and seeing the small group of people crowded together on the dacha's porch, who inescapably sailed back into the distance. The car turned and that was it.[1]

In a month and a half, on 10 October, in the middle of the night, the same thing: the noise of a car approaching, headlights slicing the dark. After conducting a search and drawing up a report, this time they took Sergei Yakovlevich Efron. The route was the same—to Moscow and the Lubyanka.

Tsvetaeva was able to receive several letters from her daughter in the spring of 1941 from a camp in the Komi Republic (Sevzheldorlag); but never a thing from her husband, not a line.

More than half a century later, thanks to Gorbachev's perestroika and a petition submitted by Anastasia Ivanovna Tsvetaeva, I was able to read the investigation files of Ariadna Sergeevna and Sergei Yakovlevich Efron.

The walls of the terrible building on Lubyanka Square have gradually lost their impenetrability. Clarity is still far away, of course; the records of the interrogations and the memories of the survivors will never create a completely reliable account of what took place there.

Yet, here is the warrant for the arrest of an employee of the journal *Revue de Moscou*, Ariadna Sergeevna Efron. It bears the black signature of Lavrenty Beria—black in the most literal sense, since a thick, black pencil was used. Here is the arrestee form that the prisoner filled out in her own hand. And here is the record of the first interrogation, which took place on the day of her arrest—27 August.

The first protocol is short, just a few lines. The prisoner was ordered to discuss her anti-Soviet activities and her collaboration with foreign intelligence agents. Her recorded answer: the prisoner knows of no such activities on her part. The question was repeated in a different way—the answer was the same. The record is drawn up in strict correspondence with the rules: it includes the time the interrogation started and ended, the investigator's surname, and—on every page—the signature of the person under interrogation.

The "dialogue" began at 2 P.M. and ended at 5 P.M. Three hours. How was the time spent? What is missing from the record, which consists of a few standard phrases? To what extent does the record reflect reality? My own experience now proved useful. Toward the end of the 1950s, on a number of occasions over the course of two months, a black Volga with several zeros on its license plate took me from work to Leningrad's "Big House" for questioning. This experience, notwithstanding its uniqueness, now helped me to read the interrogation records. I remembered clearly how different the real dialogues in the investigator's room were from the ones written down on paper; how often the record was drawn up after the "talk" was over, containing scarcely one-tenth of what was said. Even that was formulated by the investigator. (In principle, one can correct the record, but not everyone is aware of that and, even if they are, not everyone uses the opportunity.) The record does not reflect the investigator's abusive or mocking tone, his provocative lies, threats, and dirty gossip directed at friends and acquaintances. Or the hours and hours when the person being interrogated is left "to think things through properly," while the investigators go to eat, take a cigarette break, or simply busy themselves with other matters. Or, if you're stubborn, being dragged from one official to another, which adds new faces to the interrogation. None of these things will be found in properly drawn-up records. And my experience took place during our "vegetarian times," as Anna Akhmatova put it.

What was left out of the frame—that is, outside the record—at the end of the thirties is harder to imagine. The stories of those who survived and returned, and the memoirs of those who were repressed, recreate the conditions in sufficient detail. Probably no one still thinks that conversations were held over a cup of coffee. Still, all too often the protocol forms, whether typed or filled out in the investigator's hand, seemed like hieroglyphs to me, the meaning of which only the participants in the "dialogue" would be able to decipher.

Where is the truth? How true is it? Is the confession sincere or a carefully thought-out version? If there is fabrication, how was it carried out so smoothly, almost masterfully? Why a "no" one day, and the next day "yes"? How did prisoners relate to each other during the confrontations of suspects? To what extent were things done according to law? Should "methods of physical pressure" be seen behind every false accusation the prisoner brought against himself or others? And what if an accusation was not false?

Two weeks passed between Ariadna Efron's first and second interrogations. The first interrogations were conducted by Senior Lieutenant of State Security, Nikolai Mikhailovich Kuzminov. A month and a half later he would work on Sergei Efron's case. Another investigator, Junior Lieutenant Alexei Ivanovich Ivanov, conducted the second interrogation and several subsequent ones.

Ariadna was now asked concrete questions about her circle of acquaintances in Paris and whom she met with after she returned to the homeland. Had she collaborated with émigré White Guard organizations? What was her purpose in returning to the USSR? The subtext of the last question was made clear: "We know that you came here on a mission of the foreign intelligence service you worked for."

"I was not connected with any foreign intelligence service and I came here only out of my own desire," her answer reads.

The second interrogation took place at night; it lasted for eight hours, beginning at 9 P.M. and ending at 5 A.M. The third began on the following day, after a sleepless night, and again dragged on far past midnight; the fourth on the afternoon of the following day. These days were the 7th, 8th, and 9th of September. A one day break followed, and then again: the 11th, the 13th, the 14th.

Fifteen years later, in May 1954, after the Twentieth Party Congress and the condemnation of Stalin's "cult of personality," Ariadna Efron sent a petition from Turukhansk, in Siberia, where she had been exiled as a so-called "repeat offender," to the General Procurator of the USSR, Roman Rudenko, requesting a review of the case and repeal of the sentence. In the petition she wrote: "I was beaten unmercifully with rubber truncheons [*damskie voprosniki*]; for 20 days and nights I was deprived of sleep; they conducted round-the-clock 'conveyor belt' interrogations [i.e., during which investigators rotated], kept me in a cold incarceration cell, undressed, standing at attention; they staged a fake execution." Further: "I was forced to incriminate myself falsely. . . . They beat me into giving testimony against my father."

That testimony was given on 27 September 1939, approximately one month after her arrest. On that day Ariadna agreed to write a "confession." Others, much more hardened, gave in more quickly. From materials of the special commissions that were created in the late 1980s to investigate the true history of the political "show trials" of the late thirties, we know, for example, that Marshal Tukhachevsky confessed to his ties with foreign agents after a week of interrogation and torture; thirty-three days after his arrest, G. L. Pyatakov began to sign absurd confessions; and it took two months and eighteen days to break Karl Radek.[2]

The record of Ariadna's 27 September interrogation is signed by the two investigators who conducted the interrogation—Kuzminov and Ivanov. But in a petition she sent from Turukhansk on 9 March 1954, this time to Kruglov, Minister of Internal Affairs of the USSR, Ariadna Efron indicated that one of Beria's deputies was also present during her questioning, apparently on several occasions. She recognized him because she had seen him earlier, while "at liberty," when she accompanied her sick father to a meeting with him at a Moscow hotel. His surname was either Georgian or Armenian. During her investigation, according to Ariadna, he constantly demanded evidence from her against her father. His presence is not indicated in the interrogation records, however. Neither is the participation of Ya. M. Sverdlov's son, who became a NKVD investigator. Ariadna also talked about his participation to her friend A. A. Shkodina-Federolf, who also lived in exile in Turukhansk, and to Maria Belkina, the author of *Interlocking Fates*. These stories should caution us against any illusion that the interrogation records truly reflect the real conditions that existed during the interrogations.

Within a month of her arrest, Ariadna Efron confessed that she had been recruited by the French intelligence service and sent to the Soviet Union on an espionage mission. Her self-incrimination was based on facts that had figured in her earlier interrogations; Ariadna had reported them herself. But now she interpreted them as the investigator wished. She talked about her contact in Paris at the end of 1936 with Paul Merle, the editor of the journal *France–USSR*. (Ariadna was working at the time in the editorial offices of the journal *Our Union*, published under the aegis of the Union for Repatriation.) Merle proposed that the young journalist write an essay about life in the Soviet Union based on material from the

Soviet press. She did, and Merle was enthusiastic about it. New orders followed. Ariadna kept writing articles, and each time they were eagerly accepted and generously remunerated. Then, shortly before Ariadna left for the Soviet Union, Merle invited her to his home for a farewell dinner.

He was in very good spirits that evening. The conversation touched on the most diverse topics. Did Ariadna know Jakob Suritz, the Soviet ambassador? And Viktor Serge?[3] What did she think about the strange confessions of the defendants at the trial that took place in Moscow in January 1937?[4]

"In this way I became aware of Merle's connection with the Trotskyites," appears in Ariadna's deposition for 17 September. Here, and in later entries of her answers, one sometimes gets a strange sense that she is almost ridiculing the investigator. She answers absurd questions with unconcealed nonsense.

Ariadna now showed a willingness to help "unmask" others—the people the prosecution was interested in. True, the investigator became angry at descriptions that were too general: he needed concrete facts about espionage activity. Did Alya understand that even general descriptions sufficed to destroy the lives of the people they asked about? It's possible that she never fully understood, just as she didn't understand the real threat to herself. According to the testimony of her cellmate, Dina Kanel, cited in *Interlocking Fates,* in spite of the whole nightmare of what was going on, for a long time both Alya and Dina preserved the frivolous hope that their punishment would be relatively light: "The fact that they had been charged was so clearly absurd and they felt so completely innocent that they were certain that the maximum they might get was three years of exile!"[5]

The state security establishment thoroughly investigated the psychological state of a person under interrogation—one must give them their due. Many years after I had been questioned by the police, I asked my "fellow accomplices" about some of their confessions. What type of coercion had provoked them? We were discussing confessions that were clearly dangerous for people who were still free. The answers startled me. "Well, it was clear that they knew everything . . . why confuse matters?

Besides, it didn't relate to anything very serious and I thought nothing would happen if I confirmed it." Things that aren't "serious" have often turned into ruined lives—even in our times. But in the thirties they led to physical suffering and—most often—to death.

For a long time Ariadna thought her own arrest was a ridiculous mistake, the result of "sabotage" that came from within the NKVD. Even in her cell, even in the camp, she still believed that the fundamental principles of this most just system had not been affected. In a letter from the camp to Samuil Gurevich she even referred to her arrest as a "stupid accident." "I am not so stupid and petty as to mix the general with the personal. What happened to me was a minor incident, but what is great will remain great."[6]

Irony is out of place here, but isn't this an instructive example of the "unwavering spirit" we traditionally admire? Steadfastness mixed with blind faith. The fusion of these qualities is often ruinous even for people of intelligence and selfless nobility.

Let us return to the confession of 27 September 1939. At the farewell dinner Paul Merle proposed that Ariadna continue her cooperation with his journal from Moscow. In order to send materials more quickly, he gave her the addresses of two French journalists who were in Moscow at the time. Ariadna had informed the investigator about this earlier, but now she made important additions. First of all, Merle, it seems, had asked her to write about the *anti-Soviet* sentiments of the Moscow intelligentsia. Second, the addresses of the journalists were now called "secret meeting places." Ariadna claimed that it was clear to her at the time that Merle was proposing a direct collaboration with French intelligence. However, she insisted that she had not sent any material to Merle from Moscow, neither directly nor through his "spies." Nevertheless, the charge that "she was an agent for French intelligence" appeared in her sentence as if an established fact.

The Merle plot has a completely realistic basis. Such a journal did exist and Paul Merle, too. The assumption about Merle arose naturally. The topics of the farewell conversation may also have been noted correctly. It's just that everything was reflected in a deliberately distorted mirror.

The investigation was thrown a bone: if you want to play that way, go ahead.

Even after Ariadna's confession they didn't leave her alone, however. Now the investigators demanded that she unmask her father—just as they had done earlier. Finally, the record includes the sentence her torturers had waited for: "Not wishing to conceal anything from the investigation, I must report that my father was an agent of French intelligence."

2

Five days later the investigator Kuzmin drew up an order for the preventive detention (i.e., arrest) of S. Ya. Efron. Beria's signature was appended in the same thick black pencil we saw on the warrant for Ariadna.

Ariadna later claimed that her own arrest was required primarily in order to extort information that would compromise her father. Perhaps. But hers was by no means the only fabrication against Efron. On 7 August 1939, Pavel Nikolaevich Tolstoi testified about Efron's "anti-Soviet and espionage" activity. Most likely, these were not the first incriminating depositions the NKVD had at its disposal. Efron's friend and fellow Eurasianist Svyatopolk-Mirsky, who was arrested in 1937, could have named him. Efron might also have been named by other émigrés who returned from France and fell into the NKVD's hands. We are still not able to trace the entire history of this matter in the KGB archives.

It makes no sense to search for sound logic in the orgies of repression in those years. Another mysterious matter is why the investigation so persistently extorted from its prisoners possible grounds for detaining its own cadres, who in good time were themselves charged with crimes. Why was it necessary to observe the formalities of legal proceedings so pedantically, appending the prisoners' signatures to their "confessions" in the interrogation records? Whence this preoccupation with the observance of "rules," for example, rules requiring that participants in a confrontation of suspects append their signatures to each of their replies as part of the protocol? For whom was this spectacle played out—without spectators, without witnesses—and with such cruelty toward the victims?

During the ill-starred investigation of 27 September, Ariadna had to substantiate her claim about her father's ties with French intelligence. She referred to their intimate conversations in the thirties. The most "artistically" interpreted conversation was one that in content (Ariadna's forthcoming departure for the USSR) might date back to the mid 1930s.

Ariadna recounted that her father was sick that day. They were home alone. He called for her and asked her to sit down on his bed. He said that life had irreparably destroyed him and her mother. She thought he was talking about the difficult material circumstances of their life and began to comfort him. But he stopped her. He said (the rest I quote verbatim from the deposition: "You are still young, you don't know anything and can't understand me. You don't know and can't know how wretched I feel. I'm caught like a fly in a spiderweb. . . . You can go to the USSR and establish a nice life for yourself there. My situation is hopeless because I will never be able to return to the USSR in person."

"Knowing that Father was involved with Soviet intelligence," Ariadna continued, "I asked hadn't he compensated for his past [i.e., in the White Army] by his work for the USSR?"

"Not only for the USSR," Efron supposedly told his daughter.

"It was clear to me that he was talking about French intelligence," Ariadna added. With the same logic, or more precisely, analogous to the logic in her story about Paul Merle.

If all this was fabrication from beginning to end, then it was practically inspired. Alya Efron's literary talent was well known, incidentally, as was her childhood talent for fantasy that Tsvetaeva noted in her letters. But how enchantingly like the truth is this dialogue between father and daughter. The part about French intelligence is nonsense, of course, but the rest! And what if Ariadna's father while still in France had, in fact, felt guilty before his wife and sensed that he had been trapped, like a fly in a spiderweb, into a dirty business from which he could no longer get out in one piece? He certainly could have guessed as much, since from 1931 the embassy had every year been delaying the possibility of his return to the homeland.

The record of just this one interrogation takes up twenty-six pages of A. S. Efron's file. She would be left in peace for almost a month, however.

If one is to trust Dina Kanel's memory, at first Ariadna didn't realize the importance of what had taken place. She was even pleased when she came back from the investigation and said that she had finally confessed. In Belkina's rendition, the two friends were only talking about Ariadna's "guilt." But, still, why "pleased"? Evidently, the version she gave to the investigators had not matured during the questioning, but during the agonizing hours she spent in an icy cell or during breathing spells in the cycle of interrogations. Now she hoped that the most difficult part was behind her.

Her relief did not last long, however, and soon Ariadna demanded a meeting with the prosecutor in order to retract what she had said about her father. But a meeting with the procurator, Antonov, could not be arranged until March. By that time Sergei Efron had been in prison for five months.

3

It's interesting that the investigator drew up the warrant for Sergei Yakovlevich's arrest on 2 October 1939, but Beria's signature of approval appeared only on 9 October. Doesn't this indicate that, because of Efron's services, approval from an even higher level was required? In any event, Efron was given an extra week of freedom. He was able to spend his birthday with his wife and son, and then also Marina Ivanovna's birthday. Tsvetaeva was forty-seven.

After he was taken to the Lubyanka, Efron filled out the arrestee form. He gave a double-surname: Andreev-Efron; for profession he wrote "writer" [*literator*]; for last place of employment, "I was on the payroll of the NKVD"; his spouse "Marina Ivanovna Tsvetaeva, writer and poet." Next came information about his children and sisters. His internal passport had been issued in Moscow on 16 October 1937.

Efron's first interrogation began on the day of his arrest—10 October 1939 at 11 A.M. It lasted for three and a half hours, slightly longer than Ariadna's first interrogation. There was a clear difference. Ariadna's record consists of only several lines of dialogue, but Efron's deposition is extensive and informative.

Sergei Yakovlevich gave detailed biographical information about himself. He recalled his service as a medical orderly during the First World War and brief work as an actor in the Kamerny Theater. What was his attitude toward the February Revolution? "Like that of most officers," Efron answered vaguely (to give a precise answer would have taken too long, and at the time he was not very enthusiastic about his past). In addition, he was questioned about his attitude to the Bolsheviks, his participation in the White Army, his evacuation to Turkey with the White Army units that escaped, and the detention camp in Gallipoli. The investigator evidently had heard this name for the first time because he wrote "Gamporizhsky," and when Efron signed this page, he pedantically corrected the mistake.

"What did you do there?" the investigator probed.

"I was starving there and spent the winter in an unheated tent," Efron answered.

"Why did your hosts receive you so poorly, when you were waging armed struggle on their behalf?" the investigator asked sarcastically.

(The tone and direction of the investigator's questions were subordinated to the task of "establishing criminal guilt," to elicit criminal intent from every fact the prisoner reported. Dense ignorance was visible not only in the "Gamporizhsky" mistake, however. The investigation records are unique material for a psychiatrist—so obvious is the wackiness of Soviet investigators. Their brains seem to have been wired by a special circuit; the instilled Soviet cliches had replaced logic. "Not black" meant "white"; "not ours" meant "that of the imperialist sharks"; "against us" meant "done on behalf of capitalism and for money." The NKVD investigator did not hesitate to put the alogical results of his own sick inferences into the records. In the late fifties and the sixties prisoners were no longer beaten—at least not in Moscow and Leningrad—but the same type of investigator remained. And don't believe that after Yeltsin's victory in August 1991 everything inside that same organization suddenly changed.)

The investigator energetically prompted Efron. "So, you held a hostile view of the October Revolution? Were your general views during the struggle against the Bolsheviks a reflection of your association with the White movement?"

The prisoner was not evasive: "Absolutely correct. . . . Precisely."

One feature that appears here is characteristic of all Efron's remaining testimony. He did not try to smooth over the sharp turns in his biography or avoid relating incidents that were not helpful to him in his present situation. In such instances, he was reserved and stayed within the bounds of whatever the investigation knew from the other prisoners. Occasionally, he disputed the interpretation of these incidents if it strayed too far into the realm of fantasy. The records of all eighteen interrogations of Efron create a distinct picture of his firmness and his readiness to stand before Soviet justice to answer for his real transgressions.

Efron gave a detailed account of his years in emigration. In Prague he had organized the Democratic Union of Russian Students; the group had an anti-Soviet orientation, but at the same time was anti-White Guard. It did not have its own political program, but tried to develop positions that were different from those of the Whites. Efron and other former White Guardists in the group who thought like him were by then deeply disillusioned. In order to develop new positions they thought it necessary to examine more intently the actual processes taking place in contemporary Russia.

If the ungrateful investigator to whom Efron now gave so detailed an account of his life could have picked up the student journal *By Our Own Paths* (*Svoimi putiami*), he would have seen that the prisoner was scrupulously honest. Sergei Yakovlevich had, in general, spent all his time in emigration persistently trying to find a basis for bringing together the irreconcilably hostile Whites and Reds. Neither group won his full trust, but he searched into both and found fragments of his own truth. Only for a while, however. Time took its toll. What he saw, upon close inspection, too often alienated him—émigré quarrels, undiluted anger toward everything in the USSR, unrestrained praise for the White movement.

How much easier it was to idealize what was far away. By the late twenties Efron's searches for a "third position" ended with his choice of "Soviet truth." When he was questioned about his Parisian period, Efron gave detailed testimony about the Eurasian movement, which had captured the imagination of a broad segment of the emigration in the mid twenties. He outlined the principles of the Eurasian program, giving a detailed picture of the movement's diverse practical activities and its financial sources. He named the leaders of the Parisian group that he had belonged to. Almost all of them remained in France: S. N. Trubetskoi, P. P. Suvchinsky, P. N. Malevsky-Malevich, N. N. Alekseev. Two Eurasianists—P. S. Arapov and D. S. Mirsky—had returned to the USSR in the early thirties and had already been arrested.

Efron ignored the tone of the investigator's pointed questions and stubbornly tried to follow a path of trustworthy facts and circumstances. At times he seems to have been moved by a simpleminded hope that he could break through his interlocutor's denseness and explain the latter's own "errors" to him. Efron absolutely failed to take note of the fact that the interrogators had no interest in the truth.

Meanwhile, the interrogators constantly interrupted Efron with blunt questions, reminding him about just where he was giving his explanation of historical circumstances. For example, they asked: What specific anti-Soviet activity did the Eurasians conduct? What foreign intelligence agents were they involved with? What espionage missions did they—and you personally—carry out?

Efron was prepared to call the Eurasians' policy anti-Soviet, though on the grounds that one of the Eurasians' slogans in the second half of the twenties was "Soviets without Communists." But he firmly denied any recruitment by foreign agents. In addition, he persistently stressed that during 1928-1929 many Eurasians, and he personally, had reconsidered their earlier views and become staunch "supporters of the Soviet line."

"Describe your anti-Soviet activity after 1929," the investigator persisted.

"There's nothing for me to tell," Efron responded. "After 1929 there was none."

"The investigation does not believe you."

This interrogation did not forget another important part of the charge, one that was developed beforehand. Not a single political trial of these years avoided the Trotskyite connection.

P. N. Tolstoi had provided the necessary link on 7 August 1939. He reported to the investigator a fact that he, Tolstoi, said he had heard from Efron in France in the early thirties—that is, that a meeting had taken place between the Eurasians and G. L. Pyatakov, when he was the Soviet trade representative in Paris. Tolstoi called the meeting a "joint conference," as a result of which the Eurasians became a foreign branch of the Trotskyite bloc that had been established in the Soviet Union. By the time of Efron's interrogation Pyatakov had been executed. He was found guilty at the January 1937 trial, along with Sokolnikov, Radek, and others, for founding the so-called "parallel anti-Soviet Trotskyite bloc," which reportedly had intended to overthrow Soviet power and establish capitalism.

Efron must have understood the full danger of the revealed episode. His brevity in this part of his testimony is uncharacteristic. He admitted that such a meeting had taken place, but only Pyotr Petrovich Suvchinsky had taken part in it, and he, Efron, did not know the details of the conversation.

Jumping ahead, I'll say that the prosecutors wouldn't let Efron maintain this terseness. They not only interrogated Efron and Tolstoi about the ill-starred meeting, but also—and under torture—the Klepinin-Lvovs and Emiliya Litauer. The details they procured gradually forced Sergei Efron to talk more. He reported that Pyatakov himself had initiated the meeting. In January 1929 Boris Neander, editor of the Parisian Russian newspaper *Russian Herald* (*Russkii vestnik*), supposedly came to see the Eurasians on Pyatakov's behalf; Neander spoke of Pyatakov's interest in the Eurasians' program. The meeting that took place had a semi-official character—as if it were being held with the Soviet trade representative and not with a leader of the opposition. That was Efron's interpretation.

Just at this time the newspaper *Eurasia* was beginning to have financial problems. According to Efron, Suvchinsky proposed using the newspaper to propagandize the successes of Soviet society, not in exchange for financial help but in connection with the sincere desire of the leftist Eurasians to help build socialism in Russia. Efron claimed that the meeting led to nothing, however, and there was no further contact.[7]

4

Life's tragic paradoxes. First, Efron was charged with collaborating with the Trotskyites. Then charges were brought against his associates, the Klepinins, Afanasov, and Litauer—people who were energetically involved in the mid thirties in the struggle against Trotskyism abroad (and on the orders of NKVD operatives in the Paris embassy). The accused were the same people who took a secret trip to Norway in 1936 in order to verify Trotsky's residence; they shadowed Trotsky's son Lev Sedov; they took part in a whole series of anti-Trotskyite operations, the details of which we may learn some day. How did they feel when they were accused of collaborating with the Trotskyites, whom they considered inveterate enemies of the fatherland?

Did they remember how a little more than two years earlier they had discussed the shocking news about this or that prominent person who suddenly turned out to be a secret associate of Trotsky? Did they by now understand the real worth of the "confessions" heard at the Moscow trials? However, we won't understand anything about Efron and the group around him, now under arrest, unless we see them in the context of that insane time.

Today, when the policy of glasnost has permitted everything to be hashed over, it's easy to speak scornfully about people whose homesickness deprived them of a sober view of things. Dimitry Sezeman does this in his memoir *Paris–Gulag–Paris*. But how is one to categorize the simple-mindedness of a great number of European journalists, who in 1937 persistently repeated implausible gibberish about "Trotskyite Fascists" said to have found a home in Spain in the Catalonian party POUM (Partido Obrero de Unificación Marxista). This myth was created in the same police offices where the famous "trials" were prepared, but it was picked up by newspapers in Valencia and Paris, London and New York, not by nostalgic Russian émigrés. This is by no means the only time in the second half of the 1930s when the minds of the world's progressive intellectuals were mysteriously confused.

The interrogator turned a deaf ear to everything that Efron said about the Eurasian movement. However, several realistic details—distorted beyond recognition—were inserted in the fantastic version presented in the formal charge. Meanwhile, in characterizing Eurasianism in the late twenties, Efron related rather unexpected things. He avoided its history and any mention of the first books and anthologies (1921-1922) in which Russian émigré scholars were promoting a new concept of Russia's historical development. Early discussions had focussed on the peculiar geographical situation of the Russian state, which had absorbed features of Europe and Asia and had developed its own unique culture, economy, and religion. The anti-Western spirit of this concept, combined with a critique of the Russian intelligentsia's pre-revolutionary frame of mind, ensured its popularity among people forced to leave their homeland.

Efron did not join the Eurasianists until 1926, after he moved from Czechoslovakia to Paris and became acquainted with Mirsky and Suvchinsky. They were "the most interesting Parisians," Efron attested in a letter to his Prague friend Evgeny Nedzelsky. "The most interesting, creative, and lively things in emigration come together in Eurasianism."[8] The Eurasians' "approach to national self-consciousness through culture" impressed him, but its political program seemed "insignificant" at first. However, in the fall of 1926 (he admitted in other letters to Nedzelsky) he turned from being a sympathizer to a "person with the same views" as the Eurasians, and in December he took an active part in creating a Eurasian seminar in Paris. In May 1927 Efron informed Nedzelsky that Eurasian work had become the principal occupation of his life.

By this time people of a different sort had substantially replaced the intellectuals in the Eurasian movement. The newcomers called for the active participation of Eurasian ideas in contemporary political reality.

Eurasianism "was poisoned by the desire for a quick, external success," G. V. Florovsky wrote in a 1928 article. The most radically inclined group of Eurasians—Suvchinsky, Mirsky, Malevsky-Malevich, Arapov, Rodzevich, Sezeman—also included Efron.

Efron's energy helped him launch the Eurasian club in Paris. Its regular lectures and discussions drew large audiences during these years. In the fall of 1928 the first issue of the newspaper *Eurasia* was published.

Efron didn't mention any of the above material during his interrogations, however. Expounding on the Eurasians' program for Russia in the future, he identified only two points: the goal of state capitalism and a plan to replace Communists in leading positions with people of Eurasian persuasions. For the investigation, that was quite enough material to justify defining the Eurasians' mission as the overthrow of the Soviet system.[9]

For the first and last time Efron was asked about Marina Tsvetaeva at this interrogation.

"What anti-Soviet work did your wife carry out?"

"My wife did not carry out any anti-Soviet work," Efron responded. "She has written poetry and prose her whole life. Although she expressed non-Soviet views in some of her works."

In the record the investigator disagreed with Efron's remarks with a subtlety behind which one can easily imagine—at best—an unprintable shout: "The picture you present is far from the truth. It is a known fact that your wife lived with you in Prague and actively participated in newspapers and journals published by the Socialist Revolutionaries. That's a fact, isn't it?"

Ariadna had given the investigation the information about where Tsvetaeva lived and where she had been published. Materials from Ariadna's interrogation were cited (and perhaps parts were shown) to Efron that day. A copy of the deposition from 27 September was placed in her father's case file.

"Yes, it's a fact," Sergei Yakovlevich acknowledged. "She was an émigrée and did write in those papers, but she was not engaged in anti-Soviet work."

"Impossible," the investigator replied. "It has been proven irrefutably that the publications of White émigré organizations presented tactical directives for a struggle against the USSR."

(I cite only the dialogue about Tsvetaeva, omitting nothing, and not putting anything in my own words. The leaps in the investigator's logic might cause the reader to suspect an omission. But the record reads exactly this way.)

"I'm not refuting the fact," Efron answered, "that my wife published in the pages of the White émigré press, but she was never engaged in any kind of anti-Soviet political work."

And all this took place during the first interrogation.

The record of the first interrogation in Efron's file is followed by a medical certificate. As a reward for all the torment of patiently explaining his transgressions, Efron was immediately sent to Lefortovo prison. Whereas Maria Belkina managed to locate Ariadna Efron's cellmates and talk to them, the circumstances of Sergei Yakovlevich's stay in prison remain completely unknown. The reputation of the terrible Lefortovo prison is legendary, however. Today much is known about the system of interrogations that was put in practice. In 1938, M. P. Frinovsky, an official in the NKVD's foreign section, testified that,

> the people conducting the investigation . . . began the interrogations by applying physical coercion that would continue until those under investigation consented to an incriminating deposition. The interrogation proceedings and confrontations of suspects often were not arranged until the prisoners had confessed to their own guilt. It became a common practice to include many interrogations in one record, and records were also composed even when no one had been interrogated.[10]

The medical certificate was signed by the head of Lefortovo's medical office, Yanshin, a military doctor of the third rank. He certified that Efron suffered from frequent attacks of angina pectoris or stenocardia ("the heart is enlarged on all sides, with faint heart sounds"), and also a

rare form of neurasthenia. The investigators were given the following practical recommendations: to conduct their "business" during the day, for no
more than three or four hours in a twenty-four-hour period, in a location
with good ventilation and under the daily observation of a doctor.

The certificate was dated 19 October, but the investigative section's
inquiry was made earlier—on the 15th. Evidently, there was a sharp deterioration in the prisoner's condition soon (or immediately) after the first
interrogation.

On 26 October, Kuzminov, the investigator, presented Efron with
the indictment. It states that the arrested man had been "sufficiently
unmasked as one of the leaders of the White Guard 'Eurasian' organization . . . which was actively engaged in subversive work against the USSR.
At the same time he was an agent of one of the foreign services, on whose
orders he was sent to the USSR to carry out subversive espionage work. He
was a secret collaborator of the NKVD but concealed his espionage ties
with foreign intelligence from that agency."

Efron categorically denied the charge that he had acted as a traitor.
His conversation with the investigator this time, if one is to believe the
record, took only twenty minutes.

5

Kuzminov also conducted the next interrogation, on 1 November.
There was no need for more biographical information. The main themes
now were the Eurasians and foreign intelligence and the Eurasians and
their ties with the Trotskyites.

Let us note one important place in Efron's deposition. In the first
interrogation he had named Pyotr Semyonovich Arapov as the leader of
the Eurasians' secret work. Now, on 1 November, giving in to the investigator's demands, Efron confessed that Arapov was actually connected to
Polish, German, and perhaps also to English intelligence. But Arapov *had
done this on the instructions of the GPU* (Main Intelligence Directorate).
Efron said he had heard that explanation from Pyotr Semyonovich's own
lips. This account would not inspire trust were one to find it in others'

depositions. But it seems that Efron did not fabricate stories. His words probably correspond to the facts.

Toward the end of this interrogation another theme arises, one that seemed extremely difficult for Sergei Yakovlevich. It concerned his neighbors at the Bolshevo dacha, the Klepinin-Lvovs. The investigators' office was preparing to arrest them, but they were still free.

We can guess that while pressuring Efron to give incriminating testimony against the Klepinins, the investigators would provoke him with information his own daughter had given during her recent interrogation. Ariadna gave a great deal of specific information about something that possibly didn't seem very criminal to her—"anti-Soviet conversations."

It's unlikely they cited Ariadna at this time. But when specific familiar details, known only to a narrow circle of friends, came up during the investigation, the psychological impact was shocking. Efron might have felt that everyone in the Bolshevo dacha had been arrested, or were about to be.

The second medical examination certificate in Efron's file is dated 20 November; it was forwarded to the investigators' office by Senior Lieutenant of State Security Bizyukov.

The contents are frightening. The certificate states that starting 24 October (two weeks after the arrest) Efron had been placed under the care of a psychiatrist. On 7 November he was put in the psychiatric ward of the hospital in Butyrki prison. (This means that the investigation of 1 November 1939 took place during a period of remission, which was later followed by a new and severe deterioration in the patient's condition.) The certificate indicates that Efron had attempted suicide. He was likely put in the hospital to be kept under close supervision.

Sergei Yakovlevich probably made the suicide attempt soon after the 1 November questioning—a time when he might have keenly sensed the trap into which he had fallen and had dragged others into. Now he was being forced to testify against people for whom he felt responsible.

The information from conversations in the Bolshevo dacha, which clearly came from *inside*, must have been unbearable for him. He understood that these reports constituted a threat for everyone living there, including his wife and son. And what if the investigators told Efron point blank that the evidence was provided by his daughter, whom he had drawn into this terrible mess?

I quote more fully from the text of the medical certificate: "Since 7 November [Efron] has been in the psychiatric ward of the Butyrki prison hospital as a result of severe reactive hallucinosis and attempted suicide. At the present time he displays aural hallucinations: he feels that people are talking about him in the hall, that his wife has died, that he heard the name of a poem that only he and his wife knew, etc. He is disturbed, with suicidal thoughts, is depressed, has unrealistic fears and expects something terrible. His condition (severe emotional disorder) requires treatment in the psychiatric ward of the Butyrki hospital and follow-ups with the psychiatric commission (conclusion of the psychiatrist)."

The document on the patient's condition was signed on 20 November 1939, by a whole multitude of "specialists": doctor-psychiatrist Dovbiya; consultant-psychiatrist Berger from the medical division of the NKVD; Larin, the head of the medical service; Smoltsov, military doctor of the second rank and the head of the commission.

On 20 November the doctors thought that it would take thirty to forty days to treat Efron. However, Kuzminov, who was conducting almost all of the examinations of Efron that fall, ignored these recommendations. On 8 December the prisoner was again taken to the investigator's office, this time to be brought face to face with Tolstoi.

6

In the group of accused who would appear before the Military Tribunal of the Supreme Court of the USSR on 6 July 1941, Pavel Nikolaevich Tolstoi was almost an incidental figure. This in spite of the fact that he had met everyone earlier in Paris, where he had lived since the age of six, and where he had extensive contacts with the most diverse Russian émigré circles. His easy-going temper and sociable character led him first to the Eurasians, then to the Young Russians; he was also well received in the Union for Repatriation and in White Guard circles. He had friends and relatives everywhere. Tolstoi was often at Efron's home; before he left for the USSR in 1933 he was a frequent guest.

Pavel was a distant relative of the writer Alexei Tolstoi, and after he returned to Russia, he lived for about a year in the writer's home in Detskoe Selo near Leningrad. Later Pavel Tolstoi moved to Moscow. As early as 1934 he took up the offer of the secret police to become a collaborator. He shadowed Gayana, the daughter of E. Yu. Skobtsova (Mother Maria), who had come from France and soon disappeared into the Gulag.[11]

Tolstoi was arrested at the end of July 1939. After only a week he began to give the evidence the investigation wanted and needed. He was quickly summoned to face-to-face confrontations with anyone who was resisting. He unmasked his recent friends and acquaintances as participants in whatever was needed—espionage, terrorist schemes, contacts with Trotskyites, anti-Soviet activities.

Tolstoi slandered them confidently and thoroughly, calmly looking in his victims' eyes, at times admonishing them in a condescending tone: "Why be so secretive, you have to answer for your sins." I would not make this claim were it not for the poignant testimony of Tamara Vladimirovna Slanskaya. She told me (and others as well) that precisely because of Tolstoi's unbearable tone and attitude, she grabbed an inkwell from the investigator's table and threw it at the lordly unmasker.

At his face-to-face confrontation with Efron, Tolstoi claimed that Efron had involved him in espionage for French intelligence. On the eve of Tolstoi's departure for the USSR, Efron reportedly gave him the job of establishing contact with Trotskyite organizations in the USSR; Efron also gave him addresses in Moscow and Leningrad to use for making contacts with fellow conspirators. From Leningrad, through Slanskaya, Tolstoi allegedly was sending secret information to Efron in Paris.

Efron's reaction, as recorded, was extremely strong: "I absolutely deny everything Tolstoi has just stated." Further: "Whereas until this moment I thought that Tolstoi's memory had betrayed him, now I must say that what he says is simply a lie."

False testimony, like too good a memory, would not save Tolstoi. In

May 1940 he attempted to refute his testimony. But when summoned to explain, he immediately took back his denial and confirmed everything he had said earlier. When the prosecution invented the "Efron group," they attached Tolstoi to those he had helped to unmask. He became the sixth— clearly a superfluous sixth—and an alien member of the conspirators.

7

The most dramatic episode in Efron's entire case was a confrontation that took place on 30 December 1939. That day (evening and night) in order to break Sergei Yakovlevich's resistance the investigation summoned Efron's closest friends and comrades in France, Nikolai Klepinin and Emiliya Litauer.

The investigation began without witnesses. The investigator took a routine approach: "Tolstoi unmasked you completely during the confrontation. Do you intend to stop denying things now?"

Efron's answer: "I don't consider myself unmasked and I consider Tolstoi's unmasking to be false. I firmly maintain that I never engaged in any kind of espionage activity on behalf of foreign intelligence services."

The same question, put somewhat differently, was repeated several times. But the substance of Efron's answers did not change. Then the investigators brought Nikolai Klepinin into the room. More than a month and a half had passed since his arrest. The Klepinins had been arrested on the same day that Efron had been put in the psychiatric ward of the prison hospital—7 November, the anniversary of the October Revolution.

After the ritual identifications and questions to both sides about their relations with each other, Klepinin repeated the testimony he had been forced to make: yes, he was an agent of *several* foreign intelligence services, and he and Efron had actively carried out espionage work.

"Do you confirm these statements?" the investigator turned to Efron.

"I deny them," Efron answered.

Directed by Kuzminov's questions, Klepinin talked about the newspaper *Eurasia,* in whose publication Efron played a prominent role, and about the fact that the newspaper was meant for distribution in the USSR and intended to "seek out oppositional elements inside the Soviet Union." (This corresponds to historical truth only as concerns the original idea behind the publication; in practice the editors moved far to the left.)

"But none of this in any way speaks of espionage activity," Efron answered.

Next Klepinin brought in the theme of Efron's connections to Russian Masons in Paris, in particular, to Count Bobrinsky, who, Klepinin claimed, was in direct contact with French intelligence. The Masons were interested in infiltrating the territory of the Soviet Union, Klepinin said, and they thought Efron's close ties to the Soviet ambassador in Paris and membership in the Union for Repatriation could be useful.

"What will you say now?" the investigator asked Efron.

"I maintain that Nikolai Andreevich also did not take part in any kind of espionage activity."

The answer clearly was not an answer to the question. And no matter how difficult it is to construct a theory about motives of behavior on the basis of "depositions," still one has the impression that during this meeting Efron was trying to bring his friend to his senses. He wanted to help him resist the pressure of the investigation, to get him to deny the main accusation being prepared against them.

Klepinin again remembered a specific detail, however: a meeting in 1935 in a café near the École Militaire. In Klepinin's presence Efron had written a letter to Pyotr Bobrinsky and they discussed the Masons.

Again Efron avoided a direct response to what was said.

"Is that a fact?" the investigator to Efron.

"I don't understand anything," the record reads. "I only know that I was not engaged in any kind of anti-Soviet activity after 1931."[12]

"Seryozha," Klepinin finally turned to his old friend (I quote this entry verbatim), "I appeal to you again. There's no point in further denials. There are certain things that cannot be combated, because it's useless and criminal. Sooner or later you will confess anyway and you'll say . . ."

During confrontations of suspects usually a stenographer, rather than the investigator, would take down testimony. Later she would transcribe her notes and present a typed copy. Therefore, at confrontations of suspects we are better able to hear the voices of the investigated than in the depositions of other interrogations. The intonations are more natural, contradictions are not glossed over. The records of confrontations also reveal the indignant replies of the person being "unmasked" and the persuasive tone of the other side. These records dispel the contemporary reader's doubts as to the validity of the investigative files of those times.

Klepinin was led away and Emiliya Litauer took his place. Litauer had been arrested on the same day as Ariadna, and she also did not give in right away. Two weeks after her arrest at a confrontation with the same Tolstoi on 10 September 1939, she again stubbornly contradicted the absurd accusations. Now, however, she had just endured four months of ordeals, among them the Lefortovo torture chamber.

When the investigator asked Efron if he knew Emiliya, Sergei Yakovlevich answered, "Yes, she is my comrade and friend."

"Your friend," Kuzminov says, "has also unmasked your espionage activities in her testimony."

Efron's recorded reply: "I would like to hear more precisely what Emiliya Litauer testified about."

Now he would hear the same things from her lips: about their espionage work together, beginning in 1927 when Emiliya joined the Eurasian organization; how spheres of activity were distributed among the Eurasianists after their "break-up" at the end of the twenties. "I was ordered to join the French Communist Party," Litauer said, "and Efron took on espionage work in the Union for Repatriation and in Soviet intelligence."

Efron was clearly overwhelmed. He burst out, "If all my comrades think I'm a spy, including Litauer and Klepinin and my daughter, then, consequently, I'm a spy and I'll sign my name under their depositions."

He asked for a break in the interrogation. His condition is reflected in this surprisingly faithful entry in the record: "Right now I can't talk, I'm very tired."

Litauer was taken away. But the end of the investigation was not in sight: the typewritten record takes up thirty-seven pages. The investigation began at 9:45 P.M. and did not end until 2:30 in the morning.

This double face-to-face confrontation was apparently the investigators' last hope to break the prisoner. The goal now seemed close to completion. There was no doubt about Efron's depressed condition.

"Please postpone the deposition," he repeated several times. He received this answer: "Your request will be granted, but just tell us which intelligence services you worked for."

Efron requested an opportunity to ask a few more questions of Klepinin. The latter was returned to the investigator's office.

"What are you accusing me of?" Efron addressed him. "Tell me directly."

"Of being a member of the Eurasian organization. It had a plan to infiltrate the Soviet Union with the help of foreign intelligence. Svyatopolk-Mirsky came to the USSR in order to secure a position of control in the Soviet press. Bruno Yasensky and his group assigned him to organize the persecution of Fadeev."[13]

"From whom could I have learned about that plan?"

"From Mirsky, from Malevsky-Malevich, from Spalding . . ."

"Which intelligence services did I work for?"

"For several, including the French," Klepinin answered.

"Is it clear to you now?" the investigator asked Efron.

"It's clear to me," Efron's tired answer reads in the record. Perhaps now he understood everything—that no one here needed the truth. Klepinin had already pointed to the general policy of lying—lying in order to survive, as he thought.

"Which intelligence services did you work for then?" The investigator did not stop.

"I can't talk about anything now," Efron repeated.

They led Klepinin away again. Emiliya Litauer was brought into the office. Demoralized and evidently suffering from physical illness, Efron suddenly agreed to a compromise. All right, he had been involved with intelligence services, though indirectly, but he had never been a spy.

Litauer wouldn't let Sergei Yakovlevich quit halfway. She set out a version he could subscribe to. According to this version Efron had given Emiliya a mission before she left France: making use of her profession as a writer, she was to infiltrate Soviet military plants and collect secret information. She also "remembered" that Efron continued to give her instructions when he came to the USSR. It was his idea to take advantage of the fact that the editors of French publications in the USSR had a poor knowledge of French. She, Emiliya, was to "insinuate" anti-Soviet propaganda into these publications. For example, she said, Sergei Yakovlevich thought it necessary to conduct a war against "official optimism."

Only Efron, I think, could have appreciated this last detail, which was seriously included in the record. Emiliya, like Ariadna, was suggesting a mixture of fabrication and truth. For a moment a suspicion occurs: what if the former Eurasians had not completely abandoned their earlier ideas? During the mid twenties, for example, their most important goal was to get existing Soviet organizations to adopt Eurasian programs. There was no need for secret information about military plants.

The investigator demanded that Efron confirm Emiliya's statement. He answered, "I repeat, I am not able to talk about anything."

"When are we to believe you?" the investigator asked, referring to the fact that Efron had already "confessed" to a collaboration with foreign intelligence services.

"Let my friends unmask me," Efron answered. "I can't say anything."

Litauer then repeated almost the very same thing that Klepinin had said several hours earlier.

"I want to give Sergei Yakovlevich urgent advice. Tell the whole truth, don't hide anything about yourself or about your friends. I'm telling you this as a comrade and friend."

The confrontation was suspended in the middle of the night—with few gains for the investigation. But it certainly cleared up much for Efron. He saw that his friends had accepted the investigation's version as inevitable. This version had now been distinctly laid out for him.

The investigators could see that Efron was still not about to slander himself or others. His resolve in face-to-face confrontations would only shake his comrades. The investigation would no longer resort to confrontations with Efron.

8

During the interrogations Klepinin behaved differently from Efron. At first glance it might seem (as it did to the Klepinins' daughter Sofia when she first read the records and was too shaken to analyze them), that Nikolai Klepinin simply could not stand up to the ordeal—that he broke down. His behavior rather resembled something else, however: a well-thought-out line of behavior, devoid of illusions, based on a sober evaluation of the hopeless situation they all were in.

Unlike Efron, Ariadna, and Emiliya, Nikolai Andreevich was not summoned for his first interrogation on the day of the arrest, but only after a week—on 15 November. During this time he evidently had the opportunity to observe and listen to his cellmates, to come to himself, and to think. He no longer had any hope (Efron, it seems, still kept some) that the authorities would listen to him if he told the truth.

Klepinin had renewed his collaboration with the NKVD at the beginning of 1939 (and only later was given work in VOKS). He made some connections there and managed to see enough of what was going on. During his interrogations, at every convenient opportunity he found satisfaction in destroying his secret police colleagues, if only ones who he knew had been arrested and could no longer hurt him. For example, Klepinin said that Shpigelglas, in whose office he had had such strange negotiations in the spring of 1939, had intentionally sabotaged the Lausanne operation by giving extremely stupid instructions to the participants and not providing basic security measures. (In Bolshevo Klepinin and Efron had heard ample details of Reiss's murder from Kondratiev and Smirensky.)

Klepinin also gladly discussed the behavior of the NKVD employees who had come to France in the thirties on assignment: how they squandered state resources, far from the eyes of their bosses, staying in the most expensive hotels, going to the most fashionable Parisian restaurants and traveling everywhere in taxis on completely unofficial business. Klepinin didn't trust the investigators one bit. He also didn't try to out-maneuver them. He behaved as if he no longer had hope that he would be saved and was just trying to protect himself and his comrades from unnecessary suffering. (Needless to say, he did not escape that. One of Klepinina's cellmates later told Klepinina's son that during her interrogation Klepinina could hear the moans of her husband, who was being tortured on the other side of the wall.)

At his confrontations with prisoners, Nikolai Andreevich first persuaded Emiliya and later Nina Nikolaevna, who had resisted for a long time, to follow his line of behavior. He told them the same thing he told Efron: there are situations in which resistance is useless. No one will believe our denial. Sooner or later you will have to "confess." He found ways to say this that were suitable for the investigator's ears, and finally "his people" understood him. During their last interrogations his wife and Emiliya behaved exactly that way.

Klepinin practically instructed them during the confrontations about how to speak and what should be said while straying into the traps of fabrication. His prescription was simple: anyone who collaborated with the Soviet secret police abroad should be named an agent of foreign intelligence.

It was as simple as that. And everyone would be happy. He had discovered a formula that was acceptable to the investigators and that his own friends were eventually able to understand. The details that were endlessly demanded from the prisoners could be exaggerated as much as one liked, especially when the topic concerned Russians who had stayed in France.

Efron remained unyielding in the face of Klepinin's arguments, however.

From two different sources came a rumor that Efron had been taken to Beria's office and that their "conversation" was extremely stormy. While in prison camp, Alexei Eisner heard that Efron had behaved in such an unruly manner at this meeting that he was shot right in the office by one of the People's Commissar's guards.

Ariadna Sergeevna was the author of the other version. She claimed that when she was at the military prosecutor's office, the prosecutor, handing her a document about her father's rehabilitation, said, "Your father was a courageous man. He dared to dispute the charge against him in the presence of Beria himself. And he paid for that by being shot within the walls of the Lubyanka."

But Efron was not shot until 16 October 1941. At least, we know that to be true now.

All the same there's no smoke without fire. Efron probably was taken to Beria's office: the arrested man's stubbornness combined with the hopes they had placed on him as a witness (more about this later), makes such an assumption quite realistic. Since there is no reliable testimony about how such a meeting could have taken place, it seems appropriate to cite a similar episode from the memoirs of Evgeny Gnedin, head of the People's Commissariat of Foreign Affairs Press Department. He was arrested at almost the same time as Efron (May 1939), was also in Lefortovo, and then in Sukhanov prison; their sentences were handed out a day apart.

The investigators had extracted false evidence from Gnedin against Maxim Litvinov;[14] they were pressuring Efron to agree to the story that a large group of repatriates were involved in espionage and had connections to Trotskyite terrorists. Had Efron yielded, the fates of many repatriates would certainly have been affected in the worst way. Gnedin survived, however, and wrote his memoirs. If you look through them you will see clearly how distorted is the information in the interrogation records. There is no mention there of legs swollen from many hours of standing, the blinding bright lights directed at the eyes, slaps in the face and socks in the jaw, the humiliating verbal abuse, the terrible howls from the other side of the wall that could not be drowned out even by the wind tunnel that roared day and night in the Lefortovo prison yard. Gnedin's memoir, *Not to Lose Oneself,* helps us imagine that office of all-powerful "nonhumans," to whose hearts Marina Tsvetaeva would later appeal in a letter.

Gnedin had to go to Beria's office three times. In the presence of the people's commissar, acting on his special orders, two assistants (one of them was Kobulov, the head of the investigative department) set to beating the prisoner, first with blows to the head, then with rubber truncheons on the heels. He was hardly able to protest his innocence to Beria. The butchers then threw the prisoner into a cold cell with a stone floor. After a while they dragged him back into the same office. "When they sent me off a second time to the cold cell, I lost my sense of time," Gnedin writes.

> I couldn't determine, either right after the torture stopped, or later while calmly reflecting on it, how long the first series of torture lasted: three, four, five days and nights? I remember that when I first returned to the cell for a short time I was astonished to learn that days had passed. It was during the morning "toilet" of the prisoners. A former colonel, looking me over (and the torture was still far from finished), said, "I wouldn't be able to endure half of that!" I'm afraid that his familiarity with my experience had crippled his resolve."[15]

CHAPTER 3

"IN THE BEDLAM
OF NONHUMANS"

1

After Nikolai Klepinin's arrest, Tsvetaeva and her son left Bolshevo and moved into a tiny anteroom at Elizaveta Yakovlevna Efron's home in Moscow. But in December, thanks to Pasternak's efforts, they were able to move to Golitsyno, near Moscow, and settled in a house belonging to the Union of Writers.

They spent the winter and spring of 1939-1940 there, a time marked by fear and Marina's concentrated work on translations. Since her daughter and husband's arrest she was left with absolutely no means for living. Now she also had to find money for parcels to be sent to Sergei and Alya in prison. Tsvetaeva made up parcels every week: each could receive two a month. Only when the parcel was accepted could she be reassured that he or she was still alive.

The letter that Tsvetaeva sent to L. P. Beria, the People's Commissar of Internal Affairs, is dated 23 December. Very possibly a similar letter was sent to Stalin. The variants preserved in the poet's archive reveal the agonizing work of composing the text. Paragraphs and sentences were written down and then crossed out. Marina Ivanovna tried to shield her husband by recalling her father's contributions to Russian culture and the revolutionary past of her husband's mother, Elizaveta Durnovo-Efron. She added her own testimony about Sergei Yakovlevich's sacred faith in the path the Soviet state had taken. The letter points out Efron's inborn qualities: nobility, unselfishness, an incapacity for duplicity. "I swear as a witness," Tsvetaeva wrote, "this man *loved* the Soviet Union and the idea of communism *more than life.*"

Tsvetaeva's letters always have an intimate, confiding tone, no matter to whom they are addressed—that is their most characteristic feature. Even her letter to the executioner did not break this tradition. (See her letter to Stalin in the Appendix). What a multitude of illusions and hopes she must still have had—after all the drafts and variants—to settle on *such* an attempt at defense, *such* a tone.

Evil senses evil from far away: a scoundrel knows in his gut that the world is full of scoundrels pretending to be virtuous; a thief is certain that everyone steals and that some are caught and some do the catching. Marina Tsvetaeva, who wrote the narrative poem *The Swain* and articles about the rebel leader Pugachev, stubbornly believed, in spite of all the apparent facts, that the most inveterate scoundrel still had a heart. It had not entered her mind, apparently, that her addressee was one of the *nonhumans* that she did know to exist. She knew, because in the spring of 1939 she had written these lines:

> In the Bedlam of nonhumans
> I refuse—to live.

When nonhumans suddenly intrude in your life, it's almost impossible to believe it's happening. One's consciousness refuses to accept a sudden personal catastrophe. In any case, when she wrote these letters, Marina still seems to have hoped that her husband had been slandered and that the authorities had believed the lies. She counted on the tiniest part of the vampire's heart—perhaps it was capable of responding to a confiding voice.[1]

She hoped to lead the Minotaur out of the refuge of evil along a "thread of good," if only for a moment. If only for the sake of a single good deed. . . . In December 1939, a terrible year for her, she still believed. Perhaps she had a glimmer of crazy faith because, at the time of her letter, she knew from Pasternak that several years earlier a similar letter that Anna Akhmatova had written *had* helped. Akhmatova's husband and son were freed almost immediately. (They were later rearrested, but that was a different matter.)

(How did Tsvetaeva escape the fate of a "wife of an enemy of the people"? Who can answer?[2] Soviet practice attests only to the fact that there were no rules in this matter, as in many others. From Efron's closest circle the wives of Afanasov and Shukhaev had already been arrested. Marina must have known about this. Since 1937 in Mordovia, in Potma, a special division had existed in the camp for "members of the family" of repressed "enemies of the people." At the higher levels everyone was considered a potential avenger for his or her dear ones.)

Later Tsvetaeva would remember the terrible fear she felt almost every night in Golitsyno from the expectation of arrest—there was an almost absolute certainty it would eventually occur. Among all the people who had lived in the Bolshevo house only she and Mur remained free.

Tsvetaeva had good reason to be worried. Each of the prisoners from the Bolshevo house was certainly questioned about her.

On 7 January 1940, Klepinin was called in for another interrogation. He was questioned *only* about Marina Ivanovna. Usually prisoners were asked about several individuals, since material was needed for new arrests or to pressure those already in custody. But that day Klepinin was not asked about anyone else. The interrogation probably came in reaction to Marina's letter in defense of her husband, which had gone directly to the secret police. It was exactly two weeks since she had written it, the ideal time to take an interest in the author.

Klepinin said that he had known Tsvetaeva since early 1927. They had become good friends later, in the mid thirties, when Klepinin was constantly at the Efrons' apartment and Efron and Tsvetaeva would visit the Klepinins. (Nikolai Andreevich maneuvered between Scylla and

Charybdis with all his might: he clearly wanted to defend Tsvetaeva but also to sustain the investigator's belief that he, Klepinin, was disclosing everything.)

His recorded testimony reads:

> Tsvetaeva was a very original person. All of her interests were concentrated on literature. In addition, she was an extremely unconventional individual and by nature not a social being. She often said that she would have liked to live a hundred or two hundred years ago because she found everything contemporary to be alien and unpleasant.
>
> . . . Her political beliefs? It's very hard to answer that question. She usually contradicts the person she's speaking to at the moment. When speaking with White émigrés, she would repeatedly express pro-Soviet views, but with Soviet people she would defend the White émigrés.
>
> The whole system of the USSR and communism is alien to her. She said that she came here from France only because her daughter and husband were here, that she was hostile to the USSR, that she would never be able to adjust to Soviet life. She often had conversations of this sort. They should not be taken to mean that she was critical of a certain aspect of life in the USSR, but rather that the whole Soviet system, its ideology, and its spirit, were unacceptable to her and she would never be able to adjust. Although at the same time she never indicated what political and social system she would prefer.
>
> In connection with her sister's arrest, and later with her daughter and husband's arrest, her dissatisfaction took on a more specific character. She said that the arrests were unjust.
>
> As far as I know, she was completely ignorant of her husband's espionage and anti-Soviet activities, and he, again, as far as I know from his words, never let her know.
>
> [Who was she acquainted with before she arrived in the USSR?]
>
> Her contacts in France were so extensive that it's hard for me to name them all.

Klepinin was questioned two more times about Tsvetaeva: on 19

February and again on 4 July 1940.[3] Both times the interrogators persistently asked about Marina Ivanovna's circle of acquaintances—both in France and after her return to Russia. Klepinin clearly answered very cautiously. In his replies he drew psychological profiles, which allowed him to advance his own line. In essence, it was a line of defense.

Quite to the point, Nikolai Andreevich informed the investigator of Tsvetaeva's difficult character, which had caused her to quarrel long ago, for example, with D.S. Mirsky (he had been arrested by now). Klepinin stressed the fact that Efron's circle of friends was completely unlike his wife's. They socialized with completely different groups of Russian émigrés. Klepinin was convinced that the wife had no knowledge of her husband's real business.

Of the Soviet writers who came to Paris and met with Tsvetaeva, the only ones mentioned were Vladimir Mayakovsky, Pasternak, and Alexei Tolstoi. Isaac Babel and Boris Pilnyak might have been included, but they had been arrested by then. Among Marina Ivanovna's friends in France, Klepinin mentioned the politically neutral names of Vladislav Khodasevich, the Remizovs, Balmont, Volkonsky, Alla Golovina, Anna Ilinichna Andreeva, and her sons. None of these was in Soviet Russia.

Incidentally, Nikolai Andreevich maintained the same line with regard to other people. In answer to a question about the precise nature of his own wife's work after her return, Klepinin claimed that the NKVD had failed to give Nina Nikolaevna any interesting assignments and for that reason she was extremely hurt. In order not to injure her pride, Nikolai Andreevich had stopped questioning her. Therefore he didn't know her real business. When he was asked about Efron's specific activities, Klepinin complained about Sergei Yakovlevich's "secrecy mania." Efron was always playing games—it was simply ridiculous, according to the interrogation report.

Klepinin could not seriously protect Efron, however, because the version he had agreed to during his first interrogation could not hold up without the figure of a leader. The investigators had created this version with the obvious help of P. N. Tolstoi, though it might also have originated during the interrogations of D. S. Mirsky, or Romanchenko, or some earlier prisoner.

In any case, Klepinin did not resist what they thrust on him. He agreed to admit he was a French spy even during the first investigation. By the end of the second one he admitted that he was also an agent of English and Belgian intelligence. The Eurasians had joined with the Trotskyites and were agents of foreign intelligence services. Over time Klepinin even began to embellish this nonsense with a multitude of details. He said that in 1928 the Eurasians had made a plan to infiltrate the leading circles of a wide range of public institutions in the USSR and then to spy on behalf of foreign states. To sabotage and "undermine the foundations."

During his interrogation of 19 February 1940, Klepinin noted that as a prominent Eurasianist Efron had managed to gather a sizeable group of important people around him—Tolstoi, Smirensky, Larin, Balter, Tveritinov, Poznyakov, Struve, Paleolog, Eisner—over twenty people. In the thirties "the transfer" of cadres to the USSR allegedly intensified. After arriving, their first task was to get closer to journalistic circles, writers, and the military. But the entire plan failed, Klepinin claimed, owing to the NKVD's short-sighted leadership: they arrested people they would have been better off following. Nikolai Andreevich, may his soul rest in peace, was no fool. By then the NKVD leaders he denounced were already his neighbors in jail.

2

At the very end of January 1940 came the arrest of Nikolai Vanifatevich Afanasov, who had returned to the USSR in 1936. He was the last participant in the "group" that would stand before the Military Tribunal of the Supreme Court, united by a common charge and common sentence. On 29 January Afanasov was taken in a NKVD car straight from his work in Kaluga, and his family found out only much later where he had gone.

Afanasov was from the circle of Efron's old friends. As a young man he joined the Volunteer Army; after the Whites were defeated, he lived in

Bulgaria, working as a miner and a lumberman, and then moved to France. When the newspaper *Eurasia* began publication, he was in charge of distribution. He lived for some time in the editorial premises in Clamart, a suburb of Paris.

Like Efron and the Klepinins, Afanasov became a secret collaborator with Soviet intelligence in Paris. In the mid thirties he went on a special mission to Germany under the name Klaus. That now turned out to be enough to charge him with spying on behalf of German intelligence. Somewhere he had crossed paths with the prominent Russian émigré writer Roman Gul, and this qualified as the passing of secret information to the Gestapo. Afanasov's name surfaces in a clearly compromising context in the depositions of Litauer and Klepinin. Later, during the court session of the Military Tribunal, Afanasov would try to refute their testimony.

Efron was asked about Afanasov in March. As in other cases, Sergei Yakovlevich gave a dry, factual résumé, emphasizing Afanasov's past experience as a "worker."

"With what goal did he come to the Soviet Union?" the investigator asked.

"The goal of working in the homeland," Efron answered.

Unfortunately I was not able to study the case against Afanasov. He did not confess his guilt in court, however, and apparently, the prosecution did not break him.

One and a half months passed between the face-to-face confrontations with Klepinin and Litauer and the next time Efron was summoned for questioning.

How was this time spent? Illness? A new round of torture? Or was the investigation simply busy with others? We will not know. But on the deposition of 15 February Efron's signature looks terrible, almost unrecognizable. It seems to have been written with a barely grasped pen. But the statements are the same.

"Perhaps you will begin to testify? Your accomplices have already unmasked you completely."

Efron's answer:

"After 1931 I did not engage in any anti-Soviet activity. In my work I was involved with Soviet institutions and my work was of a strictly clandestine nature."

"The nature of your clandestine work with Soviet institutions does not interest the investigation," the record reads. "Tell us what you kept hidden from Soviet institutions."

"There was nothing of the sort. As a secret agent I was controlled by those individuals who were in charge of secret work abroad."

The prisoner's last sentence renders his physical indisposition: "Please stop the interrogation, because I am ill."

3

Let us note an obvious fact: the investigation clearly avoided Efron's story about his *actual* activities in the Soviet secret service in France.

There's nothing strange in that: Beria's colleagues had no more interest in the truth than the secret police had in Yezhov and Yagoda's days. Still, it's disappointing: it would have been such a valuable source for the specifics of Efron's secret work and the story of Ignace Reiss's murder. Sergei Yakovlevich was relatively candid, at least with regard to his own activities. He did not fabricate versions or juggle with facts—at most he avoided specific details.

A number of articles and even books have been devoted to the Reiss affair; in them appear many conjectures and much confusion. Only now, more than half a century later, have the real circumstances surrounding that murder become clear. A brief account follows.

After Yagoda's arrest in April 1937, the employees of the NKVD were purged on a mass scale. Yezhov was replacing the regular personnel by liquidating "Yagoda's spies" in the NKVD ranks. This policy was also applied to agents working abroad.

By the summer of 1937 approximately forty such agents had been called back to Moscow from Europe. Five refused to return, however, realizing that that meant death or—in the best case—prison. One of the five wrote an irate letter on 14 July 1937 to the Central Committee of the Bolshevik Party in Moscow. In it he declared his resolution to break with Stalin's regime, which had become stained by the murder of people devoted to the cause of the revolution.

The author of that letter was Ignace Poretsky, but his colleagues knew him as Reiss or Ludwig (secret police agents always lived and worked under code names). A Polish communist and experienced spy, Reiss had received his last assignment precisely during the summer of 1937: he became an NKVD agent in France. By this time, however, he already knew too much about what was taking place in Moscow. And he did not want to turn up obediently and face certain punishment.

"I have struggled together with you," Reiss wrote to the Central Committee,

> but not a step further. Our paths diverge. Whoever remains silent now becomes an accomplice of Stalin and a traitor to the cause of the working class and socialism. . . . The day is near when the court of international socialism will try all the crimes of the last ten years. Nothing will be forgiven. . . . There will be a public trial with witnesses—many witnesses—both living and dead; they will all speak again, but this time they will tell the truth, the whole truth. All of them will appear—the innocent who have been killed and those who have been slandered— and the international workers' movement will rehabilitate them, all the Kamenevs and Mrachkovskys, the Smirnovs and Muralovs, Drobnises and Serebryakovs, Mdivanis and Okudzhavas, Pakovskys and Nins,—all those "spies and diversionists, Gestapo agents and saboteurs." . . . I cannot go on. I am taking back my freedom. Back to Lenin, to his teaching and his cause.

The letter that Reiss handed in to be sent to Moscow was not dispatched anywhere, but opened immediately in the Paris office of the NKVD. This was during the same period when S. M. Shpigelglas, a major official in the NKVD's foreign section, had come to Paris in order to prepare the purge in the ranks of his colleagues working abroad. From the moment the letter was opened, a group of NKVD agents began a special operation. Two key NKVD terrorists joined the group—Boris Afanasiev and Viktor Pravdin. They used Monacan citizenship as a cover; in their passports they appeared as François Rossi and Charles Martignat. The group of pursuers also included a Swiss national, Renata Steiner; a Frenchman, Jean-Pierre Ducomet; and the Russian émigrés Dimitry Smirensky and Vadim Kondratiev.

The assassination of Reiss was not exceptional: political murders abroad began as early as 1926, when Symon Petliura was killed in Paris. Half a year before Reiss was murdered, the émigré Navashin, who refused to return to the USSR, was killed in the Bois de Boulogne; likewise, another "defector," Agabekov, was murdered several months later in Belgium. In the case of Reiss, however, the work was done too sloppily. The police succeeded in arresting a number of participants in the murder and during the interrogations the names of employees of the Soviet embassy in Paris were mentioned.

In Efron's records the episode of Reiss's murder came up only once. On 29 March 1940 (the eleventh investigation) the prisoner was asked about Dimitry Smirensky. Efron spoke about him as someone who took part in the preliminary preparation of the "Reiss affair" but not in the murder itself.

"How do you know that?" the investigator asked.

"From people who were directly or indirectly involved in the affair," Efron replied. "From the Klepinins, Kondratiev, from Smirensky himself."

Either they didn't ask further questions or they did not record them. Efron was true to himself: in such circumstances he answered without giving details.

In this light Klepinin's depositions are extremely interesting. Practically from the first interrogation he spoke freely about his "traitorous spy work," about treachery, double dealing, and all the rest—using the verbiage the investigator suggested to him as a rule. But with regard to the "Reiss affair" Klepinin stubbornly repeated that neither he nor Efron had any direct connection to the Lausanne operation. Efron had been given "another job" half a year earlier, and Klepinin, in his own words, had learned about Reiss's murder from newspapers in Lyons. However, Vadim Kondratiev, who had joined the group pursuing Reiss, appeared at the Klepinins' home just several days after the operation—before he disappeared from France for good. That threw a shadow on the Klepinins, who were related to Kondratiev. And Efron's ties to the Soviet ambassador were widely known. Thus, they both came under the surveillance of the French police.

Another month passed before Efron and Klepinin both received an order from their "secret" boss to leave immediately for Le Havre and board the steamship *Andrei Zhdanov*, on which they would leave France forever. The order, given by Grozovsky, was issued through an intermediary and was not open to discussion. Meanwhile, Klepinin claimed, the very haste of their "evacuation" was a stupid mistake. The Soviet secret service thereby acknowledged its direct participation both in the murder of Reiss and in the kidnapping of General Miller. On the other hand, Klepinin said, their escape, which received much publicity, was a clear source of satisfaction to the French police. They could now loudly assure the public that they had done everything possible: the real murderers had been discovered, but—alas!—they had simply disappeared. The case could be closed—or at least the process of finding out who was guilty. Such was Klepinin's testimony.

For those who truly wish to sort out "who is who" or "who did what," Klepinin's statements are extremely important. Why would Klepinin have invented things about the Reiss matter now? His testimony, repeated several times in his records, contains the true story behind the charge that stuck to Efron (and the Klepinins) for more than half a century. It was convenient not only for the French police, but for the Soviet secret services to present Efron as more or less the main culprit behind the Swiss murder: the police were able to show they had quickly completed the investigation, and Soviet intelligence concealed the real organizers and perpetrators of the crime.

In the 1970s three people who were personally close to Sergei Efron absolutely insisted that Efron's role was very different from the official version spread by the foreign press. Their statements might be considered subjective, but let's give the three a chance to speak.

First, the words of Efron's daughter, spoken to me personally: Reiss's murder came as a surprise to Sergei Yakovlevich. He was sure, Ariadna Sergeevna asserted, that the defector would be taken to Moscow to stand trial before a Soviet court.

Second, Efron's own words: "They dragged me into a dirty business. . . ." These words were reported to me in the 1980s in a letter from Vera Traill, whom we mentioned earlier, a close friend of Efron's and, like him, a collaborator with the Soviet secret police. According to Traill, Efron had told her that when they met in Paris soon after the murder.

Finally, Elizaveta Yakovlevna Efron passed on these words of her brother: "I had to take the blame for others." Efron's complete trust in his sister is well known.

Tsvetaeva had to give depositions at the police headquarters in Paris twice: on 22 October 1937 and again, several weeks later, on 27 November 1937.

The first investigation was especially long—from morning to evening. Yet the protocol of the proceedings conducted by the examining magistrate, Monsieur Beteille, is not lengthy. Tsvetaeva was shown photographs of different individuals; she was asked about her husband's official work and his political views. She identified Efron as a journalist who published regularly in *Our Union*, the journal of the Union of Repatriation. Her husband had gone to work there every day for several years in a row, Tsvetaeva claimed. His views had changed greatly since the time Efron had served in the White Army: they were already "becoming leftist" when he lived in Czechoslovakia. She added that she thought her husband "had become a supporter of the Russian regime" two to three years earlier.

Among the photographs Tsvetaeva was shown, she recognized Vadim Kondratiev, whom she had met at the home of their acquaintances, the Klepinins. She also recognized Poznyakov, her husband's fellow student at the gymnasium, who had photographed her son several times. She was also asked about others—Smirensky, Chistoganov, Steiner, Ducomet. She didn't know them. Yes, she had heard about Reiss's murder. That act had made both her and her husband angry, Tsvetaeva said, since "we both condemn violence, no matter from which side it emerges." She corroborated Efron's alibi: from 12 August until 12 September, he was continuously with her and their son in the south of France in Lacanau-Océan at Villa "Coup de Roulis."

Tsvetaeva was shown telegrams sent from Paris to Lausanne during that time and addressed to Kondratiev. She was asked to identify the hand-writing. One was signed "Mikhail" and Marina was asked if she knew who that was. She answered that she knew one Mikhail, the son of the owner of a pension in Haute-Savoie where their family often spent the summer. His last name was Shtrange (Strangue, in its French spelling).

The police archives from those years confirm the following: under interrogation Steiner, Smirensky, and Ducomet said that during the sum-mer of 1937 they were put under the command of a Mikhail, whose last name they did not know, although they had met him. The police now turned to Tsvetaeva with this question, since these three agents had all received assignments from Efron. However, all three—independently of each other—had provided descriptions of "Mikhail" that clearly did not fit Sergei Yakovlevich: "a rather sturdy build, a height of approximately 175 centimeters, clean-shaven—that is, without a beard. He wore a felt hat, appeared to be educated, and spoke French and Russian, though his Russian was not pure."

The Swiss historian Peter Huber, who worked in the police archives at the Hoover Institution at Stanford University in 1990, was inclined to think that the description precisely fit Mikhail Strangue.[4] Strangue, who safely returned to the Soviet Union after World War II, in Huber's opinion, could have been the coordinator of the group that was formed to follow and kill Reiss. But that is only an assumption. In the photos of Strangue that have been preserved, he appears as a squat man, and according to the testimony of those who knew him in his Soviet period, his Russian was absolutely pure—without the slightest accent. The infor-mation gathered later during the investigation of Efron in Moscow only confirmed the fact that Sergei Yakovlevich had recruited Mikhail Strangue to work for Soviet intelligence.

The recently published memoirs of Pavel Sudoplatov, the retired KGB general, also reject the charge against Sergei Efron in the Reiss murder. Sudoplatov personally knew Reiss's real killers, Boris Afanasiev and Viktor Pravdin. Moreover, he met with them in Moscow right after the operation was completed. He reports that Afanasiev was rewarded with a respectable position in the intelligence directorate, and Pravdin was fixed up with work in the Foreign Literature Publishing House, where he worked until his death in 1970. Pravdin's mother, who lived in Paris, also received financial compensation.

"Claims that Sergei Efron, the husband of the famous Russian poet Marina Tsvetayeva, was involved in betraying Reiss to the NKVD are false," Sudoplatov writes. "Efron, who did work for the NKVD in Paris, had no idea of Reiss's whereabouts."[5]

Let us consider one more document here, perhaps, the most important one—a memorandum that was found in Efron's file. It was composed in connection with Ariadna's request for her father's rehabilitation and prepared with material from the KGB's secret archive. Among other things, the memorandum states that in France, Sergei Efron "was utilized as a group leader and a recruiter." It notes Efron's participation in the Eurasian movement, his membership in the Masonic lodge Gamayun (on a job for Soviet intelligence), and a request to be sent to the war in Spain that was turned down by his superiors. The memorandum was intended strictly for internal NKVD use. It contains not a word about Efron's participation in the Lausanne event.

4

During the second half of the thirties the NKVD's aims and methods of inquiry were determined by a cruel standard that bore no relation at all to the arrested person's real situation. As a rule, the accusations had practically no connection to the reasons for detention. The nature of the charge was dictated by "state" considerations that almost completely ignored the specific individual and his or her biography.

The "state" plan (on the level of Beria and Stalin) regarding Efron and his comrades most likely had to do with the hope of organizing yet another noisy political trial. As is known, the NKVD had already tried to charge Rykov and Bukharin with criminal links to the Russian emigration in Paris, and Pyatakov had been incriminated by a link to Trotsky and Trotskyites abroad.

How tempting it would have been to continue this theme. Stalin and Beria viewed the former émigrés who had returned to the Soviet Union as soiled by their participation in the Eurasian movement and especially by such a trump card as the fact that one or several of the movement's leaders had met with Pyatakov himself—wasn't that a catch and good luck? It wouldn't have made sense to release them. They were such good material for another show trial.

It was natural that Efron should appear as the head of the "criminal group" of émigrés ("who were sent to the USSR by foreign intelligence services and acted here in close collaboration with Trotskyites still on the loose"). His role as organizer, including the permission he received from the Soviet embassy in Paris to go to the Soviet Union, were outlined in sufficient detail during all interrogations.

Using well-tried methods, the investigation continued to expand its incriminating material on Efron. With the help of P. N. Tolstoi it fabricated links between Efron and a circle of the Leningrad intelligentsia that was dissatisfied with Stalin's regime and supposedly had planned a terrorist act against the leader. They wrung "confessions" from three Leningraders who were arrested on the basis of Tolstoi's slander (A. V. Vvedensky, Ya. I. and A. Ya. Strelkov), and these confessions confirmed the criminal plans. However, in addition to these plans, there was talk about intelligence information that Efron supposedly was forwarding from Leningrad to Paris through T. V. Slanskaya, a worker at the Leningrad seaport. Slanskaya denied this charge during her interrogations as pure fantasy on Tolstoi's part.

The nature of Efron's interrogations changed after February. By this time the investigation probably had lost hope of obtaining the self-incrimination they wanted. The scenario for a new show trial fell through: in any case, Efron was clearly not suited to play the role of a sincerely repentant ringleader of a "band of émigré spies and Trotskyites." After February he was basically questioned about specific individuals. The investigator named one after another of the repatriated émigrés, demanding information about their anti-Soviet views and activities. Most had already been arrested.

The testimony that Efron gave was as cautious as possible and unfailingly well intended. It was exclusively factual information: the history of an acquaintance, the biographical data he knew. At each convenient opportunity he underscored the pro-Soviet inclinations of the individuals and their pure desire to return to the homeland.

On 2 April the investigators proposed that Efron list everyone he had personally recruited for clandestine work in the Soviet secret services abroad. Efron cited a long list—of twenty-four families—with the specific dates on which they were recruited. Among the first were Konstantin Rodzevich and his wife Maria Sergeevna, the Klepinins, and Vera Suvchinskaya (Traill).[6] They all had been Eurasianists and Efron's personal friends. Most of those recruited, he indicated, maintained their connection to the representatives of the Soviet secret police through him, Efron, and only a few found a connection of their own.

In this interrogation he gave the names of the employees of the NKVD in Paris to whom he was directly subordinate: above all, Kislov, and, in addition, Zhdanov, Azarian, and G. I. Smirnov. It's hard to say if these were their real names or code names.

"Inform us of whom you recruited for French intelligence," Lieutenant Kopylov asked Efron.

"I never recruited anyone for any foreign intelligence service," Efron answered.

"You're lying. The investigation has at its disposal sufficient materials that refute your claim."

The recorded part of the interrogation breaks off here.

In Efron's file there are eighteen interrogations, but we can be certain there were more. We know that investigation records were not made in many instances. Even the complete publication of all the records would not give a realistic picture of what took place within the walls of Soviet prisons of that time; in fact, it might even distort it. Too many important and terrible things remained offscreen.

The last record, the eighteenth, is dated 5 July 1940. On 13 July the final charge was filed, approved by Deputy Military Procurator Afanasiev.

Why was the sentencing delayed for a whole year? It's hard to find an answer. The sentence was pronounced only on 6 July 1941, a little more than three weeks after the war began. Of course, they were also working overtime at the Lubyanka in 1940-1941, although the work had slowed down a little.

Did the investigation search for someone to replace Efron in the role of leader? If they had given up their plan, why did they continue to keep him in Moscow?

In the spring of 1941 Tsvetaeva was asked to bring things for her husband's transit. She handed them in. But why was this request made if his sentence had still not been pronounced? Many things are not clear.

We will return to the day of sentencing.[7]

5

It is incomparably more difficult to determine what is truthful in Ariadna Efron's testimony than in her father's. After the ill-starred interrogation of 27 September she took up the investigators' suggestion of "a version for survival" (like a great many of those who turned up in the NKVD's torture chambers). This decision compelled her, like others, to mix reality thickly with fantasy, not only regarding her own biography, but in descriptions of the people she was questioned about. It's not for us, who have been made wiser by all we know, to now condemn this twenty-seven-year-old young woman. But all the same let me relate the impression that arose as I read Ariadna's case.

This impression concerns illusions that Efron's daughter had grown quite accustomed to in her youth and that prompted her return to the

Soviet Union in the spring of 1937, earlier than the other family members. She so strongly believed in the "great experiment" her native land was undertaking in order to create the most just society on earth that she could not free herself from that vision. The illusions kept their hold on her even when she found herself caught up in the relentless investigation machine.

The example of her father likely played a decisive role. From early on she saw him as the model of chivalry, courage, and nobility, practically identified (in the years when he participated in the White movement) with the icon of Saint George, who had battled the evil dragon. A cult of her father developed; he ruled in their home—and in her mother's verse during the Civil War. Its power continued in emigration.

The daughter *could not but believe* in what her father believed; for her it was more than the authority of truth—it was the authority of a *pure heart*. Alya was witness to his enthusiasm and unselfishness; she had been raised on them, and clearly considered herself his comrade-in-arms.

Efron's undercover collaboration with Soviet agents in Paris was no secret for her. At some point he had informed Alya about his special mission with the Union for Repatriation in Paris. And he helped her to become involved—to unite the new generation of Russian émigrés under the Union's auspices. This was a source of pride for the daughter—a feeling that lasted until she died. Her father's collaboration was secret and thus dangerous, and it was noble to participate in something dangerous as long as it was dedicated to a high ideal. She never thought to question the greatness of the idea that inspired her father. Precisely for that reason she thought that what happened in 1940 was a horrible mistake, but only an individual instance.

"I could not understand for whom and for what reason this was necessary," A. S. Efron wrote in a petition she sent from Turukhansk to Minister of the Interior Kruglov fifteen years later. "Only the unmasking of Beria gave me an answer . . ." (Alas, this is the voice of an absolutely ordinary person of the thirties, so eager to grab at an instance of "sabotage." Although it might also be a prisoner's absolutely conscious gamble on the unmasking of the latest enemy.)

There has been little discussion about the destructive influence that the cultivated obsession with saboteurs exerted on the morals and psyches of contemporaries. A morbid suspiciousness began to corrode human ties. I recall this because elsewhere in her writings Ariadna Efron exhibits signs of the displacement of values that Stalinism instilled into people's consciousness. At times, for example, Efron's daughter seems to have been sincerely convinced that Soviet people who criticized the country did pose a real danger.[8]

I draw attention again to one important detail the reader might have missed. Today we utter the words "GPU agent" and "NKVD agent" with a contempt that demands no explanation. They signify participation in the bloody crimes of a sinister organization—inside the country and abroad. But on Ariadna's lips, and on her father's, on the lips of Afanasov, the Klepinins, and Emiliya Litauer "intelligence agent" (*razvedchik*) meant something else. If we want to understand the tragedy of émigrés caught in the net of "collaboration," we must take that into account—in order not to mix the deceived with the scoundrels. To learn certain lessons from history one needs to reject a black and white picture of the world and rash denunciations. Those are also the heritage of Bolshevism.

6

A special, closed session of the Military Tribunal of the Supreme Court of the USSR weighed the charges against Efron, Klepinin, Klepinina, Litauer, Afanasov, and Tolstoi on 6 July 1941. Bukhanov, a military lawyer of the first rank, presided.

The prosecution "established" the following: the accused had participated in the White Guard organization Eurasia, which planned to become the center of all anti-Soviet elements abroad and in the USSR and to overthrow the existing regime in the Soviet Union; Eurasia kept contacts with intelligence agents from other foreign states in order to get their help in sending counterrevolutionary literature and emissaries to the Soviet Union; in 1929, through Pyatakov and Sokolnikov, Eurasia established ties to the Trotskyite underground and conducted criminal activities together with the Trotskyites. Finally, the members of Eurasia had gained the confidence of the NKVD organs in Paris in order to penetrate the USSR with the help of the latter and to carry out espionage and terrorist work there.

Only Klepinin and Litauer acknowledged their guilt during the court session. Efron and Klepinina admitted their participation in the Eurasian organization but categorically denied any connections with or work for foreign intelligence. Tolstoi did not admit to any charges and disclaimed all the testimony he gave during the preliminary investigation. Afanasov strongly denied all the charges.

Efron's last statement was entered in the records of the judicial session: "I was not a spy. I was an honest agent of Soviet intelligence. I know only that from 1931 on all my activities were designed to benefit the Soviet Union."

All six of the accused received the same sentence: capital punishment. An addendum was included: "The sentence is final and not subject to appeal."

In Efron's investigation file, following the minutes of the court session there is a pencil mark at the bottom of the page. The mark indicates the sentence was carried out: for N. V. Afanasov on 27 July; for the Klepinins, Emiliya Litauer, and Tolstoi on 27 August 1941.

Efron is not mentioned here. He was shot later than the others—on 16 October 1941. That date was entered in Efron's file only on 8 August 1989; the form certifying the date was signed by I. M. Denisenko, head of the Central Archive of the KGB.

7

When all is said and done, Efron's behavior in prison helps us to understand the attitude Marina Ivanovna displayed toward her husband during her interrogation by the French police in October and November 1937. In a letter to Ariadna Berg, written in October, Tsvetaeva quotes from her conversation with the investigator about Efron:

He is the most honest, most noble, most humane person.

But his good faith might have been abused.

Mine in him remains unchanged.

During this period Tsvetaeva sent Ariadna Berg an old poem dedicated to her husband, which had two dates beneath it: "Koktebel, 3 June 1914–Vanves, 1937." I remember one of its stanzas:

True to him, to Chivalry I am true—
To all of you who lived and died without fear!
Those who—in fateful times—write poems—
Those who mount the scaffold.

Tsvetaeva was certain—at least while she was in France—that Efron had been falsely and unjustly accused and that he was not guilty of anything before the French government. "Don't believe it," she told everyone who still continued to see her.

People who are quick to denounce others—and they are legion—will question this steadfast devotion of a wife during a time of tribulation. "She knew everything and covered it up!" they will declare, regardless of evidence, ignoring the character of Efron, who worshipped and protected his family, and likewise ignoring the rules of secrecy in the milieu of the secret police. "She had to know." Well, what can one do? You can't stop people from talking.

Sergei Efron and others like him suffered dearly from starry-eyed credulity and a neutralized capacity for independent judgment. Even in the early thirties the "apolitical" Tsvetaeva thought that her husband's passion for "the building of socialism" in the USSR verged on elementary blindness. In a letter to Anna Tesková on 16 October 1931, she wrote: "S. Ya. has completely gone over to Sov. Russia, he doesn't see anything else, and sees only what he wants in it."[9]

Efron's courage and his morally irreproachable behavior in prison and under interrogation is indisputable, however. In the face of torture and death he remained a man of honor until the end. Not only did he not slander anyone, but he did not turn away from duty and truth as he understood them. He consistently rejected lies and did not take part in the dirty business the prosecution proposed. He cannot be put in the same category as his "colleagues" in Soviet intelligence who coldly and cynically carried out crimes, knowing very well whom and what they were serving.

There is another matter: people lacked sufficiently developed spiritual qualities that could protect them from the network of refined lies emerging during the 1930s. Efron was not the only one deceived by the poisonous sophistry about the "good of the fatherland." The secret police counted on people who were innocent and ready to sacrifice themselves for a higher ideal. We have yet to learn the real number of victims.

CHAPTER 4

YELABUGA

Any suicide is a mystery shrouded in unbearable pain. Rare are those cases when notes or letters written before the act explain what actually prompted it. At best we can identify a specific external stimulus that triggered the event, but we won't find the key in external events alone. It always lies buried within the heart of the person committing the act. The most important factor is the emotional state of the suicide at the fatal moment.

It is almost impossible to see inside a person who is in this extreme state, however. All the more so when it's an individual as exceptional as Marina Tsvetaeva. Yet our duty to the great poet's memory is to bring all the details and circumstances together in order to present a more complete picture of the tragedy that took place on 31 August 1941 in the small Tatar town of Yelabuga. There are totally blank places in this picture, which explains why so many versions of Tsvetaeva's death exist: each one is essentially an attempt to alleviate some of the anxiety that surrounds every secret.

Despite the claims of some experts who have tried to end the speculation, snags—or omissions—continue to turn up. We won't pretend, then, that everything in our narrative is definite, for new information may appear. Therefore, it makes sense to me to examine Tsvetaeva's last days carefully, to point out the questions that remain, and formulate new ones for which there are still no answers, in the hope that the answers eventually may be discovered.

1

Everyone who saw Marina Ivanovna in the month and a half between the beginning of the war and the day she and her son were evacuated share the belief that she was in an extremely tense and depressed state.

There were good reasons for this even before 22 June 1941. Still, according to many witnesses, Tsvetaeva viewed the German attack and the swift advance of Hitler's army deep into the country as a global catastrophe with an almost predetermined outcome. The fate of Czechoslovakia and the rapid fall of France remained open wounds in her heart. She had close acquaintances in Prague and Paris, and could visualize places there where she had been happy and sad, where she had agonized over a difficult line and paced for miles over every path and small street. Now all of this—familiar faces in Prague and its hilly outskirts and the crooked narrow streets of Meudon—had fallen beneath the shadow of the insane Führer.

Since she believed that myth was a necessary element of existence that was present in daily life, Tsvetaeva may have sometimes thought that she could hear the approach of the Bronze Horseman's steed. The clatter of hooves could be heard in Moscow then.

In the middle of June 1941 Tsvetaeva spent twelve days outside the city, near Kolomna, at the dacha of literary friends. But on June 24, she was back in Moscow. The raids of German bombers had already begun. Sirens sounded air-raid warnings daily. Building management committees organized brigades to stand guard on the roofs during the raids in order to extinguish the incendiary bombs. The city was transformed beyond recognition: windows of buildings were covered with strips of newspaper to keep the glass from flying out during the bombing. Loudspeakers hung at many intersections; and in the evenings cumbersome clumps of balloons would rise into the sky.

In those days people would often meet Tsvetaeva in the small square in front of the Rostov building on Vorovsky Street (formerly Povarskaya) where the board of the Writers' Union was located. Here the young Marina had once heard the inspiring speeches of Andrei Bely. But now the anxious Moscow literary crowd came here to hear and exchange news from the front lines and the city.

The word "evacuation" was a constant refrain everywhere. The first echelon of Moscow writers and their families left Moscow on 6 July 1941, the same day the Military Tribunal sentenced Sergei Efron to death.

Lists were being drawn up of those who would be in the next group, scheduled to leave on 27 July. Tsvetaeva sought advice from almost everyone with whom she was even the least bit acquainted: should she go or stay? If she left where should she go? And with whom? She had needed a traveling companion and guide even during calm days in the past when she traveled from the Czech countryside to Prague on various business. Now she needed someone to help her decide about the terrifying and unknown evacuation. She knew all too well how unfit she was for the practical matters of life. Moreover, in those trying days there was no one nearby who could make a decision for her and do what needed to be done. "I don't have friends and without them I'm lost," Marina wrote in her journal as early as May 1940. Over the next year the situation did not change. She had many acquaintances, but no one who was right there.

Mur was now sixteen; he was smart and well read, but he was least of all fit to be a support for his mother. That was her own fault—she wouldn't let him grow up. She treated him like a silly little boy, forbidding him this, allowing him that. She became completely flustered when he exerted his own will. Now he had fallen in love and didn't want to hear anything about a departure. In the evenings he took walks with his friend, a girl from the ninth grade, and during air raids he sometimes stood guard on the roof.

The guard duty was the essential thing that pushed Tsvetaeva to hurry with the departure: she was terribly afraid for her son. How could she not be? She would have been afraid even if her whole family had been there. But now he was the only one she had left. Pasternak was living outside Moscow, in Peredelkino, for almost the whole time, and the faithful, decent, and friendly Tanechka Kvanina (to whom Tsvetaeva had become close a year earlier at the Writers' Home in Golitsyno), had not shown up for more than a month.[1] Tsvetaeva couldn't call her—she didn't have a telephone. Nikolai Vilmont had joined the militia, and Tarasenkov had been at the front since the first week of the war. Her new acquaintances lacked authority for Tsvetaeva in the matters that had to be decided now. She didn't even have much trust in the sincere young poet Yaropolk Semyonov. He had appeared on her horizon a bit too suddenly and accidentally. "Why is he so nice to me?" she asked Alya's friend Nina Gordon. "Could he be from the NKVD?"[2]

Certainly Tsvetaeva trusted Nina Gordon and also Samuil Gurevich. Along with her husband's sister, Elizaveta Yakovlevna, they were the people closest to her. But they all had their own troubles, concerns, and duties. Moreover, the telephones often didn't work just when some quick decision had to be made.

Every bombardment caused Tsvetaeva genuine horror. "I thought I was brave," Marina Ivanovna once told Shur-Gelfand, who shared an apartment with Elizaveta Yakovlevna, "but it turns out I'm a terrible coward who panics during the raids."

Tsvetaeva's neighbor at the apartment on Pokrovsky Boulevard, not the one who was her enemy but another one—Ida Shukst (later Shukst-Ignatova), who was a student in the ninth grade at the time and the daughter of an engineer who had gone to the north—recalled that during an air-raid alert she once found herself in the bomb shelter of the building. Marina Ivanovna sat beside her. She was like stone, like a statue, sitting stiffly with her hands as if glued to her knees and staring straight ahead with unblinking eyes. Ida couldn't look at her—it was too painful—and she tried not to go to the shelter with her again.

Tsvetaeva's constant inner tension was visible even on relatively calm days, however. She was like a string stretched taut, Shukst-Ignatova recalled; any kind of casual touch was dangerous. "It was clear that she was restraining herself the whole time—her nerves were at the breaking-point."

People came to see her, but not often. Ida didn't remember seeing any women guests. There was no one she could relax with if only for a while, no way to escape her emotional burden. "She kept everything held in, behind an inner gate, and a nervous breakdown was always looming."[3]

Tsvetaeva and her son left Moscow on 8 August.

On the very eve of her departure Tsvetaeva made a visit to the writer Ilya Ehrenburg, who had returned from France a year earlier. We don't have any reliable accounts of this last meeting between two people who were never bound by sincere friendship.

There is an account that is not particularly reliable. In his book *Paris–Gulag–Paris* Dimitry Sezeman discusses the Ehrenburg-Tsvetaeva meeting on the basis of what Mur had told him. No other sources are available, and one can only hope that the general tone of the meeting has not been distorted.

Sezeman writes:

> Marina began to reproach Ehrenburg bitterly: "You've explained to me that my place, my native land, and my readers are here—well, now my husband and daughter are in prison, my son and I are without means, we're on the street, and no one wants to publish anything or even speak to me. How am I supposed to live?" And how did Ehrenburg answer her? Mur told me this story on the platform of the Tashkent railroad station, where a train with passengers evacuated from Moscow University had been kept standing for hours. He spoke in his usual ironic, even sarcastic way, far from making any kind of moral judgment. . . . Well, Ehrenburg answered Tsvetaeva like this: "Marina, Marina, there are high state interests that are concealed from you and me, in comparison with which the personal fate of every one of us is worth nothing. . . ." He would have made his sermon even longer but Marina interrupted him. "You're a scoundrel," she said and left, banging the door.[4]

It is always hard to believe in the accuracy of dialogues reproduced from memory, even more so after several decades have passed, and even more so when they are third or fourth hand. Ehrenburg's meeting with Tsvetaeva was probably not solely taken up by a dialogue of this sort. If we keep in mind the date of this meeting, it's clear that Marina had not come for the purpose of reproaching him, but most likely with her most pressing questions: Should she join the evacuation? What destination was best? With whom? Yet, it's possible that she was trying to get Ehrenburg to clear up her husband's fate. After all, Tsvetaeva still had no idea where he was or how his fate had been decided. Or if it had been decided. It was not clear how she would continue to get news about Sergei once she left Moscow. (In accordance with the procedures of those years the family had received no news about the court session of 6 July at which Efron was sentenced to death.)

The evening of the departure from Moscow is described in Nina Gordon's memoirs. She characterizes Tsvetaeva's decision to leave with the next writers' echelon on 8 August 1941 as a sudden one, made hastily, in a state of extreme tension: "She was just like a spring—tense, sharp, abrupt. . . . I clearly remember her eyes that day [7 August, the eve of departure]: they would glare, wander, and be absent. She would seem to be listening to you and she even answered to the point, but all the same it was obvious that her thoughts were occupied with something else, something private."[5]

Something else is more obvious from Gordon's description: in making her decision to leave on 8 August, Tsvetaeva hadn't consulted either Nina Gordon or Alya's husband, despite all her trust in them. When they came to see Marina Ivanovna on the eve of her departure, they both tried to convince her to stay, not to act hastily, and to make careful plans. She would still be able to leave. Tsvetaeva seemed to agree . . . but she left the next morning anyway.

Pasternak, Lidiya Libedinskaya, and Lev Bruni went to see her off at the port. Does this mean that Marina had found the time to call and inform them? Or that the departure was not such a sudden one, not just decided the previous day? We know that early in the morning of August

8, the Literary Fund truck stopped at the house on Pokrovsky Boulevard to pick up the passengers' belongings. The truck entry had been made earlier. All these factors make one again feel Tsvetaeva's terrible loneliness.

2

August 8 marked the departure from Moscow, from the river station, on the steamship *Alexander Pirogov*. In Kazan Marina and Mur transferred to another ship, which was to travel on the Kama River. Yelabuga is located at the confluence of the Kama and Toima rivers.

When she was in Yelabuga, Tsvetaeva mailed a postcard to the Tatar Writers' Union. On the card she requested help in moving from Yelabuga to Kazan; the Tatar Writers' Union might be able to use her as a translator. Tsvetaeva mentioned that she had a letter of recommendation from P. I. Chagin, the director of the State Literary Publishing House. She even had two letters of his—one to the Writers' Union and one to the Tatar Publishing House. This detail does not correspond to the version of Tsvetaeva's sudden, panicky departure. She was very familiar with the steamship's itinerary and had consulted with Chagin and even enlisted his support.

"Tense, sharp, abrupt," writes Gordon. But there were completely natural reasons for this—all the things to do on the eve of departure. Her son's rude behavior would have been explanation enough. Mur opposed the departure until the last moment.

The trip to Yelabuga took ten days. During this time Tsvetaeva became reacquainted with the wives of many writers. Some of those with whom she managed to become friends during the journey disembarked in Chistopol—a small town that had become one of the centers for evacuated writers and their families. It was overcrowded, however, and the Moscow Litfond was sending new groups further on to Yelabuga. The only people who could get off in Chistopol were those who had relatives there.

Let's turn our attention to an episode of Tsvetaeva's further journey.

A new passenger appeared on the ship. Mur would write about her in his diary. Flora Leites had been living in Chistopol for several weeks and was now going to Bersut, which was on the way to Yelabuga, in order to pick up some of the writers' children who had been vacationing at a Pioneer camp there and to bring them back to Chistopol. Flora spent almost the whole short trip to Bersut talking to Marina.

The conversation seemed so sincere and personal that when they parted Flora gave Tsvetaeva her address in Chistopol and promised to help if Marina Ivanovna decided to try to get permission to move from Yelabuga. Flora got off the boat in Bersut and Tsvetaeva had the rest of the trip to Yelabuga to think about what she had heard.

Flora strongly supported the idea of not staying in Yelabuga. Her information about Chistopol was first hand. Certainly she would have told Tsvetaeva that the town had a voluntary council of people who had been evacuated under the auspices of the Writers' Union, and that this council helped the newly arrived with living arrangements. She would have told Tsvetaeva that the poet Nikolai Aseev, with whom Tsvetaeva was on somewhat friendly terms, lived there as well as the families of Boris Pasternak, Ilya Selvinsky, Konstantin Fedin, Leonid Leonov, and Konstantin Trenyov. It would be much easier for Marina Ivanovna to be in a literary milieu than in a place where she would be a complete outsider.

This encounter en route explains the otherwise strange fact that on the day after she arrived in Yelabuga Tsvetaeva sent a telegram to Flora asking her to begin making efforts on her behalf. She made this decision, it seems, while still on the way to Yelabuga.

Maria Belkina suggests another explanation in *Interlocking Fates*. She thinks Tsvetaeva was frightened by the very sight of the small provincial town. "Overwhelmed by Yelabuga," Belkina writes, Marina hurried to send a telegram.[6]

One interpretation does not exclude the other, but rather supplements it. We shall propose still another explanation for the haste. A mystical one. I won't insist on it, but I find it completely realistic to conjecture that in that state of extreme tension Tsvetaeva had been in for several weeks, she might have felt a tremor in her heart as soon as she stepped on the Yelabugan soil. An inexplicable tremor of fear or horror. For she had stepped on the ground in which her body would be buried only two weeks later.

On 17 August the ship moored in Yelabuga. The next day Tsvetaeva sent the telegram to Flora Leites.

I saw Yelabuga for the first time more than half a century after that tragic autumn of 1941. The city grew enormously after 1951 (oil was discovered in the vicinity). In the eastern part of Yelabuga a completely new district appeared, built up with the usual Soviet buildings. But the historic center had been well preserved—with the inevitable Soviet architectural innovations, of course. Thank God there were few of these. A modest statue of Lenin still stood in the central square; Lenin Street and Communist Street had kept their Soviet names, but another main street had regained its old name of Kazanskaya. At its far end, however, some Soviet signs remained—for many years Kazanskaya had been Karl Marx Street.

Without hurrying, you can walk around the center of the old city in an hour or so. All the buildings I searched for turned out to be close to one another: the Librarians' School building where the Muscovites who arrived with Tsvetaeva were first put up, the former city administration building where evacuees were helped to find housing and work, the children's library, which Marina visited two or three times, I learned.

On two or three main streets of the old town there are comfortable and stylish two-story brick villas that were built in the nineteenth century by Yelabugan merchants and factory owners. But take two steps out of the old center and you'll find yourself in the realm of single-story log houses, sometimes trimmed with bright paint, or decorated with fanciful wood-carving on the shutters and gates. Behind the fences you see the heavy branches of apple trees everywhere. I went to Yelabuga in August shortly after the Feast of the Savior, or Apple Feast, which takes place on August 19. The local housewives, seated comfortably on benches and stairs, were selling apples near almost every store.

Old-timers remembered that during the fall in which Tsvetaeva arrived, there had been no apple harvest: almost all the apple trees were killed by frost in the winter of 1939-1940 (the "Finnish winter"). There were no asphalt roads then either. During the bad weather in the fall shoes stuck in the mud and people could only walk around in boots.

The house where Marina Tsvetaeva lived now bears a memorial plaque stating that she lived here in August 1941. The small street has also regained its old name. It is no longer Voroshilov Street, as it was during the war, and not Zhdanov Street, as it was later called: now it is Malaya Pokrovskaya. From Pokrovsky Boulevard in Moscow to Malaya Pokrovskaya in Yelabuga! The renaming left a legacy, however. "The Protection of the Mother of God" Church (Pokrov Bozh'ei Materi) had not given shelter. On Malaya Pokrovskaya Street near the church (which now has been restored) you can still see sturdy signs reading "Zhdanov Street" that even seem rather new. Like a burdock the past clings to its former supports.

Incidentally, Yelabuga has its own glorious and ancient history, though it is no longer reflected in any names. In 1870 Ivan Vasilievich Shishkin, twice chosen the mayor of Yelabuga, and the father of the celebrated Russian painter Ivan Ivanovich Shishkin, wrote an extensive history of Yelabuga.

In the pre-Christian era the Persian king Darius I was here, and beginning in the tenth century a Bulgarian state flourished for three centuries. In the early thirteenth century Tamerlane's army passed through and laid waste to the area. Pugachev and his troops and Radishchev were here in the eighteenth century; Radishchev was returning to Petersburg from exile in Siberia. In the nineteenth century the famous "cavalry maid," Nadezhda Durova, lived here. Disguised as a male soldier, she had fought in the Napoleonic Wars and later wrote her memoirs. In her honor the town erected a statue and established a museum, as was also done for the painter Shishkin. Yelabuga was probably as proud of both Shishkins —father and son—as it was of its cultured and talented merchants who traded all over the world.

Today Marina Tsvetaeva is also honored here. The house where she lived is still privately owned, but every year at the end of August the town holds Tsvetaeva readings. There is a memorial service at the cemetery where poems are read. Still, I had occasion to hear unfriendly words from some people in Yelabuga: "she defamed the town"; "other people came and lived here and nothing happened, but now Yelabuga is to blame—we didn't help her." These are usually voices of older people who are offended that today everyone knows Yelabuga primarily as the place where a great poet died.

3

Three serious accounts of Marina Tsvetaeva's suicide exist today.

The first, which her sister Anastasia Tsvetaeva supported, has been widely circulated in the many editions of Anastasia's *Reminiscences*. This version holds that Marina died in order to save her son's life, or at least make it easier. Having become convinced that she could no longer help him and was actually even harming him because of her reputation as a White Guardist, she made her fatal decision in the hope that people would sooner help Mur if she were not there. Especially if she were to die in *that way*.

In 1941 Marina's sister was still in exile. She would learn about her sister's death much later, and collect information about Marina's last days indirectly—at second or third hand. Anastasia was a true believer and she wanted to justify her sister's suicide at all costs.

Maria Belkina has made the strongest argument for the second version. On the one hand, she believes that emotionally Tsvetaeva had long been ready to die, and that this is attested to by a large number of her poems and diary entries. Belkina introduces another reason, however; one that she doesn't name directly but puts forward with conviction—that Tsvetaeva suffered from a mental illness, which became more acute after the war began. Belkina relies on her own personal impressions and meetings, and therein lies both the strength and weakness of her evidence. "She had already lost her will while still in Moscow," we read in *Interlocking Fates*. "She wasn't able to decide about anything, she yielded to anyone's influence, she was no longer in control of herself. . . . Even her appearance had changed in Moscow when I saw her during the time of the air raids; she had become thin and had aged; she was, as I've said, extremely confused, her eyes roamed, and the cigarette in her hand shook. . . ."[7] In this light, Tsvetaeva's last step seems natural and inevitable—the act of someone ill.

Finally, in recent years a third version of the poet's death has appeared. This version assigns a fatal role to the organs of the Yelabugan NKVD. The author of this account is Kirill Khenkin, who advanced the theory in his book about the spy Rudolf Abel, *The Topsy-Turvy Hunter (Okhotnik vverkh nogami)* published in Frankfurt-am-Main in 1980 and in Russia in 1991.

Based on autobiographical materials, the book appeared in Moscow in the 1980s. Like other products of *tamizdat* (works published outside the USSR), it circulated among dissidents and their acquaintances. Since I always traveled from Leningrad to the capital for only short periods of time, I wasn't able to get my hands on it for a long time. My friend Lev Levitsky in Moscow gave me a detailed account of one episode concerning Tsvetaeva. It did not seem very plausible, especially because it seemed too much part of an epidemic then in fashion—to seek the hand of the NKVD here, there, and everywhere. Especially because, if I understood Levitsky correctly, there was no evidence to support this account. The story was based on the testimony of a certain Maklyarsky, whose name meant nothing to me at the time, like the name Khenkin itself.

The Topsy-Turvy Hunter was not to be found in the special reserves of Leningrad and Moscow libraries, and quite a few years passed before I was able to read the book myself. The subject that I had been told about took up only six small pages; I read them and once again found them lacking in substance. The author's style alone made it impossible to put great trust in his account. Khenkin chose a semi-fictional approach, and he constantly guesses at the motivation behind others' actions—a Chekist's, Tsvetaeva's, Pasternak's, Aseev's. He misses things at every turn. There are obvious simplifications or distortions both of individuals and circumstances, strained interpretations, and an ignorance of facts. I'll cite the most significant passage:

But even then [the winter of 1941] I knew that Marina Ivanovna's trip to Chistopol hadn't been for money—it was for sympathy and help.

Maklyarsky told me the following story . . .

Immediately after Marina Ivanovna arrived in Yelabuga she was summoned to the local NKVD authorities who proposed that she "be of help."

The provincial Chekist had most likely reasoned in the following way: this woman has come from Paris. That means she'll be unhappy in Yelabuga. Since she'll be unhappy, other malcontents will be drawn to her. They'll strike up conversations, and that always allows one to "expose enemies," that is, to concoct a criminal case. Or maybe the "case" of the Efron family was transferred to Yelabuga with instructions to link her to state security. I don't know . . .

They suggested that she become an informer.

She expected that Aseev and Fadeev would become angry the way she had and that they would protect her from these vile proposals. . . . Fearing for themselves, fearing that having mentioned them, Marina would destroy them, Aseev and Fadeev said (or one of them said—maybe even Aseev, who feared Fadeev) the least harmful thing that people in their position could say under such circumstances. That is: everyone should decide for himself—to collaborate or not collaborate with the police, that this . . . depended on one's political maturity and patriotism.[8]

This version certainly never occurred to anyone before. But, as it turns out, Fadeev was not in Chistopol at the time, and the speculation about who feared whom and what they could have said sounds unconvincing in any case. It was beyond any Maklyarsky to confirm exactly what Aseev thought and exactly what he told Tsvetaeva, or whether or not such a conversation took place in Chistopol. And nothing can be done with even a trustworthy element when it is so dissolved in conjecture. In general, such testimony should be disregarded—and yet this touches on too important a matter. Whatever the case, this third version appears stronger than the earlier ones.

At first I found Khenkin's version unreliable from many points of view. How could someone in Moscow in the winter of 1941 have learned about what was going on in a secret office in far-off Yelabuga? And who in the capital would have become so interested in Tsvetaeva's fate at this time, except someone in the very narrow circle of people who knew her personally? After all, she only gained the reputation of a great poet forty years later.

However, with time, when the character of both participants in the winter conversation had taken a more concrete shape, my doubts began to fade. Newly published memoirs and documents confirmed Khenkin's closeness to Tsvetaeva's family while still in France. Kirill and Ariadna (almost the same age) had, in fact, become friends and even corresponded with one another after Alya went to Moscow. In Mur's diary there is an entry about the Khenkins' arrival in the USSR (entry of 28 February 1941). In one of Ariadna Efron's recently discovered letters E. A. Nelidova-Khenkina (Kirill Khenkin's mother) is described as a person well acquainted with the details of Sergei Efron's secret work for Soviet intelligence. And from his book we now know that Khenkin was enlisted in the ranks of NKVD collaborators "on the recommendation of Efron."

By the winter of 1941 Khenkin was serving in the Fourth Department. His direct supervisor was none other than Mikhail Borisovich Maklyarsky. The specific sphere of interests entrusted to Colonel of State Security Maklyarsky included figures from Soviet literature and art—during both the pre-war and war years. Later, after the war ended, a second side of the colonel's talents was brought to the foreground and recorded in the Soviet film encyclopedia. In peacetime he became a screenwriter. The film scripts he worked on are well known: "A Spy's Heroic Deed" (*Podvig razvedchika*, 1947), "Secret Mission" (*Sekretnaia missiia*, 1950), "Conspiracy of Ambassadors" (*Zagovor poslov*, 1966), and others of this sort. In 1960 Maklyarsky was head of the Institute for Screenwriters. Today many Muscovites from circles of film and literature still remember Maklyarsky well (he died in 1978) and even claim that his direct connections to the NKVD-KGB were widely known.

But if such was Maklyarsky's occupation then, he of course *must have known* about the poet who had recently returned from emigration and whose sister, husband, and daughter had all been arrested right before the war. The news of her tragic end *must have reached* him through completely natural channels, since Tsvetaeva fell into the sphere of his "wards." With all this in mind, a biographer of Tsvetaeva cannot disregard Khenkin's version as a conjecture on a fashionable theme. His version has still not been examined seriously by researchers—at best it is mentioned in passing, probably because it is difficult to verify and corroborate with either a document or at least some additional evidence.

My searches for a file on Tsvetaeva had come to a dead end. By the logic of things, there *had* to be one. But the Yelabuga NKVD responded that one had to look for wartime archives in Kazan, who denied they had anything. Moscow referred me back to Kazan, in evasive language. Losing hope, I sought to learn from well-informed people—officials in the KGB archive—if any traces of recruiting, that is, a "proposal to collaborate," would be preserved in a prisoner's file? Not necessarily, it seems. Especially if the person being recruited refused. Why preserve traces of bad work?

So we found and find ourselves left with the choice of either trusting or not trusting Khenkin's story. After all, there is a good possibility that Maklyarsky invented things. Perhaps in order to impress subordinates. It is also possible that Khenkin interpreted the colonel's "speculation" as reliable information.

There is nothing implausible in Khenkin's account, however. The NKVD had its own production plan for recruiting secret agents from the population: it was known as "prophylactic work." In order to "have a talk" with Tsvetaeva in the aforesaid spirit, the Chekists in Yelabuga would not have had to wait for the arrival of official mail with personal files. Certainly the personnel department of the Writers' Union was forwarding everything necessary to Chistopol and Yelabuga with one of the people traveling there.

Let us assume that depression and provincial rot ruled in the Yelabugan NKVD. And suddenly such good luck: a former White émigré (this was precisely the term used then) arrives, whose entire family is in jail. Her husband had fought with the White army. And there's a son—the only member of the family nearby.

Such vulnerability is a godsend. There was a large opportunity for warnings, threats, and blackmail. I've heard this objection—why would they need her? To watch whom? Inform on whom? What could she have reported that would have been of use? But the secret police has never subscribed to the bounds of reason and logic. There could be many answers: a "production plan"; or direct orders from Moscow; or curiosity; or the desire to intimidate, the pleasure in the feeling that everything is permitted; or, simply, why not? She had a very suitable background.

Our difficulty does not lie in the availability of suitable reasons but in the fact that we are forced to operate without documentary evidence. The conscientious biographer can only *keep in mind the real possibility* of this version and compare the established facts with it, as well as new evidence. That is what I propose to do.

4

In the chronology of Marina Tsvetaeva's last twelve days of life (from disembarking in Yelabuga to 31 August) much is unclear. Even in Belkina's superb book, which is based on a large body of collected evidence, inconsistencies and omissions remain. Belkina alludes to some of these herself, if a bit cursorily. What follows is an example.

What does one live on when the food provisions sent from Moscow run out and the things you've brought with you have been eaten? Where and how can one earn money? This worry tormented Tsvetaeva on the boat even before they got to Yelabuga.

Upon her arrival, however, if one believes T.S. Sikorskaya's memoir (which Belkina cites), Marina Tsvetaeva refused to go to the city hall and look for work: "I don't know how to work. Once I begin I'll confuse everything immediately. I don't understand a thing in any office, I'll be so scared I'll confuse everything." "She was especially frightened," Sikorskaya writes, "by the thought of those forms one has to fill out at work."[9]

This claim does not fit with information we have today, however. Tsvetaeva *was looking for work* in Yelabuga, and very energetically. According to her landlady, A. I. Brodelshchikova, Marina Ivanovna was almost never at home. She is known to have stopped at the district department of state education several times. She offered her services to the secondary school that trained elementary school teachers. Two or three times she went to the children's library on Toiminskaya Street. She didn't take out any books, she didn't bring her son with her, and each time she went by herself to the director's office—wasn't this in order to get a job?

Tsvetaeva constantly had to overcome her fear, even in such matters as showing a passport or filling out a form. Evidently she had had to do this in Yelabuga. Otherwise how would people in the small town know that she had come from abroad? Or that her husband was in the White Army? She wouldn't have spread this around on her own.

In one place she was refused work right away. She turned down another job herself after she learned the conditions and nature of the work and understood that she couldn't manage it. Tsvetaeva had recognized her unfitness for office work in 1919, during the Civil War, when she had to work for several months at the Committee of Nationalities. She describes this in her autobiographical essay "My Jobs." She also knew that she was completely unfit to be something like a kindergarden teacher. This point needs no elaboration—it's enough to remember her nervous state at the time.

Here's a clear example of inconsistency. Sikorskaya writes: "All urgings to go to the city hall were of no help . . ." But according to an entry in Mur's diary, *Tsvetaeva was at the city hall.* Perhaps this only means that Tsvetaeva didn't go there with Sikorskaya. Did she go alone? Possibly, though in the past she always asked someone to accompany her, the more so in a strange city.

There's more. Mur's entry is not quoted in full in Belkina's book. The entry is both strange and significant. Unfortunately, I know it only through a copied excerpt. It's completely believable, however. One detail catches your attention. The entry by Tsvetaeva's son says that on that day (20 August) Marina Ivanovna *was at the city hall and there was no work for her except for a position at the NKVD as a translator from German.*

Nota bene! A position as a translator was Tsvetaeva's best dream. The solution to all problems! Why keep on searching then? But here's what's strange: the city administration could not offer work for the NKVD. That was simply impossible. State security never entrusted anyone to select its personnel.

In Yelabuga I recently found a woman who had received exactly such work during the war. She was a translator from German at a Yelabugan camp for prisoners of war. The camp sprung up at the beginning of 1942, and it's quite likely that in the fall of 1941 they were beginning to pick a staff in preparation for its opening. But Tamara Mikhailovna Grebenshchikova, with whom I spoke, was sent to this job on special orders of the NKVD in Tataria. She remembers this clearly. She confirms that the city administration had nothing at all to do with the selection of these employees.

What's left for us to think? It's impossible to dismiss this strange entry. Mur wrote the entry on the same day—while his memory was still fresh. Could Tsvetaeva have been at a different place that morning, not at the city hall at all, but at the NKVD? Isn't that why she went alone? But why? Was she summoned there? And so soon? The Moscow Litfond group had only arrived in Yelabuga two days earlier. They weren't even settled in apartments yet but living together on the premises of the Librarians' School.

Such efficiency seems unlikely: it's not Soviet style. But couldn't Tsvetaeva have gone to the police on her own, without a summons? She still didn't know anything about her husband's fate, for example. In May the NKVD had requested his things; it was natural to think that they were finally preparing to send Sergei Yakovlevich into exile. But where was he now? It was essential for Tsvetaeva to find out his address for letters and packages and also to inform him of her new address in Yelabuga.

On the other hand, to go voluntarily to the NKVD when the terror of his arrest had stayed with her for a year and a half . . . Yes, but she had gone to prisons in Moscow—four times a month—with parcels and in search of information.

There's another possibility, however. At that time, the secret police had the habit of cleverly disguising their work. The person they wanted would be called to the local police station, for example, or to the district administrative building, or city hall, or simply to the housing office under the most innocent pretext—in connection with a permit, for instance. Once there, secluded in a special room, they would hold their frightening conversations. Perhaps at the time Tsvetaeva was actually summoned to city hall on some such pretext and then cornered by the worst kind of Chekist boor.

Did Tsvetaeva tell her son the whole truth about this conversation? Not likely, especially if the police had proposed collaboration in exchange for work. And even if Marina *had told her son the whole truth*, it's doubtful he would have written it down—in black and white—in his diary. After the arrest of Mur's sister and father, he knew all too well what kind of country he lived in. I think she did not tell him, however. Otherwise it would have leaked out later, through some close friend of Mur's, Dimitry Sezeman, for instance. I wasn't able to find the slightest support for such a supposition in Mur's diary and letters. But the diary entry under discussion is extremely important: unclear as it is, it unexpectedly strengthens Khenkin's version.

5

My trip to Yelabuga in the fall of 1993 turned cautious suppositions into near certainty. I talked to Batalov, then head of the KGB, and Senior Captain Tunguskov. They both answered my blunt questions the same way: such a "conversation" with Tsvetaeva in August 1941 seemed most realistic.

They didn't have any documentary corroboration but that did not exclude the possibility of such a meeting. But really, I asked, wouldn't the facts of Tsvetaeva's biography (as recorded in her file) have excluded her as a possible collaborator, even if a secret one? Wouldn't it have been more natural for them to have watched her and not to have charged her to spy on others? As far as I understood their answer, one did not preclude the other.

The recollections of old Yelabugans were even more substantial, though most often they spoke about the general practices and atmosphere of those years, and not about Tsvetaeva's case. But when a former math teacher in the city told me how the NKVD in Yelabuga had tried to recruit her as a secret agent I took her story as relevant material.

Anna Nikolaevna Zamoreva was persistently asked to spy on another teacher, German Frantsevich Dik, who had arrived from Bologoe at the start of the war. They advised her to take notes on whom he associated with and precisely what he said. Zamoreva also told me that they knew how to take revenge for refusal or disobedience.

This certainly wasn't the only such case in Yelabuga. Provincial towns were full of informers, just as larger cities were. An unprecedented wave of arrests had taken place here during the years 1937 and 1938. The best people in the town disappeared into the Gulag camps. The few who returned spoke in whispers—and only to the very closest family or friends—about what they had seen and lived through in the prisons and camps.

I also found some people who had seen and could remember Marina Ivanovna and her son. There weren't many of these still alive now, and their stories were fragmentary and sparse. One recurring note in particular struck me. It was all the more believable because I heard it from people who weren't acquainted with one another.

Tamara Petrovna Golovastikova, who was then quite young, had once seen Tsvetaeva in the middle of the marketplace. She realized many years later that it *was* Marina Tsvetaeva after she chanced upon a book with a picture of her. "I had the absolutely clear sense that she was the one I had seen then!" It would have been impossible for her to ignore the unusual woman she saw standing in the middle of the market, wearing some kind of jacket over an apron and speaking angrily in French to a handsome young man—her son. Tamara Petrovna knew a little German and said that she could easily distinguish French from other languages. The woman was smoking and the way she flicked the ashes was also memorable. Tamara Petrovna found it strangely beautiful. She had an eye for such details and was training to be an artist. The son answered the woman angrily in the same language; then he ran off somewhere, apparently at the mother's request. The pair didn't look like anyone else, and Golovastikova remembered them for a long time.

The woman's face was unusual, as if carved from stone, and she looked totally exhausted. Like someone who had just suffered great sorrow. That was the recurring note I heard—the exhausted face, as if they'd all agreed on it. People remembered different details: Tsvetaeva's clothes, the severity with which she walked past the young librarian and went into the director's office. And each time I heard the obligatory, "Her face looked ravaged . . . tormented."

Tsvetaeva's appearance was made even more unusual by her hair, which she wore pushed back from her forehead and hidden under a beret, then covered with a shawl that she tied in the style of a nun. In addition, she wore glasses. At first these details made me think it wasn't Marina. But the description was repeated in a second account, and a third: it was precisely Tsvetaeva. The glasses were also mentioned in notes made by people who spoke to her landlords, the Brodelshchikovs. And the shawl was mentioned by the young librarian, who knew the visitor's name.

Another former resident of Yelabuga testified about a personal acquaintanceship with an order that directly affected Tsvetaeva. This man, Nikolai Vladimirovich Leontiev, had a clear memory of the order's contents. It contained a description of Tsvetaeva and also strict instructions about the measures needed to protect the citizens of the town from the harmful influence of the memory of Tsvetaeva's stay in Yelabuga. Leontiev knew about this order owing to his job as "second secretary" of the Yelabugan Party committee. He headed the Department of Propaganda and Agitation, as I believe it was called at the time, not during the war, but shortly after. The war had ended, but the order reflected the same spirit that existed when Tsvetaeva arrived in Yelabuga on 17 August 1941.

"Who composed the circular," I naively asked Nikolai Vladimirovich, "the authorities from Yelabuga or Kazan?"

His response was almost pitying—it was so obvious that I didn't understand a thing. But when he began to expound the essence of the order my naïveté vanished. The Yelabugan authorities could not have invented such a thing. The description of Tsvetaeva had clearly been composed in the highest offices of state security, that is, the Moscow NKVD. Tsvetaeva was presented as "an inveterate enemy of Soviet power": a person not only disposed against the Soviet regime, but one who had actively fought against the regime even abroad. She had been published in White Guard journals and newspapers. She had joined White Guard organizations, and so forth, in the same vein. In short, the person was not only alien to socialist society but also very dangerous.

Leontiev asserted that there was definitely nothing about Tsvetaeva's husband in the circular. Apparently, for provincial Yelabuga extra information was unnecessary. After all, Efron wouldn't be able to show up there. Through Leontiev's help I got hold of many circulars from those years. He remembered there were lists of books that were subject to destruction in all the town libraries, including the very smallest; he remembered orders about portraits of Politburo members—which ones were and which were not to be carried during the May Day demonstrations.

An article that appeared in the journal *Rodina* added reliable facts to my meetings and conversations. Its author, A. Litvin, became acquainted with the file of another Yelabuga visitor—the celebrated singer, S. Ya. Lemeshev. Lemeshev came to the town several months after Tsvetaeva's death and spent two months there, from the end of May through July 1942. The documents Litvin revealed conclusively refute the idea that it was easy to hide from the secret police in the Russian interior. A circular quickly followed Lemeshev and his wife from Moscow to Kazan and from Kazan to Yelabuga. It was addressed to Senior Lieutenant of State Security, Kozanov, head of the local NKVD. The circular ordered that vigilant control be maintained over every step of the renowned tenor and his wife, since the police were preparing a case against them as presumed spies.

Litvin's description of the file makes a strong impression. It is full of information about the recruiting of Lemeshev's neighbors and friends of his friends, and about the diligent reports that they and others made.

Czechoslovakia, 1923. Sitting (*left to right*): Marina Tsvetaeva, Ekaterina Eleneva, Konstantin Rodzevich. Standing (*left to right*): Sergei Efron, Nikolai Elenev.

Marina Tsvetaeva in
Prague, 1924.

Ariadna Efron and her mother,
Marina Tsvetaeva, Czechoslovakia, 1925.

Tsvetaeva with her son, Mur,
Clamart, 1933.

Sergei Efron in Paris, 1937.

Ariadna Efron in Paris before her return to the USSR.

Prince Dimitry Svyatopolk-Mirsky under arrest, June 1938.

Ariadna Efron before her arrest,
Bolshevo, 1938.

Sergei Efron in the
sanitorium, 1938.

Marina Tsvetaeva
in Moscow, 1939.

Georgy Efron in Christopol,
September 11, 1941.

Nina Klepinina.

Nikolai Andreevich Klepinin.

Alexei Sezeman.

NKVD dacha in Bolshevo.

Yelabuga.

Yelabuga. The house where Tsvetaeva
lived and died.

Tsvetaeva's landlords in Yelabuga,
A.I. and M.I. Brodelshchikov, 1960s.

Left, the cross that Anastasia Tsvetaeva put up in 1960 in the presumed area of Tsvetaeva's burial.

Below, in 1970, the Tatar Union of Writers erected a monument over the grave. There is no certainty, however, that Tsvetaeva is buried there.

Anastasia Tsvetaeva with her son Andre 1963.

The Lemeshevs were thoughtfully supplied with partners for card games and companions for his beloved hunts, and he most likely didn't suspect that they were all intently memorizing his every word in order to report them to the right place. What small crime had attracted such energetic police activity? The German surname of the singer's wife, it seems. The reports about Tsvetaeva must have been guarded much more carefully.

Let us return to the narrative of Tsvetaeva's remaining days in Yelabuga. On the day after she visited the city hall, Marina and Mur took up residence in the Brodelshchikovs' house on Voroshilov Street. It was a single-story log house like many in Yelabuga. It is quite impossible to think that the lodging came as help "from above," so wretched was the tiny room in which they settled. The room was only about six meters long; the partition that separated them from the landlords' part did not reach the ceiling, and there was a curtain in place of a door. To have agreed to this poverty Tsvetaeva must have been unbearably tired—or confident that she would only have to live there a very short time.

There is an entry in Mur's diary for the next day, 22 August. Tsvetaeva had decided to go to Chistopol by herself, without her things or her son. The goal of the trip was briefly mentioned: Flora Leites had still not replied, and it was essential to find out if they could move to Chistopol. The motives were understandable. The only strange thing, again, is the hurry. Only three days had passed since the telegram was sent. It was only their fifth day in Yelabuga. Why not wait a bit longer for an answer? But on 24 August Tsvetaeva was on the boat on her way to Chistopol.

Let us spend a bit more time in Yelabuga, however. A half century after Tsvetaeva's death, in 1991, at an evening celebration in her memory, another eyewitness of those years unexpectedly turned up—Alexei Ivanovich Sizov. As a young man, at the start of the war, he had taught physical education and military science at the Yelabuga secondary school for teachers. One day, at the end of the summer of 1941, before classes began, he met a woman in the institute courtyard who looked totally exhausted. She asked him if he was a local person and when he said yes, she asked for help in finding a room for herself and her son.

Sizov realized that she was an evacuee and advised her to go to the city hall: that's where newcomers were given help in finding places to live. The woman answered, "We already have a room, but I'd like to move. We don't get along with the landlady."

After he found out where the newcomer had settled and who her landlady was, Sizov thought that indeed it wasn't easy to get along with Anastasia Ivanovna Brodelshchikova. She had a difficult character. Alexei Ivanovich knew that because he had gone fishing several times with her husband and was a welcome guest at their house. During the conversation it became clear to Sizov that the newcomer was a writer. He remembered that he had heard about her. She had come to the institute to find work. But her past was unsuitable because she was a White Russian émigré. A "foreign element," as they said. They didn't take her, even though there was an opening.

Alexei Ivanovich began asking the woman if she had been abroad and which of our writers and which French writers she had met there. They spoke a short while. Sizov, though a military instructor, had been an avid reader since his youth. I saw his library when I visited his home. He had a reverential attitude toward literature and writers. At the end of his conversation with Tsvetaeva, he promised to look for housing.[10]

"How did you know," I asked Alexei Ivanovich, when I met with him in August 1993, "that she had come from abroad? Did she tell you that herself?"

"Of course not. But I heard people gossip about her in the office."

Brodelshchikova supported what Sizov said when I met her. She had wanted other lodgers, not Marina and Mur.

"They don't have rations," she had explained to Sizov. "And also the Naberezhnaya people come [in Yelabuga NKVD headquarters was located on Naberezhnaya Street] and look at her papers when she's not here and ask me who comes to see her and what they talk about. It's just trouble. I told them to find another room."

At first I doubted this detail in Sizov's recollections. Wasn't this haste on the part of NKVD officials invented later when such stories became fashionable? But after my meetings in Yelabuga and in light of people's recollections, everything seemed different. What would have been simpler, in fact, than to make the landlords into informers?

Within a day or two Sizov found a room for Marina Ivanovna on Lenin Street, near the Tatar cemetery. A friend of his family lived there. He even took Tsvetaeva there so that she could negotiate, but he didn't stay. He had things to do, Sizov said; it was August, he was working on a threshing machine in the outlying districts of Yelabuga.

Another two or three days passed. (These breaks— "a day or two," "two or three days"—are hardest of all to remember half a century later, whereas for Tsvetaeva in Yelabuga the days were numbered. And in the middle was the trip to Chistopol. When did the Sizov business begin? If it happened—and apparently it did—it must have started before the trip and continued after Tsvetaeva's return from Chistopol.)

Sometime later, the porter at the secondary school handed Alexei Ivanovich a note. There in Tsvetaeva's large hand was written: "Alexei Ivanovich, the landlady whom we saw turned me down." Sizov set off for Lenin Street and there he found other lodgers moving in. The landlord's explanation was simple: "Your woman doesn't have a ration card or wood. And she's a White Guardist too. And these promised to fix my stove."

"White Guardist," "foreign element," "came from abroad"—the Yelabugans and the evacuees who were there before the writers' group arrived immediately remembered Tsvetaeva by these labels. She alone was such a marked person. This trait attracted the young and curious Sizov, but it scared away older people. Tsvetaeva was "different," not like others, "not ours." In the provinces it was sufficient cause for unfriendly feelings.

"But why did it matter to the landladies," I asked Sizov, "how tenants would make ends meet—with rations or without? Why would they care about it?" It turns out they cared a lot. It was an established custom for lodgers to invite their landlords to tea every evening and offer them food. That meant, Sizov said, that the newcomers had to share their rations. In addition, the city administration allocated firewood to people with rations. And by this time winter was not far off.

Why didn't Tsvetaeva have a food ration? Had the authorities not yet managed to register her or did they deprive her of it? I wasn't able to find out for sure. But there's another possibility: on one page of the house register only Mur's name appears. Perhaps Tsvetaeva put off her registration because she hoped to leave? The residence permit might have been a prerequisite for a ration card.

I'll return to the Sizov theme, but for now I'll merely note that he introduces a correction into the recollections of those people who managed to speak about Marina Tsvetaeva with the Brodelshchikovs in Yelabuga. In those recollections the landlords with whom Tsvetaeva spent her final days appear as very decent people. Nice, sweet, good, "with an innate noble aversion to gossip and to prying in others' affairs."[11]

Nevertheless, one can sense concealed resentment in some of the landlady's recorded remarks: the newcomer was *very* quiet, she never said anything about herself. For the simple Russian, that was arrogance. "She just smokes and keeps quiet." That's what Tsvetaeva did while sitting next to her landlady on the porch.

Brodelshchikova remembered one phrase uttered on that porch that is very important for us. In the evenings Red Army soldiers who were undergoing military training in the town would march past the house. One time Tsvetaeva blurted out: "They're singing victory songs, and *he* keeps on advancing . . ."

6

On the day Marina Tsvetaeva left for Chistopol, Mur wrote in his diary: "She's in a foul mood, as pessimistic as you can be."

In Kirill Khenkin's version this trip is presented as an important link. Khenkin is convinced that Tsvetaeva had been frightened by the secret police in Yelabuga and went to Chistopol above all "for sympathy and help." Let us note, by the way, that if indeed "city hall" is a euphemism for the NKVD, the date of the "conversation," 20 August, fully corresponds with what Maklyarsky told Khenkin: "Immediately after Marina

Tsvetaeva's arrival in Yelabuga the local agent of the NKVD summoned her to his office."

The following chain of events emerges: 17 August, arrival in Yelabuga; 20 August, the conversation with the NKVD in the city hall; 22 August, Mur's entry about his mother's decision to go to Chistopol; 24 August, her departure. Psychologically, in this variant the impetuous departure from Yelabuga is more than logical. To be alone in such a situation is a crisis, especially for a person whose nerves are exhausted. You need someone close, not a new acquaintance, no matter how likeable, but one of your old friends, someone trustworthy, who knows all the peculiarities of your situation and doesn't require explanations.

It was natural for Tsvetaeva to think first of all of Nikolai Nikolaevich Aseev. He was in Chistopol, and he was not an ordinary person or an outcast; not a small fry, but a famous poet, one of the most influential members on the board of the Writers' Union. He had authority and connections and was someone who mattered.

I don't believe that Tsvetaeva was really counting on an active "defense" (as Khenkin states ironically). She was hardly so naïve. She needed support and advice. What should she do? How should she behave in the future? For if we assume that the meeting with the NKVD did take place, we can well imagine the tone; offers of help would have been quickly followed by threats in the event of a refusal or even vacillation.

"Agree to collaborate with us and we'll help you find a place to live, and here's the job as a translator you were dreaming about. No? Well, then no one will take you on anywhere. . . . So, you don't want to think about the fate of your son?" This was a well-known, standard tactic, and once we allow the possibility of such a "plot" we need to think it through to the end.

The simplest (although truly naïve) thing that might have come into Tsvetaeva's mind would have been to leave Yelabuga right away in order to be near Aseev and the writers' organization, where she wouldn't feel like a needle lost in a haystack. She had stayed away from associations and groups her whole life, always standing *outside*, but now she had to join some community to find help.

Incidentally, there was no particular warmth in Tsvetaeva's relations with Aseev. In the spring of 1941 something resembling friendship had existed and Marina and her son visited the Aseevs. The friendship was never very close, however, if only because Aseev's wife, Oksana Mikhailovna, strongly disliked Tsvetaeva.

I had to speak with Aseev's wife once and she let me know immediately that she had nothing good to say about Marina. Tsvetaeva had been to their place in Moscow, more than once. "And she used to walk right by me, as if past a piece of furniture, barely nodding. She only wanted to talk with Aseev, the others didn't interest her . . ." Aseev's wife wasn't able and didn't want to make any allowances for the tragic nature of Tsvetaeva's circumstances at the time. On the contrary, these circumstances reinforced her hostility, for she belonged to the cream of Soviet society. The only ones who survived were those capable of turning their backs on others' misfortunes.

Tsvetaeva's son, apparently, didn't register these hidden undertones. On 3 June 1941, he wrote to his sister, "During the last two or three months we've become friends with Aseev, who won the Stalin Prize for the narrative poem 'Incipit Mayakovsky.' He's a simple and likeable person. We go to his place rather often—he appreciates and respects Mama very much."[12]

Tsvetaeva stayed in Chistopol for two days—the 25th and 26th. On the morning of August 27, she returned to Yelabuga on the next boat.

In Chistopol she undoubtedly set out for Aseev's at once, unsure even of his address. But we know almost nothing about this meeting, which was likely the most important of her encounters in Chistopol. We know that two or three days before her arrival the question of Tsvetaeva's possible move from Yelabuga was discussed at a meeting of the evacuees' council, probably at the request of Flora Leites. Flora had been to Aseev's and, while trying to convince him, had promised that she would lodge Tsvetaeva and her son at her place. Aseev agreed to put the matter on the meeting's agenda.

The playwright Konstantin Trenyov took a strongly negative stand, however. A year earlier, together with Samuil Marshak, he had given

Tsvetaeva either fifty or a hundred rubles on some occasion, and now he spoke angrily about the "freeloader moods" of the recent White émigré. (Trenyov's play *Lyubov Yarovaya* was playing in many theaters in the country at the time, feeding its author well.)

Aseev didn't stand up to defend Tsvetaeva's interests. Perhaps he was afraid to argue with Trenyov's line ("her husband is a White Guard, she herself is a White emigrant, and Chistopol is crowded enough as it is"). Perhaps, he was protecting his own peace: if Tsvetaeva turned up it would be harder to avoid further troubles and efforts on her behalf.

The distraught Flora was about to send a telegram to inform Marina Tsvetaeva about the meeting's distressing result, but she was talked out of it at the post office by the writer, Lydia Chukovskaya, who by chance turned up right beside her.

"One shouldn't send such a telegram," she told Flora. "You yourself say that Marina Ivanovna is in a bad state."

"Well, what do you think can be done?" Flora asked.

"Insist! Plead on her behalf! What difference does it make to the Writers' Union where Tsvetaeva lives? She had a residence permit in Moscow or Moscow oblast, so why shouldn't they register her here?"[13]

Tsvetaeva found out about the meeting after she arrived in Chistopol. She went to Aseev's, and when he saw her, the poet was ashamed. With the excuse of feeling sick—an exacerbation of his tuberculosis—he didn't go to the next meeting, but, apparently, precisely through his efforts, on the day after Tsvetaeva arrived in Chistopol the board took up the matter again. Aseev sent a letter, and this time it supported Tsvetaeva's request.

(Many years later Aseev's wife claimed that in his letter Aseev simply quoted from "Lucerne," a famous story by Lev Tolstoy whose moral is that people should know how to value an artist while he is still alive. It was probably the following: "Such is the strange fate of poetry. . . . Everyone loves it and looks for it, it is the only thing in life that men want and seek, and yet no one recognizes its power, no one values this best treasure in the world, or values or thanks those who give it to people.")

Was Tsvetaeva at Aseev's only once? How did this meeting turn out? What topics were discussed, besides permission for the residence permit? And—what is especially important—*were they left alone*, without Oksana Mikhailovna, so that they might discuss sensitive topics? We don't have any reliable information about this and can only say for sure that Aseev didn't give Tsvetaeva any additional reason for cheer. He didn't promise her any serious support and didn't embellish the situation in Chistopol.

Very likely he intimidated her by emphasizing the impossibility of finding literary work, which in general, was not true. The writers who had settled in Chistopol gave lectures to audiences of workers and peasants and organized literary evenings; they published poetry in local and distant newspapers; they did extra work in the editorial offices of the local radio station. But it's true that none of this was for Tsvetaeva. I can't picture her traveling to give lectures or bringing poems of topical interest to the editorial office of the Chistopol newspaper.

Only in November 1941 would Konstantin Fedin come to Chistopol as a plenipotentiary representative of the board of the Soviet Writers' Union. The evacuees would then receive more protection.

Tsvetaeva might have felt that the most Aseev would do for her was write a letter to the board. That's the only thing he was capable of doing. But you can be sure that when they met, Tsvetaeva did not voice any reproaches or complaints. Otherwise before her suicide she couldn't have written the letter in which she entrusted to Aseev the care of her son.

Tsvetaeva spent the nights in Chistopol in the building of a secondary school for training teachers, which had been turned into a dormitory for evacuees. She spent the first night (25 August) in Valeria Navashina's room (she was the writer Konstantin Paustovsky's wife at the time). The next night (26 August) was spent in the room of Zhanna Gauzner, the daughter of the poet Vera Inber. Marina Ivanovna knew her slightly from Paris.

Everyone knew each other here—and knew about everyone's experiences. In two days time there was sufficient opportunity to collect information about Chistopol. Did people scare Tsvetaeva with the difficulties, or did they cheer her up, promise help, inspire hope? It's hard to measure someone else's experience—so many people, so many evaluations and opinions. However, it seems that Tsvetaeva saw many more minuses here than she had expected.

7

Almost everyone mentions Tsvetaeva's deathlike rigidity in Chistopol. According to Flora Leites, it was hard to look Marina Ivanovna in the eye: her glance was full of such hopelessness. Tatyana Alexeevna Evteeva-Schneider repeated this almost word for word.

When Tsvetaeva was introduced to Lydia Korneevna Chukovskaya on the street, Marina's words were friendly. But the words "weren't accompanied by a friendly smile," Chukovskaya writes. "There was no smile, either of the eyes or the lips. Neither an artificially polite, nor a sincerely friendly smile. She made her own kind of polite greeting in a soundless voice and toneless phrases."[14] Another writer, Pyotr Semynin (also in Chukovskaya's essay) described Tsvetaeva's voice as lifelessly "mechanical," repeating phrases that seemed to have been learned by rote.

On 26 August, the second day of Marina's stay in Chistopol, Chukovskaya met her in the hall of the city administration building, across from a room with the nameplate "Party Office."

> Marina Ivanovna stood pressed against the wall, her eyes fixed on the door, and totally gray.
>
> "You!" she threw herself at me like that and grabbed my hand, but immediately jerked her own hand back and settled into her former place. "Don't leave! Stay with me!"
>
> Right at this moment, behind the door, the question of Tsvetaeva's relocation to Chistopol was being reconsidered. They had already listened to Marina Ivanovna; now she had been sent out to the hall to await the decision.
>
> "My fate is being decided right now," she told me. "If they deny me a permit for Chistopol, I'll die. I'll throw myself in the Kama."[15]

It should be noted that these minutes in front of the Party office were fatal in Tsvetaeva's eyes. The decision that would be taken would determine—no more, no less—the question of whether she would remain in this world.

"Here, in Chistopol, there are people, there there's no one. Here there are brick houses, in the center at least, but there it's just country."

"I reminded her," Chukovskaya continues, "that even in Chistopol she and her son wouldn't be able to live in the center or in a brick house. They'd be in a wooden village hut. Without plumbing. Without electricity. Just like Yelabuga."

"But there are people here," she repeated unclearly and in an irritated manner. "In Yelabuga I'm afraid."

Soon Vera Vasilievna Smirnova would come out of the Party office and inform Tsvetaeva that a favorable decision had been reached. Tsvetaeva could go and look for housing right away. It wasn't so complicated, and as soon as she found something everything would be signed once and for all and she could move. Smirnova returned to the meeting in the room, and Chukovskaya and Tsvetaeva left the city council building and went out to the square.

I was amazed that Marina Ivanovna seemed completely unhappy about the favorable outcome to her troubles with the residence permit.

"Is it worth looking? I won't find anything anyway. It's better if I give up right away and go to Yelabuga."

"No! It's not that hard to find a room here."

"It doesn't matter. Even if I find a room, they won't give me work. I won't have anything to live on."[16]

Let us emphasize another thing: "they won't give me work." She might have said, "I won't find," but she said "they won't give." After all, what she had called her fate had just been decided, and decided in the best way. She could move to Chistopol right away, where everyone knew her and would *support* her, where Aseev lived and where the society organized by the evacuated writers would offer some protection.

Chukovskaya observed that her companion showed no joy, however. The obstacle that seemed insurmountable had barely disappeared when another one took its place. The feeling of hopelessness didn't disappear, punishment was simply delayed. That meant that new efforts were needed.

Chukovskaya agreed to go and look for housing with Tsvetaeva, since Marina Ivanovna was easily disoriented in unfamiliar places. On their way they had a conversation that is exceptionally important in understanding Tsvetaeva's emotional state. (I remind the reader that Chukovskaya's essay "Before Death" was based on material from the personal diary she kept for many years, including her years in Chistopol. Chukovskaya was scrupulously and pedantically devoted to the truth, which she never embellished with fabricated details. Her authority adds invaluable importance to *her testimony* about a meeting with Tsvetaeva several days before the suicide.)

"Tell me, please," here she came to a stop, stopping me also, "tell me, please, why do you think that it's still worth living? Don't you really understand what's coming?"

"Worthwhile or not—I stopped debating that long ago. They arrested people close to me in '37, and in '38 they shot my husband. Of course, life's not worth living for me, and in any case it doesn't matter any more how and where I live. But I have a daughter."

"But don't you really understand that everything's over? For you, for your daughter, and altogether."

We turned into my street.

"What do you mean—everything?" I asked.

"Altogether—everything!" She made a large circle in the air with the strange little bag she carried. "Well, Russia, for example!"

"And the Germans?"

"Yes, the Germans too."[17]

Let us focus on this: "the Germans too." I asked Lydia Korneevna about these phrases again. That's how she remembered them, how she wrote them down at the time, how she had heard them: "the Germans too," and "Well, Russia, for example." It's clear enough that the matter was not just one of the Germans alone and not just in Russia.

I'll risk taking this thought to its conclusion. In Tsvetaeva's eyes the catastrophe that was going on was worse than the nightmare of war. A disaster of global proportions was underway, swallowing Russia too. The dark forces of the world had incarnated into "nonhumans"; they held absolute power and were pitiless toward man. The swarm of Hitler's army, which was swallowing the Russian land, was only one of the faces of triumphant evil. It seems to me that it was precisely this—and nothing less—that Marina Ivanovna was talking about on 26 August 1941, four days before her death.

She was speaking to the only person she had met since leaving Moscow in whom she could sense a person like herself. She spoke, at last, in her own voice, without caution. Because it was *her scale of appraisal,* her characteristic viewpoint about what was happening: "from the roof of the world," as she wrote in one of her poems.

During the period when the Fascist army swallowed Czechoslovakia in practically one hour, Tsvetaeva wrote a poem that expressed the tragic feeling of a contemporary. "Verses for Bohemia" stuns with its uncommon power of personal feeling and its enlarged vision:

> I refuse—to be.
> In the Bedlam of nonhumans
> I refuse—to live.
> With the wolves of city squares
>
> I refuse—to howl.
> With the sharks of the plains
> I refuse to go—
> Down—in a stream of spines.

I don't need earholes
Or prophetic eyes.
There's just one answer to your
Senseless world—refusal.

This was only the spring of 1939! But for Tsvetaeva the bell had tolled. A year earlier her daughter had left France for Moscow; and half a year earlier, following the orders of the head of the NKVD in Paris, her husband had fled there in secret. When her husband and daughter were arrested in the fall of 1939, Tsvetaeva probably thought that her own freedom was based on some mistake and strange oversight. She viewed the freedom of her small circle of friends the same way.

Tsvetaeva completely lacked that aptitude for self-protection that ordinary people have: to adapt to the unbearable, to fuss, to make arrangements, to hold out—even at the foot of a volcano. She tried to do something and sometimes even displayed unexpected foresight (the letters from Chagin that she brought from Moscow, for example). But she couldn't become another person. She couldn't stop hearing what she heard, stop experiencing everything with an intensity that tore her heart.

"Lightning keeps striking you, but you have to live," she had written to Boris Pasternak seventeen years earlier [11 February 1923]—practically another life.[18] Tsvetaeva never resorted to beautiful metaphors for the sake of beauty alone, particularly when addressing a fellow poet. She was speaking about something that he was as familiar with as she: *the nature of the true poet.* You can be sure that she selected the most exact words so that he would recognize this immediately.

"Lightning keeps striking you, but you have to live . . ." In any case, it was that way with her.

If she had felt the approach of destruction so distinctly in the spring of 1939, and her sense of involuntary complicity in the growing treachery, baseness, and violence in the world was so unbearable at that time, what must she have felt now? The world was rapidly falling under the black shadow that covered the entire horizon.

At times she felt this so strongly that later, when she got hold of herself, she was ready to attribute it to illness. "I'm terribly ill," she wrote in a diary entry four days before her death—"it's no longer me." That's just what she had written Pasternak in that letter almost twenty years earlier (as well as in her essay "Art in the Light of Conscience"). The poet admits all elements, lightning keeps on striking her—and she can repulse it only in her creative work. But what if creative work had disappeared from her life?

8

Chukovskaya took Marina Ivanovna to her new friends the Schneiders. Lydia Korneevna had met them very recently, on her way to Chistopol. They received the unexpected guest very warmly. It turned out that they knew and loved her poetry and were sincerely happy to see her.

After tea and some conversation Tsvetaeva recited "Homesickness" (*Toska po rodine*, 1934).

> Homesickness! A darkness
> uncovered long ago!
> I don't care at all
> *where* I'm all alone,
>
> on what stones I drag myself
> and my market bag home
> to a building I don't know is mine—
> like some hospital, or hostel.

And further:

> Paralyzed, like a stump
> remaining from an avenue,
> I care about no one, I care
> about nothing, and maybe what I care

least about is what was once most mine.
All the signs, all the tokens,
all the dates—just gone like that:
A soul that was born—somewhere.

What would the penultimate stanza have conveyed at the time?

So little did my land protect me,
the most vigilant sleuth
will spy no birthmark in my soul,
the whole of it—length and breadth!

She didn't recite the poem to the end. Now it only expressed renunciation, absolute sorrow, the utter pain of abandonment—with no suggestion that tenderness had softened her feelings for her native land. At the Schneiders' home she didn't recite the abrupt ending:

But if along the way a bush appears—
especially the rowan-berry…

They asked her to read "Verses to Blok." She dismissed it—"old stuff!" She only wanted to recite what was still in her heart. Neither the Schneiders nor Chukovskaya knew her talent in full bloom; their admiration was confined to the work of the young, almost novice, poet, whom she had long ago left far behind. Tsvetaeva promised to recite *Poem of the Air* later that evening.

Her terror seemed to diminish a little. She relaxed in the atmosphere of a friendly home. Chukovskaya writes that Marina changed before her eyes. "Her gray cheeks acquired color. Her eyes turned from yellow to green. She drank her tea, moved to the rickety couch, and started smoking. She sat very straight, looking at the new faces with curiosity. . . . With every minute she got younger."[19]

Four days after this tea at the Schneiders came the fatal day in Yelabuga. I asked Lydia Korneevna about the idea that Tsvetaeva's breakdown bordered on mental illness. Chukovskaya strongly objected. Yes, there had been depression, endless exhaustion, despair that was hard to alleviate. But there was an energy that flowed from Tsvetaeva when she spoke, even if contrary to the sense of her words. She was nearing the end of her physical and mental strength, of course, but that was a completely different matter.

Later that evening Marina had planned to recite from memory her *Poem of the Air*, one of her most complex works.

At the Schneiders Marina spent several hours in friendly company. They listened with genuine interest to whatever she talked about and offered her practical help—dinner and lodging that night and help with the search for housing the next day. Tsvetaeva felt that she could trust these people, even though she had just met them a few hours earlier.

Then suddenly she remembered. She had agreed to meet someone. Who? Where? Chukovskaya recalls that Marina told the Schneiders (Chukovskaya had left the apartment for a short time) that someone was expecting her at the hotel. But several decades later Tatyana Alexeevna gave a different variant, according to which Tsvetaeva allegedly said she was going to see Aseev and she would return by eight o'clock. But she didn't return.

The word "hotel" sounds a warning. In those days officials from state security liked to arrange meetings in hotels. I don't think that was the case here, however. Tsvetaeva had just gotten to Chistopol. In principle, of course, it was possible for the police to search for her and fix an official meeting. But why? It was much easier to "get" her in Yelabuga.

Most likely Marina referred to the dormitory where she had been staying as a hotel. She really did go there, though very late in the evening and in a state of exhaustion. Another detail (which Belkina found): she had terrible pains in her legs. People heated up some water for her in the room where Zhanna Gauzner and Natalya Sokolova's family lived, and Marina Ivanovna sat on a bench, put her feet in the basin, and lowered her head. . . .

Where had she been in the meantime? Why was she tired? Why

hadn't she returned to the Schneiders? There's nothing so strange about the last point: Tsvetaeva hadn't left her son in Yelabuga (this was the first time she had been apart from him in Russia) just to read poetry and have pleasant social conversations with a cultured family.

Another version of that same meeting in the Schneiders' apartment was recorded in 1965 by L. A. Levitsky. It is based on the account of Tatyana Alexeevna, who became Paustovsky's wife around this time. The story has several new nuances; I'll repeat the main points.

When she heard the last name of the woman whom Chukovskaya had brought, Tatyana Alexeevna didn't at first realize that she was looking at the very same Tsvetaeva whose poetry she had known and loved for a long time. The guest's clothing looked shabby: a faded jacket and old skirt. At first Marina spoke in a confused way; her thoughts jumped around. Then Mikhail Yakovlevich Schneider appeared and unexpectedly began speaking to Marina in a cold and severe, almost mocking, tone. Tsvetaeva recoiled, and Tatyana Alexeevna shouted at her husband. He began to speak more gently.

The conversation didn't go well, however. They sat down to eat. Gradually Marina warmed up. After dinner she insisted on helping the hostess wash the dishes. The expression in her eyes struck Tatyana Alexeevna. They seemed dead, the eyes of a person people would describe as "not long for this world." The details in Levitsky's account help explain why Tsvetaeva preferred to spend the night in the Litfond dormitory rather than the relatively safe Schneider home.

9

Marina Ivanovna might have gone back to Aseev's, perhaps in order to thank him for his plea on her behalf; and now, after the main hurdle had been removed, to speak about the possibility of work in Chistopol; perhaps about *that other matter*—the threats—if that *was* a real factor. Maybe she hadn't discussed it in her earlier conversation with him and she hoped that circumstances would be more favorable now? Couldn't she have been in a despondent state, feeling that *that* shadow would continue to hang over her?

We don't know and we'll never find out, it seems, unless Nikolai Nikolaevich shared his memories with someone outside his own family circle. Then the topic might arise some day, though it will have lost virtually all its authenticity. As for authenticity, something else is known: Ariadna, Tsvetaeva's daughter, until the end of her life paled whenever Aseev's name was mentioned.

In her letter to Pasternak, written on 1 October 1956, we find these merciless lines: "These names [Tsvetaeva and Aseev] are linked only as are the names of Cain and Abel, or Mozart and Salieri. . . . For me Aseev is not a poet, not a human, not an enemy, not a traitor—he's a murderer and this murder is worse than that of D'Anthès."[20]

Sharp opinions and absolute judgments were typical of Tsvetaeva's daughter. But Ariadna knew the details of Marina Ivanovna's last days, in part, from the diary of her brother, whom she never saw again after they parted in August 1939. (She was released from prison camp after Georgy had been killed in the war.) Also, twenty-four years after her mother's death, Ariadna Sergeevna reported in a letter to V. N. Orlov (31 August 1965): "During a brief interlude between the camps and exile I managed to get in touch with people who were in Yelabuga at that time, and I recorded in their words what they still remembered well—only six years later."[21]

They didn't remember very well, we know now, despite the short period of time separating the recollections from the suicide. In the stories Ardiana wrote down there are many mistakes in memory.

Regarding Aseev's role at the time, there is one important thing that almost everyone who lived in Chistopol at the time agrees about. After the news of Tsvetaeva's death there were rumors about his guilt: he was indifferent and callow, he didn't help, didn't give her encouragement, didn't persuade her.

He did help, though, didn't he? At least with getting permission to move. But the Muscovites who were living in Chistopol at the time remembered the Stalin Prize winner as a sybaritic and stingy person. Aseev's spouse may have helped him get this reputation, but there were many reasons why people didn't forgive Aseev; among them, the fact that he put his father, who came later, in separate housing, some seedy little room, and the father had to eat in the substandard dining hall supported by the Writers' Union, while his son carried home fat geese from the market. Oksana Mikhailovna stocked up with honey there—not in small cups or glasses, as did those who needed it for the sick, but in huge cans that couldn't be hidden in a bag. "Our Geeseevs are getting their supplies," the spiteful and half-starved Muscovites joked behind their backs.

Aseev knew about Ariadna's attitude and her uncompromising refusal to forgive him. Something else is now known: Nikolai Nikolaevich didn't forgive himself for his behavior toward Marina Ivanovna. We would like to know for precisely what. He wasn't an inveterate scoundrel, he was just *indifferent* in those days and cowardly. He also didn't like to irritate his powerful and heartless wife. These qualities were enough to deflate Tsvetaeva's last hope for support.

Nadezhda Pavlovich's story, which Belkina cites, confirms that Aseev did not have a clean conscience with respect to Marina. Pavlovich accidentally met Aseev (shortly before his death) in the small Latvian town of Dzintari. He was in a small church near the writers' House of Creativity. Aseev was on his knees, praying and crying. He confessed to Pavlovich what was tormenting him: he was guilty before Marina, he was to blame for many things. Pavlovich conveyed what she remembered of Aseev's confession in 1979, when she was on the verge of death. Aseev probably gave no other details.

Tsvetaeva spent her last night in Chistopol in the dormitory. On the morning of 27 August she was back at the port. A port on the Kama River during the war years was a frightening place. Ships were transporting wounded soldiers from the front to hospitals in Sarapul and Perm. The stops dragged on indefinitely, and during stopovers the heavily wounded soldiers were carried out and placed on ground sheets on the shore. The men who could stand got off the boat by themselves, often dressed only in their underwear; they would try to buy vodka and cigarettes on the shore. Hoping to find their sons who had gone to war, local women would run down to the port. Their cries and sobs would resound long after. A unit of recruits on its way to the port was accompanied by the same unceasing and heartrending moans.

While at the port, waiting for a ship to Yelabuga, Tsvetaeva had a chance to talk with Elizaveta Loiter, who was on her way to Kazan. Loiter remembered that Marina Ivanovna seemed unhappy about the prospect of moving to Chistopol. She was upset and depressed. But about what?

10

Tsvetaeva returned to Yelabuga—there's an entry in Mur's diary about this on 28 August. A sentence from a letter Sikorskaya wrote to Ariadna Efron—"She returned quite encouraged and hopeful"—doesn't have any authority for us, since it is not based on the author's personal recollections. Sikorskaya was not in Yelabuga then. The story told by Brodelshchikova, Tsvetaeva's landlady in Yelabuga, which R. A. Mustafin recorded in 1964 (the very earliest of the Yelabuga records), is different: Marina Ivanovna returned defeated and downcast. That version better fits with the other details.

On the day after his mother returned, Mur's diary notes that a decision had been made: the following day, that is, 30 August, they would move to Chistopol. The decision seems to have been unusually hurried.

It's easy to guess that Mur terribly wanted to leave Yelabuga as quickly as possible. No matter what sobering details Marina Ivanovna might have given about Chistopol, he was convinced that no place could be worse than the Yelabugan hole. More than anything, however, he wanted to return to Moscow. Mur and his friends at the time, Vadim Sikorsky and Sasha Sokolovsky (they had become friends during the ten days they traveled together on the boat from Moscow), literally tormented their families at this time with demands to go back. Sasha

Sokolovsky even threatened suicide and actually made an attempt that September.

Still another circumstance was pressuring Tsvetaeva to make a decision about the departure and not put it off. September was quickly approaching. It was time to enroll Mur in school.

The rumor that the Brodelshchikovs' lodgers were planning to move probably spread when Tsvetaeva was in Chistopol. But it might have started earlier: let's recall A. I. Sizov's testimony.

It was after Tsvetaeva's return that the young Nina Brovedovskaya turned up at the house on Voroshilov Street. She had just come from Chistopol, and may have traveled on the ship with Tsvetaeva. Nina was from Pskov, and had come with her mother to Chistopol by chance and didn't like it there. Independent and energetic, Nina had set out for nearby Yelabuga to look around and search for housing, if things seemed better there. Immediately upon her arrival she was given the Brodelshchikovs' address. An evacuated teacher lived there, Nina was told, but she was planning to move, something didn't suit her. Nina remembered the landlords' name (however, incorrectly, as the Brodelnikovs) because it sounded a little like her own, Brovedovskaya. She also remembered the date of her arrival in Yelabuga, 28 August. It was her cousin's birthday and Nina had already sent a letter to her mother from Yelabuga, reminding her that the cousin had celebrated with them in Pskov exactly one year earlier.

At the Brodelshchikovs' house Nina found just the "teacher" at home. Judging by a number of details, it was on either 29 August or 30 August. The conversation with Nina Georgievna Molchanyuk, born Brovedovskaya, was recorded in 1984 by L. G. Trubitsyna from Naberezhnye Chelny, who worked for many years on a collection of materials about Tsvetaeva's last days, and Lilit Kozlov from Ulyanovsk, the author of several books about Tsvetaeva. Molchanyuk also had conversations with Anastasia Ivanovna Tsvetaeva and with staff members of the Moscow Museum of Fine Arts. In a handwritten letter, Molchanyuk gave a detailed account of her meeting with Tsvetaeva.

There are almost no discrepancies between the letter and the recorded conversation, and to avoid omitting important details, I'll offer a composite version.

When Nina arrived at the house, she was met by the lodger whom, for some reason, people had described as a teacher. Nina did not ask her name. The "teacher" was dressed strangely: she wore some kind of flannel robe and her legs were wrapped in thick puttees.

The wrapped legs suggest that on the eve of her departure from Chistopol Tsvetaeva had not taken a hot bath at night simply out of tiredness. Apparently, the pain in her legs continued. Incidentally, according to Mustafin's notes, Anastasia Brodelshchikova also remembered that Marina was ill in her final days (apparently, after her return from Chistopol) and that she had lain down. Because of this, she was not able to go with the others on 31 August to clean up the airfield. Everyone, the local people and the evacuees, was supposed to go work that day.

In answering the young woman who had turned up unexpectedly, Tsvetaeva confirmed that she and her son were indeed planning to leave. She named Chistopol, a city where they had friends who would "help us get settled there." Now the fact came out that Nina had just come from Chistopol.

Nina told Marina that she and her mother had not been able to find either a place to live or work there, and that the main thing for Nina was to get her mother settled because she herself would be leaving for the front. She had already finished her training as a medical attendant.

Tsvetaeva tried to talk the young woman out of these plans. It was impossible to live in Yelabuga, she said. There were "terrible people" here, and it was much worse in every way than in Chistopol. Besides, the front was no place for a young woman. The war was dirty and horrible, it was true hell, and death was not the most terrible thing that might occur there.

"All the more so because you have a mother," Tsvetaeva added. "I have a son, he's also dying to go somewhere all the time. He wants to return to Moscow, that's my native city, but I hate it now. . . . You're lucky your mother's with you. Take care of her. I'm alone."

"But you have a son," Nina countered, not understanding.

"That's completely different," was the answer. "It's important that you have someone older nearby, or someone you grew up with, with whom you can share common memories. When you lose such people, there's no one to whom you can say, 'And do you remember?' That's just like losing your past—it's worse than death."

These words struck Nina, as did the woman's language, her very speech, so out of place with the ordinary clothing.

Let us note that Tsvetaeva was composed, calm, perhaps even sober-minded in their talk. But the theme of war and infinite loneliness revealed an open wound.

For a long time Nina often thought of what she had heard—it seemed so meaningful to her. The woman had captured her affection and sympathy. The tragic events caused her to remember all the details of their conversation.

Nina was still in Yelabuga when news of the suicide spread around the town. As chance would have it, she was even at the cemetery in Yelabuga on the day of Tsvetaeva's burial. Only then did she realize that the suicide was the woman she had recently talked to. Afterwards her name was mentioned—Marina Tsvetaeva.

From childhood Nina had heard this name in her home: Tsvetaev. Precisely Tsvetaev and not Tsvetaeva. Nina's grandfather, an instructor of drawing in the Pskov gymnasium, had carried on an active correspondence with Ivan Vladimirovich Tsvetaev, Marina's father. Tsvetaev had sent him either an album or some kind of book with a dedicatory inscription. But Nina didn't know anything about the poet Marina Tsvetaeva. She heard about her only after she returned to Chistopol. It turned out that as a young woman Nina's mother had loved Tsvetaeva's verse. She had heard Marina and her sister Asya read; she had seen the sisters at literary evenings in the Crimea. Needless to say, Nina now gave her mother all the details of her meeting and Tsvetaeva's death. The shock preserved the details in Nina's memory for a long time. I have no doubt about the authenticity of her testimony.

I immediately felt that the external circumstances of their meeting seemed authentic, as did the dialogue itself, although it is extremely hard to believe in the reproduction of direct speech more than forty years after the event. My trust was immediate, however: those are Tsvetaeva's words! Tsvetaeva could have spoken exactly *that way and about those things*. Molchanyuk's testimony fits with absolutely everything—Marina Tsvetaeva's character, the peculiarities of her worldview, and the peculiarities of her situation at the time.

I found confirmation of this story in a recent publication of Ariadna Efron's letters. In two letters, addressed to different people at different times, Tsvetaeva's daughter repeats in the same words an idea familiar to us: "On 9 April I attended the funeral of the last person, it seems, in Russia to whom I could say, 'And do you remember?'—the husband of my old friend Nina Gordon; I don't know if you know her. I became friends with him in France, and with her in the first days after I arrived in the USSR." A letter of 28 August 1974 says almost the same thing: "What happiness when troubles are shared. But for a long time I've had no one to whom I could say 'And do you remember?'—if only I could say that!"[22] This unexpected echo is an important indicator. In Yelabuga Tsvetaeva was clearly repeating to a young stranger something that was often said in their home and that Alya, who was raised under her mother's forceful personality, had instinctively absorbed.

This episode refutes the version of Tsvetaeva's suicide as an act completed in a disturbed mental state. Chukovskaya and Molchanyuk's testimony, together with Tsvetaeva's three suicide letters—which were carefully thought out and calmly written—exclude that interpretation.

Let us also add that the ingenuous Sizov, speaking about the impression that Tsvetaeva had made on him, emphasized that it didn't seem that she was preparing to do something terrible. On the contrary, he sensed that she wanted to escape her trouble—to do something about it. "She had determination," Alexei Ivanovich insisted.

Why didn't Tsvetaeva and her son carry out their plan to leave for Chistopol on 30 August? Perhaps, simply because there was no ship going to Chistopol that day or the next day. At the time ships did not run regularly, according to Nina Molchanyuk. Nina was stuck in Yelabuga for precisely that reason, even though she was in a hurry to return to her mother.

In another entry in Mur's diary, however, on 30 August, he mentions two "literary ladies"—Rzhanovskaya and Sakonskaya, fellow passengers on the earlier ship. They discussed with Tsvetaeva whether or not she should go to Chistopol. They were the ones, Mur writes, who were talking Marina out of going. Since there was nothing definite in Chistopol, they reasoned, she should also look for work in Yelabuga.

Tsvetaeva found the strength to make a last attempt to drag herself and her son out of the hopeless situation. She walked—despite the pain in her legs—to a state produce farm on the outskirts of Yelabuga. She had been told she might arrange work there. She went and offered her services to the chairman of the state farm—to do correspondence and fill out papers.

"We're all literate here!" the chairman snapped.

A few days later a young woman doctor happened to talk to the chairman. The news of the suicide had already reached the state farm. The chairman realized that the tired, middle-aged woman who had recently come to see him had killed herself the following day. "I gave her fifty rubles then, just so as not to let her go without anything," the chairman said. "But she left, and left the money on my table. I couldn't give any more." The doctor wrote to Ehrenburg about this many years later.

Alms given to a great poet in hard times—didn't this, too, play a role? Who will venture to reconstruct Tsvetaeva's thoughts and feelings as she returned to Voroshilov Street empty-handed?

There is one other report, which has still not been verified, about a walk shortly before the fatal day. Alexander Sokolovsky (he was still quite young then, but a lover of poetry) later recounted that one day Tsvetaeva proposed a walk around Yelabuga. They circled the town several times and the whole time she spoke on one topic only— Mayakovsky's suicide. We don't know exactly what she said, and Sokolovsky is dead now.

Whenever her friends pitied her, Tsvetaeva immediately would let go of the tension that usually helped her to maintain her self-control: tears came to her eyes, she couldn't hold them back. The kindness of others made her weak; it exposed all her vulnerability—another reflection of those times.

One warm August day while taking a walk, a ten-year-old boy named Stanislav Romanovsky, also one of the evacuees, wandered into the empty building of the Church of the Protection of the Mother of God, whose half-destroyed cupolas could be seen from the windows of Tsvetaeva's home. He had come here many times to study the frescoes that were preserved on the walls. On that day he saw a woman with cropped half-gray hair. Squinting, she was examining the paintings on the walls, and the boy noticed that she was studying a fresco of a subject he knew. On it Saint Nikolai of Myra ("the Wonder-Worker") was restraining the arm of an executioner who had raised his sword above the condemned.

"He will save them," the boy told the woman. "They're not guilty of anything."

"I know that," the woman answered, turning toward the boy.

They started to talk. Her face was very unusual.

"Where do you live?" the boy asked.

"Here, nearby, near the *fontal*—do you know it?" the woman said and smiled. The word "fontal" sounds like the Russian word for "fountain," but the boy knew what she was talking about—a place where the women of Yelabuga rinsed their linen. An ordinary water pipe stuck out of the ground and let out a stream of babbling water. The boy understood her because he lived close by, also on Voroshilov Street.

They left the church together and talked a while longer.

Within a day or two the boy saw a horse-pulled carriage on their street carrying an open coffin. The boy had heard that a woman had hanged herself and he went closer to the coffin; looking down, he saw a familiar strange face with a thin nose. He recognized her right away, and ran off in a state of shock. It was the first death he had seen.

Romanovsky, who has lived in Moscow for a long time, told me that he could add much more about the circumstances of Tsvetaeva's tragic end. But why? Let God's judgment decide, he said, not man's. He spoke only about their meeting in the church, because there could be no falsification about that matter.

What was the last straw? The poet's sister, Anastasia, thought that it was a quarrel with Mur on the evening of August 30. But this wasn't the first time mother and son had spoken in raised voices. Whether or not it was a quarrel, no one can say. They always spoke in French when they quarreled; the landlady couldn't understand what they were talking about.

In comparison with what Tsvetaeva had gone through, the failures of the last days were no worse than mosquito bites. However, they meant that the next day and the day after that and for many days (and maybe months) on end, she would have to go on struggling. In Yelabuga or Chistopol. To search for lodging and work. To get humiliating rejections. To search again—and again be refused.

The advice of the two well-wishers, who caused Marina Ivanovna to waver in her decision to leave immediately, came at a moment when she *no longer had the strength* to try out new alternatives.

11

What about the NKVD theme? There seems to be no place for it in the last days, at least in external events.

After she returned from Chistopol, Tsvetaeva wavered: was it worth it to leave Yelabuga? She had seen the limits of Aseev's devotion; perhaps she even naïvely believed that he couldn't do anything for her except write letters to the board. She saw a dirty city, not all that different from Yelabuga, in which she didn't believe she could find literary work. All the same, she reached that conclusion too quickly, because it's possible that later, after Fedin's arrival, something would have been found. Marina Ivanovna hurried back to her son and had been too dispirited to learn about things in more detail. Had Aseev told her, for example, that she couldn't count on earning anything through literary work, she would have believed him completely.

"I don't know how to do anything else," she repeated many times to different kinds of people. And, indeed, she didn't, and was not capable of it. Sizov reported that Tsvetaeva had tried to be a dishwasher in Yelabuga. Whether this was before or after the trip to Chistopol is hard to establish. A waitress from a small restaurant in the court building on Karl Marx Street told Sizov about this attempt soon after the sensational story broke about the "woman who hanged herself." The waitress had heard customers talking at the table and interrupted. "I saw her, that evacuee of yours. She was here to work as a dishwasher. And all she did was half a day's work. She felt bad and left. And never came back." This account likely belongs to folklore. Experts claim that it was not so simple to get even that kind of job in those days. But if she could only find a job as a dishwasher in Chistopol, even in a dining hall for writers' children and wives, was it worth moving?

Let's suppose, though, that fear, and the hunger for advice and support, were the main impulses behind her trip to Chistopol. Then it becomes easier to understand why Tsvetaeva's gloomy state didn't disappear after the board of writers made its favorable decision. If Tsvetaeva had been looking for protection in Chistopol, she didn't find it there. She probably didn't even have a chance to discuss *that* concern with anyone.

She had new acquaintances in Yelabuga. What about old ones? She had no reason to seek advice from Zhanna Gauzner, a person from another generation. After the Chistopol trip she would have understood that she couldn't escape the all-seeing eye.

To agree to be an informer was out of the question for Tsevetaeva. But if she refused, what had she to fear? She didn't get the translator's job, in any case. A friend of Brodelshchikov, who spoke to me in Yelabuga about Tsvetaeva's landlords, recounted their words: "They didn't take her as a translator because of her past history." But the state security knew all the particulars of her biography when they proposed such a job. Wasn't this their first response to her refusal? What more could she expect from them? For herself and her son?

Here, indeed, is where the specter arises of that "dead end," about which Marina writes in the suicide letter to her son: "Tell Papa and Alya— if you see them—that I loved them until the last moment and explain that I *had come to a dead end*."[23] Tsvetaeva underlined the last words.

If we evaluate the situation calmly, there was no other dead end at this time. If the goal was permission to move, the trip to Chistopol had been a success. Everyone said finding a place to live was a problem that could be solved, and good people had promised to help her find work. An outsider's eye won't find a dead end here. But the unknown circumstances remain. As for our understanding of Tsvetaeva's complete loss of inner calm, how can the outsider's eye judge?

Two years later Mur confessed in a letter to Gurevich that shortly before her tragic death his mother had "completely lost her mind," and that he had become angry at her "sudden transformation." I cite four important sentences from that letter, which Mur wrote on 8 January 1943: "I remember M. I. in the days of evacuation from Moscow and the days before her death in the Tatar Republic. She completely lost her mind, lost her will. She was pure suffering. I didn't understand her at all then and got angry at her sudden transformation."[24]

Mur, who was at his mother's side all these months, thought that her state shortly before death was a "sudden transformation." But he would only become aware of that later.

In Yelabuga, during the last days of August when his mother's strength was declining and her emotional stress was aggravated by physical pain, the sixteen-year-old adolescent, who was annoyed by the new delay in leaving, couldn't find a single drop of sympathy. He was angry and cruel.

In his diary this entry appears on 30 August: "Like a revolving door, Mother absolutely doesn't know whether to stay here or move to Ch. She's trying to get me to say the 'decisive word,' but I refuse to utter the 'decisive word' because I don't want the responsibility for mother's gross mistakes to fall on me."

Less than twenty-four hours later, still bearing the burden of his responsibility, Mur's legs would give way and he would collapse onto the dusty road when the landlady told him that his mother was dead.

12

August 31, 1941. A bright sunny day. Everyone had left the house except Marina, and she knew that they wouldn't be gone long. The three notes left on the table were laconic, but every word was precise.

She died on the last day of summer. She saw herself about to be bridled by forces to which her spirit could not submit. Tsvetaeva always had her own peculiar attitude toward death. In her mature years she constantly thought and wrote about *voluntary death*. Death as protest—if there were no longer any hope of overcoming coercion. Death, if it was impossible to *be*, to live according to her own higher laws.

> You can't take my glow—
> As vital as overflowing rivers!
> You're a hunter, but I won't be caught,
> You are chase, but I am flight.
>
> You won't take my soul alive!
> Like an Arabian steed,
> At the full speed of the chase
> Bowing and biting
>
> Into a vein.

She wrote the proud words of "To Life" in 1924, and she bore that victorious feeling throughout life. Her life derived its strength from two sources: the duty, which she took upon herself with her whole heart, of caring for those close to her, and the splendor of creativity.

Tsvetaeva needed little in Yelabuga: minimal work in order to feed her son and from time to time to send parcels to her daughter and husband in the camps, and a chance to write for several hours a day. (When did she write her last line of poetry, or the last sentence in her diary?

"I stopped writing—and I stopped *being*," which sounds like a death sentence, was entered in her working notebook in 1940.)

She always called herself a survivor. She would have had enough strength to resist all the security officers in the world, as well as other troubles, if both the anchors of her existence had not been removed.

On 31 August she stepped into the realm of freedom.

Did Tsvetaeva remember on that last morning that one year earlier, on the same day, 31 August, she had been at the Party Central Committee? Not likely. She had been invited there in response to the telegram she had sent to Stalin several days earlier.

Tsvetaeva appealed to the leader a second time. No answer followed the letter, if, indeed, the letter was sent. Now the matter no longer concerned her husband's fate, but hers and her son's. By this time Marina Ivanovna had used all the channels she could think of and that her friends had suggested in order to find housing.

In the city of Moscow, which she had once celebrated in her poetry, there was no place for her to put her suitcases. There were a lot of them now, for in August 1940 customs finally released the baggage that had arrived from France. Tsvetaeva's library comprised an enormous part of it. Without luggage, without things, she and her son might still have wandered from apartment to apartment of various people. But with the luggage there was simply nowhere to go. They stored it at friends of Nikolai Vilmont, the Gabrichevskys, on Herzen Street, but the latter were expected to return from the Crimea any day. Tsvetaeva had sent letters to the Writers' Union to Alexander Fadeev and Pavlenko, she put notices in the newspaper, agreed to use a broker (who disappeared along with the advance), and turned to the Literary Fund for help—all with no results.

On 27 August 1940, Mur wrote in his diary that his mother was in a suicidal state. That was the day the telegram was sent, out of absolute hopelessness, to the Kremlin. "Help me, in desperate situation. The writer Tsvetaeva," were the words recorded in the diary.

On 31 August she was summoned. Not to Joseph Vissarionovich, needless to say. The agents had a friendly conversation with Tsvetaeva in one of the Central Committee departments. While she was there, they called the Writers' Union with an order to find housing for "the writer Tsvetaeva."

In a little garden nearby, Mur and Nikolai Vilmont waited patiently for Marina Ivanovna. There was a drizzling rain. When she appeared, all three were happy just because they were together again.

In less than a month the problem with housing was solved: A. D. Ratnitsky, an employee at Litfond, found a room, which the engineer Shukst, who left to work in the north, leased to Marina Ivanovna for two years. It's hard to say if this was a result of the call from the Central Committee. First of all, Ratnitsky had tried to help Tsvetaeva earlier; secondly, Marina Ivanovna had to collect on her own the huge sum required for a year's advance on the room. (Pasternak gave Tsvetaeva the lion's share of it.) It is likely the phone call from the Central Committee to the Writers' Union was a pretense. The usual lies temporarily relieved the stress, however. Mur's diary notes that that evening in celebration they drank Georgian wine, first at the Vilmonts, and then later at the Tarasenkovs.

On the same day (in the morning? or very late in the evening?), 31 August 1940, Marina Ivanovna wrote a bitter letter to the poet Vera Merkurieva. She wrote that there was no room for her in Moscow, that she couldn't rid herself of the outraged feeling that she had a right to be there. The Tsvetaevas had "lavished gifts upon Moscow." Through the efforts of her father the Museum of Fine Arts was established, and in the former Rumyantsev Museum were "three of our libraries: that of my grandfather, Alexander Danilovich Mein; my mother, Maria Alexandrovna Tsvetaeva; and my father, Ivan Vladimirovich Tsvetaev." Later Marina Ivanovna listed more of her rights: she was a native of the city, and she had the right of a Russian poet—the right of the author of "Verses about Moscow."

The humiliation provoked a powerful wave of wounded pride. "I gave Moscow my birth there!" she wrote in another letter to Merkurieva.[25] She directed it to the wrong person. But who was the person responsible for tormenting her and her friends and family, who took away the possibility of even the most modest existence? To whom could she have expressed everything that smoldered in her heart? I think this letter was written right before *a conversation with the authorities,* perhaps, in expectation of the appointed hour. With pen in hand Tsvetaeva was articulating arguments that she understood she could not make to them.

13

When Tsvetaeva quarreled with her husband and daughter in France about what was taking place in the Soviet Union, she thought they had been blinded and fooled, and that her evaluation, in contrast, was sober. How far she was from sobriety, however! What layers of illusions must have burst open as soon as she arrived in her fatherland! She had been prepared for a lot, but not for this.

What had she feared? That they wouldn't publish her, that they would clutter up Mur's head with Communist rubbish, that they would have to live in an atmosphere of physical-culture parades and loudspeakers on streets. Such were the nightmares she was heading for, since she had been left without a choice: her family had made it for her.

She couldn't imagine herself in Soviet Russia—with her love of freedom and fearlessness, which she called "the first and last word" of her being.[26] With this fearlessness could she envision signing congratulatory addresses to the great Stalin? After all, she had once discovered with horror Pasternak's signature in such a context in a Soviet newspaper.

But even in her sleep she couldn't have dreamed up what actually awaited her in the USSR. She didn't have to sign a congratulatory salutation, but, instead, petitions and supplications for help to the leader who inspired and controlled the lawlessness and who was responsible for her daughter and husband's torture.

Fearlessness . . . it becomes a cardboard word from the lexicon of knightly romances when what's at stake turns out not to be your own salvation but the life of those close to you. It turns into its opposite—constant fear. For those close to you. And for yourself, too, because they try to turn you into a means of crucifying the people you love.

"Yesterday, the 10th, my teeth were already chattering in the streetcar—long before," Tsvetaeva wrote in January 1941 in a working notebook, not finishing, swallowing bits of her sentences. "Yes, by themselves. And from their knocking (which I finally realized, and perhaps heard) I understood I'm afraid. I'm so afraid. When they took it, in the little window— they gave me a token—(No. 24)—tears began to flow, as if they'd only been waiting for that. If they hadn't taken it, I wouldn't have cried. . . ."

Is this translation into common human language clear? She's going to the prison with parcels for her husband, about whom she hasn't heard a thing for half a year. The only way of knowing if he's still alive is the parcel: they took it—that means he's alive.

A short note in another place in the notebook: "What's left for me, except fear for Mur (health, the future, his approaching sixteenth year, with his own passport and all the responsibility)?"

Another note, absorbing every detail: *"Fear. Of everything."* The words are underlined.[27]

In the winter and spring of 1940 the nights in Golitsyno tormented her—beaming headlights and the sound of cars passing by. She told Tatyana Kvanina nonchalantly, "If they come for me, I'll hang myself."

Her letters of 1939-1941 contain a scattering of confessions in which fear of her arrest, perhaps Mur's arrest also, can be distinctly noted. Hadn't they already arrested Andrei Trukhachev, her sister Asya's son? And Alexei, the son of the Klepinins?

Before Tsvetaeva departed with the evacuees, she needed to get a certificate from the housing office. She was afraid to go by herself. If she went for the certificate by herself, they would seize her immediately, she thought. She asked Nina Gordon to do it. Tsvetaeva was afraid of her passport—it was "marked." She was afraid of Mur's passport. She was afraid, according to Sikorskaya, to fill out forms. Whatever the question, it could catch you: where is your sister, your daughter, your husband, where did you come from?

Ida Shukst, her neighbor (still a ninth-grader then) in the apartment on Pokrovsky Boulevard, remembers that Tsvetaeva was afraid to answer the telephone and would ask her to find out who was calling.

Once—after the war started—the building manager came to the

apartment without warning. "Marina Ivanovna stood against the wall, her arms stretched out, as if prepared for anything, strained to the breaking-point. The manager left but she kept on standing that way."[28] It turned out that he had only come in order to test the blackout. However, Tsvetaeva remembered all too well the commandant's appearance at the Bolshevo dacha in the fall of 1939. Each time there was a routine search—and an arrest.

She was afraid to trust new acquaintances. Sikorskaya writes about this rather harshly: "She thought everyone was an enemy—it was like a persecution mania."[29] Were these fears exaggerated? Not at all. People also said that Anna Akhmatova exaggerated the attention the secret police paid her. However, we now know for certain that she did not exaggerate. Akhmatova's file, which was discovered in the recesses of the former NKVD, was established in 1939 and comprised three volumes.

Let us note an important difference in the tragic experiences of the two poets. Akhmatova had lived in her fatherland her entire life. Tsvetaeva found herself there after more than a seventeen-year break. Of course, she had not suspected that *such* a monstrous outburst of lawlessness and hypocrisy would have permeated the country. That's why her family's fate here elicited such shock.

I think that the world would have seemed much more stable to her if there had been an order for her own arrest. But they took away Alya and her husband—people who throughout the thirties had only words of praise for the Soviet land.

"My strongest passion—justice—was wounded and bloodied," Marina Ivanovna wrote in her notebook (the entry dates from the beginning of 1941). She still did not suspect that to take so strongly to heart the flouting of justice in her fatherland in these years was like grieving over the absence of snow in the Sahara.

Three letters were left on the table in their small room.

To her son:

> Murlyga! Forgive me, but it would have been worse to go on. I am *terribly* ill, I'm no longer myself. I love you madly. Please understand that I

couldn't live anymore. Tell Papa and Alya—if you see them—that I loved them until the last moment and explain that I *had come to a dead end.*

To the evacutated Muscovites:

Dear comrades!

Don't abandon Mur. I beg whoever can to take him to N. N. Aseev in Chistopol. The steamships are terrible, I beg you not to send him off by himself. Help him with his luggage too—with packing and getting it to Chistopol. I count on the sale of my things.

I hope that Mur will live and study. *With me he would be done for.* Aseev's address is on the envelope.

Don't bury me alive! Check well.

To Nikolai Aseev:

Dear Nikolai Nikolaevich![30]
Dear Sinyakov Sisters![31]

I beg you, take in Mur in Chistopol—*simply take him in as a son— and see that he studies.* I can't do anything more for him and I'll only kill him.

I have 150 r. in my purse and if you try you will sell all my things . . .

In the small trunk there are several manuscript books of poetry and a packet with offprints of prose.

I entrust them to you, take care of my dear Mur, he is in very frail health. Love him like a son—he deserves it.

And forgive me—*I couldn't bear it.*

M. Ts.

Don't ever leave him. I would be insanely happy, if he could live with you.

If you leave—take him with you.

Don't abandon him.

Indisputably, and without evidence "on paper," we will name the NKVD a direct accomplice in Marina Tsvetaeva's suicide.

The black deed didn't begin in Yelabuga; or in the fall of 1939 when Alya and Sergei Yakovlevich were arrested; or in the fall of 1937, when Reiss was killed near Lausanne, Efron fled France, and the French police twice interrogated Tsvetaeva. Perhaps it began in June 1931 when Sergei Yakovlevich took his application for repatriation to the Soviet consulate in Paris? Perhaps even earlier, in the twenties, when, after being given assignments in the offices of the GPU, the first spies in civilian clothes were sent to infiltrate the Russian emigration.

In the end it's not all that important to know at precisely what moment the web of lies and blackmail that caught Sergei and Ariadna Efron became a mortal danger to Tsvetaeva. Certainly there's another consideration: the threads of that web were tightly intertwined with the fatal Yelabugan noose.

Nikolai Gumilyov was shot; Osip Mandelstam and Nikolai Klyuev perished in the camps; Vsevolod Meyerhold and Isaac Babel were stood against the wall. . . . The proud, independent, brilliant Marina Tsvetaeva remains in the company of these writers, another victim of the Great October Socialist Revolution.

NOTES

Chapter 1. Bolshevo

(Notes are by the author unless otherwise indicated.)

1. Prince Dimitry Petrovich Svyatopolk-Mirsky (1890-1939). For more about him, see the recently published biography by G. S. Smith: *D. S. Mirsky: A Russian-English Life, 1890-1939* (London: Oxford, 2000). (trans.)

2. Vera Traill (Suvchinskaya), b. Guchkova (1906-1976). See Kudrova's note 6 in ch. 3, and Smith, *D. S. Mirsky.* (trans.)

3. Sergei Efron was involved with the Union for Repatriation of Russians Abroad in Paris, an organization promoted by the NKVD, the name of the secret police during the 1930s and World War II. (trans.)

4. Mikhail Koltsov (1898-1940), writer, worked as a journalist abroad and in the USSR for *Pravda.* In Europe he was an Soviet agent. Also caught up in the purges, he was arrested and shot in February 1940. (trans.)

5. Ignace Reiss (1899-1937) (real name: Poretsky), high-ranking official of the Soviet secret police who defected and was later assassinated by Soviet agents in September 1937 near Lausanne, Switzerland. (trans.)

6. Tsvetaeva was a friend of the poet Maksimilian Voloshin (1877-1932), who lived mainly in Koktebel in the Crimea. Tsvetaeva had met Sergei Efron at his house there. (trans.)

7. General Evgeny Miller (1867-1937), a Russian military leader, fought against Bolsheviks in the Civil War; after emigrating he became head of the Russian-All-Military Union in Paris. He was abducted there by Soviet agents in 1937, taken to Moscow, and shot. (trans.)

8. Nina Gordon quoted in *Bolshevo. Literaturnyi istoriko-kraevedcheskii al'- manakh.* 2nd ed. (Moscow: Pisatel', 1992), p. 282. Cited hereafter as *Bolshevo.*

9. Victoria Schweitzer, *Byt i bytie Mariny Tsvetaevoi* (Paris: Sintaksis, 1988), p. 461.

10. Il'ya Isidorovich Fondaminsky (1880-1942) (pseudonym Bunakov), journalist and editor of the émigré journal *Contemporary Notes* (*Sovremennye zapiski*) in Paris. (trans.)

11. Anna Tesková (1872-1954), journalist, translator, and president of the cultural section of the Czech-Russian Society in Prague. She became friends with Marina Tsvetaeva in Prague in the 1920s. (trans.)

12. From the personal archive of Marina Katseva (Boston).

13. The French is from Maria Razumovsky, *Marina Tsvetayeva: A Critical Biography*, trans. Aleksey Gibson (Newcastle upon Tyne, 1994), p. 265. For more on Tsvetaeva's interrogation by the French police, see the protocols in the Appendix, and Peter Huber and Daniel Kunzi, "Paris dans les années 30 sur Serge Efron et quelques agents du NKVD," *Cahiers du Monde russe et soviétique*, vol. 32, no. 2 (April-June, 1991), pp. 285-310. (trans.)

14. The Eurasian movement was started by Russian émigré intellectuals in the 1920s, foremost among whom were P. P. Suvchinsky, N. S. Trubetskoi, G. V. Florovsky, and P. N. Savitsky. It investigated Asian elements in Russian history and culture and promoted the view that Russia and Asia formed an integral ethno-geographical unity. The Eurasians published a large body of books and documents and also the newspaper *Eurasia*. At first the movement was not pro-Marxist. In the late 1920s, as Stalin was consolidating his power in the USSR, the émigré Eurasian movement was taken over by pro-Soviet figures. (trans.)

15. Veronika Losskaia, *Marina Tsvetaeva v zhizni: neizdannye vospominani-ia sovremennikov* (Moscow: Kultura i traditsii, 1992).

16. Prince Sergei Volkonsky, director of the Imperial Theater in St. Petersburg and writer who later emigrated to France; Konstantin Balmont, Russian symbolist poet, emigrated to France in 1920; Sophia (Sonechka)

Holliday, actress at the Vakhtangov Theater in Moscow who had a love affair with Tsvetaeva there in 1919; Anna Andreevna, wife of the writer Leonid Andreev; Ariadna Berg, friend to whom Tsvetaeva corresponded (her letters to Berg (1934-1939) have recently been collected and published); Mark Slonim, writer and one of the founding editors of the journal *Freedom of Russia* [Volia Rossii]; Elena Izvolskaya, Russian émigré journalist and translator who lived in Paris. (trans.)

17. A. I. Zhelyabov (1851-81), revolutionary, one of founders of the People's Will; N.V. Kletochnikov (1846-83), spy for the People's Will. (trans.)

18. Maria Belkina, *Skreshchenie sudeb. Popytka Tsvetaevoi, dvukh poslednikh let ee zhizni. Popytka vremeni, liudei, obstoiatel'stv,* 2nd ed. (Moscow: Rudomino, 1992).

19. Maria was the religious name of Elizaveta Yurievna Skobtsova-Kondratieva (1981-1945?), a nun in the Russian Orthodox Church in Paris. She was arrested by the Nazis for helping Jews, and died at Ravensbrück concentration camp. (trans.)

20. *Peterburgskii zhurnal* (1993), no. 1-2: 177.

21. The All-Union Agricultural Exhibition (VDNKh) opened in 1939 at Ostankino in Moscow. (trans.)

22. *Bolshevo,* p. 284.

23. Ibid., pp. 255-56.

24. The International Writers' Congress in Defense of Culture opened in Paris in June 1935. Organized by André Malraux, André Gide, and Ilya Ehrenburg, it was intended to support the left-wing cultural forces in their fight against Fascism. Ehrenburg hoped it would help to support the liberal camp in the Soviet literary world. Pasternak was a Soviet delegate to the congress. (trans.)

25. Belkina, *Skreshchenie sudeb,* pp. 29-30.

26. Stalin made a mysterious phone call to Pasternak in June 1934 reportedly because of the poet Mandelstam's attempted suicide. The call was probably part of Stalin's intrigues against Bukharin and the liberal wing of the Communist Party. See Lazar Fleishman, *Boris Pasternak. The Poet and His Politics* (Cambridge, MA: Harvard, 1990). (trans.)

27. Count A. A. Ignatiev (1877-1954), Tsarist officer who supported the Bolshevik regime after the Revolution, diplomat, writer. (trans.)

28. Cited in N. Gordon *Vospominaniia o Marine Tsvetaevoi* (Moscow: Sov. pisatel', 1992), p. 443. Further cited as *Vospominaniia.*

CHAPTER 2. LUBYANKA

1. Letter to V. N. Orlov, 28 August 1974. In *A dusha ne tonet* (Moscow, 1995), p. 382.

2. Mikhail Tukhachevsky (1893-1937), career officer in the Imperial Army who later supported the Revolution and rose to the rank of Commander in Chief of the Red Army in 1928. He became the army's principal strategist but was secretly tried and shot in 1937 along with other military leaders. Grigory Pyatakov and Karl Radek were both prominent Bolshevik activists who were arrested and tried at the second Moscow show trial (trial of the "Anti-Soviet Trotskyite Bloc") in 1937. (trans.)

3. Viktor Serge was a French anarchist and novelist who went to Russia as a revolutionary in 1917. He sided with Trotsky, was arrested and exiled to Central Asia. He was released and left the USSR in 1936. Serge's cause was taken up by left European writers, especially during the International Writers' Congress in Paris in 1935. See chap. 1, n. 24. (trans.)

4. The 1937 show trial in Moscow of the "Anti-Soviet Trotskyite Bloc" included the defendants G. Pyatakov, K. Radek, G. Ya. Sokolnikov, and L. P. Serebryakov. They were charged with sabotage and espionage on behalf of the Germans and Japanese. (trans.)

5. Belkina, *Skreshchenie sudeb,* p. 404.

6. Ibid., p. 422.

7. The date of this meeting remains unclear. The trade representative G. L. Pyatakov was in Paris in 1927. The years 1928 or 1929 were cited in the interrogation. However, the newspaper *Eurasia* only began to be printed in November 1928 and by September 1929 it had ceased publication—precisely because of a lack of funds.

8. "Letter of Sergei Efron to Evgeny Nedzel'sky," Turku, 1994, p. 6.

9. Kudrova's work in the KGB archive provided her with information that did not fit into the narrative frame of this book. She included the material in an

appendix to the Russian edition, but it has been incorporated into the notes in this edition. Almost all of the supplementary material, Kudrova writes, is based on generally inaccessible facts. The following excerpt is the first of several in this chapter (trans.):

Efron, who was pressed with questions about the Eurasians' practical activities, reported very interesting information. His descriptions reveal a broad area of the Eurasians' work that was hidden from the eyes of general sympathizers.

He reports that their work was divided among three sections. The first one was in charge of dispatching Eurasian literature to the USSR, using the Polish diplomatic bag, in part. Two men organized this activity—Konstantin Rodzevich and Pyotr Arapov.

The second section was engaged in sending emissaries to the Soviet Union. This was done with the help of the well-known organization called the "Trust." For a time many Eurasians sincerely believed that the Trust was an organization of like-minded thinkers that was formed and was acting illegally on Soviet territory. Even after the first revelations of a direct connection between the Trust and the OGPU [Unified State Political Directorate or Soviet State Security], people in Eurasian circles stubbornly maintained that an infiltration of individual Cheka employees did not discredit the entire organization. The Eurasians were not capable of believing that the Trust had *initially* been conceived in the offices of Dzerzhinsky and his secret police and then resourcefully staged with the goal of large-scale provocations. For months, even years, the Eurasians confidently insisted that they knew how to take advantage of the secret police's persistent attempts to establish contact with them. We know how these naïve hopes turned out.

Pyotr Arapov, according to Efron, completed three or four trips to the Soviet Union; he left Paris the last time in 1930 and didn't return, having disappeared forever in the gulag.

According to Efron, the third unit spread Eurasian propaganda in France, arranging meetings and talks of a completely academic nature. Soviet citizens who were living abroad were also invited.

According to P. N. Tolstoi's testimony, Efron had assumed the main role in the group of "left" Eurasians after Arapov disappeared. Klepinin reported the same thing under interrogation.

In 1931, through the Soviet embassy in Paris, Efron petitioned VTsIK (All-Russian Central Executive Committee) for permission to return to the homeland. There was no hidden agenda in this step. Efron, like many in his closest circle, gradually made a complete reevaluation of events in Russia. He became a sincere supporter of "socialist construction" and wanted to participate in it directly. His enthusiasm, his passion for the latest belief and idea, and willingness to serve it so unselfishly and blindly, were taken full advantage of by the bureaucrats at the Soviet embassy who had more power to deal with the Russian émigrés than VTsIK.

The change in attitude among Efron and his circle was by no means a revolution of 180 degrees, as is sometimes alleged by poorly informed authors. It was a gradual and even almost natural evolution of people who were not born political thinkers or activists. These conscientious and caring people could not resign themselves to what they considered a destructive course of events in Russia. The evolution of their views proceeded from the extinguished halo of Volunteerism, which in the end was destroyed by malice and greed (Efron wrote about this in his article "O Dobrovol'chestve," published in 1924 in *Sovremennye zapiski*, Paris, no. 21), to a reconsideration of the creeds of the "fathers" (the old intelligentsia of revolutionaries), and then to a search for *their own* path toward a reformed society. A revision of the view of the 1917 Revolution signified a major change: blind resistance was replaced by an acceptance of the revolution as an elemental social process that had to be taken into account as a reality. As time went on, they tolerated the slogans of October, and began naïvely to trust the proposed plans for agricultural reform and the New Economic Policy. It was at this time that clever and flattering people, disguised as innocent workers, appeared in the Paris trade delegation or at the embassy. There was no abrupt and sudden turn, but rather the powerful pull of a holy vision, a seduction by the "image of good."

10. *Izvestiia TsK/KPSS* (1989), no. 9, p. 40.

11. The interrogation records reported that P. N. Tolstoi had shadowed Gayana; this was unlikely to have been known earlier.

In 1935, however, one Soviet writer who traveled to Paris for the International Writers' Congress in Defense of Culture told Efron other news: Tolstoi had written a denunciation against his famous relative, Alexei Tolstoi, whose hospitality he had enjoyed. However, he didn't realize that Alexei Tolstoi had good friends in the Leningrad NKVD. Not only did they refuse to pass on the paper, they informed the writer about his guest's zealousness.

After he arrived in the USSR, Sergei Yakovlevich absolutely avoided meetings with Pavel Tolstoi and warned people to be extremely cautious around him.

12. Beginning with Efron's first interrogation, the question of ties with Masonic organizations (the investigator spelled it "Massony") was introduced in passing. At the time Efron spoke very explicitly: yes, he did have such a link with them, but *on the direct instructions of the NKVD* in Paris, "for I was their secret agent." His admission was similar to one mentioned earlier: P. S. Arapov also had contact with foreign agents on the orders of the GPU. But at the face-to-face confrontation Klepinin suggested a new approach: the tie with Russian Masons in Paris precisely amounted to Efron's direct work in French intelligence. This allegation was apparently composed with the prompting of investigators; they somehow had to make the espionage charge stick to Efron.

Klepinin's files contain more—in this case, reliable—information about Efron's contacts with one of the Masonic lodges. Sergei Yakovlevich, Klepinin claims, gave a report there (or even reports) and finally was "initiated into the highest order." The official certificate in Efron's file names the Masonic lodge (Gamayun) that Sergei Yakovlevich entered.

13. Bruno Yasensky (Jasienski) (1901-1941), a writer of Polish origin, who was politically active as a Communist in France and later emigrated to the USSR. Alexander Fadeev (1901-1956), a novelist who became a leader of the proletarian writers and a major figure in the Soviet literary establishment.

14. Maxim Litvinov (1876-1951), an émigré who worked for the Soviet foreign service in London and recruited the English for espionage work. He later returned to the USSR and became People's Commissar for Foreign Affairs (1930-1939). (trans.)

15. *Novyi mir*, 1988, no. 7, p. 181.

CHAPTER 3. "IN THE BEDLAM OF NONHUMANS"

1. In Tsvetaeva's long poem, *The Swain*, inspired by a folktale, the heroine falls in love with a swain who turns out to be a vampire. Tsvetaeva's ending differs

from that of the tale, in which the vampire dies. In her version the heroine follows the vampire and abandons her family. (trans.)

2. Isn't it quite clear why Nina Klepinina was given permission to go to
Russia with her sons almost immediately after her husband while Tsvetaeva was
not let out of France for another year and a half? Before the publication of
Tsvetaeva's correspondence with Ariadna Berg [*Pis'ma Mariny Tsvetaevoi k Ariadne
Berg 1934-1939*, (Paris: YMKA Press, 1990)], it was not so obvious that Marina
Ivanovna was not deciding on her own during these months whether to return
with her son to Russia and precisely when to return. From the correspondence it
is absolutely clear that from the moment her husband fled, Tsvetaeva's fate no
longer belonged to her. She submitted documents for departure at the end of
1937, approximately a month after Sergei Yakovlevich's disappearance. And from
the summer of 1938 she was expecting to depart literally any moment. But for
some reason she was kept in France. Because they simply forgot about her—or
were they waiting for the "right time"?

In fact, wasn't it more convenient to keep her and her son in France—in
the role of a hostage—as a check on Efron's behavior in the USSR? If he doesn't
cooperate, we won't let in his family. Or something else might happen. Wouldn't
Efron know about that?

But by the summer of 1939 Sergei Yakovlevich's arrest evidently had been
decided upon. And—for the same reason—Tsvetaeva and her son were needed in
Moscow. That way during his interrogations Efron could be blackmailed with the
threat of their arrest. We know the NKVD often acted this way then.

Incidentally, someone who knows Russian ways might explain Tsvetaeva's
delayed departure from France more simply, as Maria Belkina does in her
book. Let's imagine someone slipped a forgotten piece of paper into the hand
of an administrator in the early summer of 1939. He took it to the right person
and the poet was permitted to return to her homeland. Why not? Everything's
possible.

3. Emiliya Litauer was interrogated about Tsvetaeva on 19 February, and no
other topics arose that day. The investigator asked: "What anti-Soviet organizations was Tsvetaeva connected with in France? Which individuals hostile to the
USSR did she meet?"

Litauer named the journal *Sovremennye zapiski* [Contemporary notes], the newspaper *Eurasia*, the SR's Bunakov-Fondaminsky and Lebedev, "agents of foreign intelligence services" Svyatopolk-Mirsky, Traill, the Klepinins. Tsvetaeva's anti-Soviet sympathies, Emiliya said, were expressed in her poems about the White Army and the Tsar's family. The investigator recorded that upon her arrival in Bolshevo, Tsvetaeva "was not ashamed to declare in her circle that she came here as if to a prison and that any kind of creative work was impossible for her here."

4. See *Cahiers du Monde russe et soviétique*, vol. 32, no.2 (Avril-Juin 1991), pp. 285-310.

5. Pavel Sudoplatov and Anatoli Sudoplatov, *Special Tasks: The Memoirs of an Unwanted Witness—A Soviet Spymaster* (Boston: Back Bay Books, 1994), p. 47.

6. The name of Vera Alexandrovna Traill surfaces several times in the depositions of the prisoners from the Bolshevo house.

The daughter of A. I. Guchkov, the former Minister of War in the Provisional Government, Vera was married as a young woman to P. P. Suvchinsky, one of the most prominent Eurasianists in the Russian emigration in the 1920s. The Suvchinskys met Tsvetaeva at the end of 1925 or at the very beginning of 1926. In a letter of 24 November 1979, to the present author, V. A. Traill recalled this meeting:

> We became acquainted—yes, almost immediately after their [Tsvetaeva and Efron's] arrival in Paris. . . . We saw each other often. I was nineteen or twenty. Early on I discovered her poems for myself, and I was stunned. Then I read in Mirsky—"an undisciplined Muscovite"—and when he came from London (he had been spending the holidays in France), I created a scandal: "Ah, you, the great critic! You understand absolutely nothing! She's a brilliant poet." He humbly reread her and said that perhaps I was right. And when she appeared in Meudon (she had earlier lived at some Chernovs, I don't remember where) we all set out to meet her—Pyotr (my husband), Dim (Mirsky), and I.

Soon after the meeting the idea of a joint edition of the journal *Mileposts* [*Versty*] arose; the journal came out half a year later and elicited an extremely negative reaction from right émigré circles.

At the time Vera Alexandrovna played the role of the wife of a prominent man, but even then Tsvetaeva noticed her intelligence and originality. "She wrote to me rarely," Traill remembers in the same letter, "as we saw each other too often—the 3 or 4 letters I had were lost in a fire. I remember a phrase (compliments stay in one's memory!), 'A big ship needs a big sea.' I.e., she thought I was very smart. And I knew that she was an extraordinary poet. . . . I can't see how she is any less than Pasternak, for example."

One of the letters from Tsvetaeva to Vera Alexandrovna that survived (the fire) was published in the journal *Zvezda* (1992, no. 10). It contains a generous recognition of the young Suvchinskaya's indisputable merits in Marina Ivanovna's eyes: intelligence, pride, and even "spiritual purity."

Several years later, however, Tsvetaeva's attitude to Vera changed decisively, in part because Vera was trying to involve Ariadna in political controversies, and this furthered the already deepening estrangement between mother and daughter.

After Vera's divorce from Suvchinsky, Efron drew her into the Soviet intelligence work he had been involved in since the early thirties. Here she apparently found an outlet for the activeness, energy, and love of adventure that she inherited from her father. And also the ability to charm people from all circles.

In the summer of 1936 we find Vera Traill in Moscow. She was living in the Moskva Hotel and having meetings in the Café Natsional with former friends and accomplices who were arriving from Paris: Ariadna Efron, Emiliya Litauer, Nikolai Afanasov. She also saw Dimitry Svyatopolk-Mirsky, who had come to the USSR earlier than many others. During her interrogations Emiliya Litauer spoke about Vera Traill's dominant— indeed, commanding—position: not only Emilya, apparently, unquestioningly followed her advice, which was like an order.

"Why did Traill come to Moscow?" Ariadna Efron was asked during one interrogation. "The authorities summoned her to discuss her future work for the Foreign Department of the NKVD," Ariadna answered. Ariadna readily displayed her knowledge during such questions, presenting it as if it were a "safe conduct" for her. The safe conduct didn't work, however; Ariadna was interrogated in the fall of 1939—two years after Traill's departure from Moscow. Ariadna had to deal with Beria's investigators, not Yezhov's gang. Yezhov, who insofar as can be judged, protected Traill and other "cadres" recruited by the secret police from the emigration, was by this time a political corpse and an "enemy of the people."

The interrogations clarify the story of Guchkova's second marriage: at a joint meeting of Mirsky, Litauer, and Suvchinskaya it was resolved (and Efron supported this decision from Paris), that for espionage purposes Vera Alexandrovna would marry Robert Traill, an English journalist, Scottish by ancestry, who was situated in Moscow at this time. The plan was put into effect, and from that moment her role as a messenger between Moscow and France was facilitated by a foreign passport.

After her marriage, the Moscow superiors intended to send Traill to Great Britain for further work. However, they unexpectedly ran up against the energetic opposition of a restive subordinate. Traill gained access to Yezhov and was able to show that her work in France would be of incomparably more use to the NKVD, since she had numerous contacts there.

In the USSR, she spent a little more than a year, though it's impossible to say for certain whether or not she left the country during this period (from summer 1936 to September 1937). But she certainly left Moscow, for she regularly visited the school for NKVD agents outside Moscow. In his book *The Topsy-Turvy Hunter*, Kirill Khenkin states that she did not study in this famous school (as I thought initially, when I first read about it in the interrogation files), but *taught* there.

In 1979 Traill wrote me the following about Efron:

I don't know, if you know and want to know about the Reiss affair. People think that S. was mixed up in this, but I'm certain he wasn't. Marina, of course, didn't know anything and wasn't interested in politics at all.

I returned from Moscow around the 15th—maybe the 10th of September 1937. Seryozha came almost every day. He said that he'd fallen in love with a young aristocrat, 24 or 25 years old and didn't know what to do. I said, "I know what to do," but he let out a sigh and answered, "No, I cannot leave Marina."

My daughter was born on 20 September. And 3 to 4 days later S. showed up at the hospital: "I've gotten involved in a dirty business, I didn't have anything to do with it but I have to leave."

Let us note that this letter confirms the fact that Traill arrived in France "no later than 15 September," and actually, as we'll see later, about ten days earlier.

The transcripts of the interrogations of Sergei and Ariadna Efron, the Klepinins, Litauer, and Afanasov unambiguously clear up the nature of Vera Alexandrovna's activities. And now, when we know a lot more about this, we can read her personal letters, which various of her correspondents have revealed.

In the book *Agents of Moscow* (*Agents de Moscou. Le Stalinisme et son ombre*, Paris: Gallimard, 1989), which abounds in factual inaccuracies and mistakes, the French author Allain Brossat told, in part, about the contents of a suitcase that was discovered among the articles of the Russian émigré K. B. Rodzevich, who died in a geriatric home in Paris. Among other things, there was a packet of letters from his old lover and comrade, V. A. Traill. They were completely honest with one another, of course, and one can only regret that they didn't find it necessary to inform each other of certain circumstances familar to both.

Nonetheless, the epistolary texts cited in Brossat's book clearly indicate that both participated in Soviet espionage.

A letter from Vera Traill to Emiliya Litauer's brother, Alexander, is a new find. In the thirties she was also a close friend of his. I cite two excerpts from a letter of 27 September 1984.

Ah yes! Why do I think that Yezhov can save my life. Because I spent 4 hours with him—from midnight till 4 a.m.—I went to try to persuade him to stop the terror—and handed him a list of my friends who had been arrested—20 people. He said that he needed their dossiers and told me to return in 3 or 4 days to discuss them with him. But I didn't wait four days.

The next midnight (the Chekists only woke up then) there was a phone call: "The Kremlin is calling. A message from Comrade Commissar: 'Leave immediately.'" I was frightened for a second—(that is, my heart managed to give a little jump—why "immediately"?), but I suddenly remembered and got mad: "I can't leave in the middle of the night." The cop with a deep voice sounded annoyed: "Not in the middle of the night, but on the first train. At 9:30, I think. If you don't make it, there's an evening train."

I continued to get mad and to argue: "But he promised to show me . . . mmm . . . some papers." "Yes," the Chekist growled. "You didn't let me finish.

The papers will be in our Paris consulate. After the birth—we wish you the very best—drop by there." I didn't leave the next day but the day after, it seems. Masha was born . . ." (The last page of the letter is missing.)

And here's another excerpt, from a letter to the same addressee:

I don't remember that I led you astray politically. It would be shameful if I had been such a naive fool. But people smarter or in any case more learned than I am also got caught and paid for it with their life. Milya [Emiliya Litauer]—and Mirsky.

How I survived there in 1937 is not completely clear, but some people suspected that Nikolai Ivanovich Yezhov himself fell in love with me. That he saved my life is a fact, but that he fell in love—I don't think so. Unlikely. He barely came up to my waist and I was in the ninth month of pregnancy. What kind of love is that?

The last sentence in this letter was written next to a drawing by Traill of Yezhov standing beside her.

Alexander Litauer, who still lives in Paris, continues to believe the version that Yezhov was in love and played the role of savior. As for me, I would interpret the episode differently. It seems to me that the People's Commissar of the NKVD found a clever way to avoid answering the obstinate Traill's demanding inquiry about her arrested friends. Of course, it would have been more natural for him simply to have given an order to arrest her, and from this point of view Nikolai Ivanovich does appear as a benefactor. However, even such a "good deed" is doubtful.

Most likely, she had gone to see Yezhov then not for her friends' sake but because she was summoned. Yezhov, evidently, had prepared Traill as an emissary—for carrying money and instructions to Paris quickly. And because of her insistent and extremely inconvenient request regarding her arrested friends, he speeded up the date of her departure.

Let's compare dates, in fact. The conversation between Traill and Yezhov most likely took place at the very beginning of September. I make this assumption on the basis of information from the Swiss historians P. Huber and D. Kunzi, who worked in the archives of Hoover Institution. Citing documents in the police archives, they discuss several circumstances surrounding Traill's return to France, particularly the fact that soon after her arrival in Paris the police appeared at her apartment with a search warrant. There they unexpectedly found K. B. Rodzevich, who had just burned some papers in a hurry. The police documents established that Traill had brought a check in a large amount from Moscow for the mother of Viktor Pravdin (also known as François Rossi, one of Ignace Reiss's murderers).

Under questioning by the French police, Traill convincingly proved her own alibi regarding that murder. She produced her passport in which the customs service had recorded that on the precise day Reiss was killed near Lausanne (4 September), Traill was crossing through Poland.

However, if she was traveling through Poland on 4 September, then she must have left Moscow on 1 or 2 September. At that very time Yezhov knew that the task force that had been searching for Reiss for a month and a half (from the time he gave the Parisian consulate his "Letter to the CC of the Party") had discovered him in Switzerland. The murder would take place soon. Perhaps it was better not to wait for the final report and to dispatch the prepared emissary a bit earlier, particularly to avoid disappointing her with distressing news about her friends.

Toward the end of her life Traill had lost her illusions about the great socialist homeland and considered herself, as we read in one of the above letters, one of its deceived victims. Nevertheless, in her memoirs (now in Leeds Russian Archive), which she dictated into a tape recorder during the last years of her life and which were transcribed by Professor G. S. Smith, there is no mention about her work for the NKVD, as far as I know.

V. A. Traill died in Cambridge, England, in April 1987, at the age of eighty.

I once managed to have a brief conversation with her during a trip she made to Moscow—in 1980, I think. The meeting was arranged by A. V. Eisner, at one time a close friend of Vera's. Traill was energetic, ironic, and cheerful, despite her age and a recently broken leg. Unfortunately, at the time I knew too little to ask the important questions. But it's not likely she would have been candid with me, even though she appeared to be extremely helpful and open.

7. After Ariadna's meeting of 14 March 1940 with the prosecutor Antonov, her case was treated separately.

From the text of the resolution composed by the investigation, it appears that this step was taken because of the failure to establish A. S. Efron's espionage ties. Nevertheless, the prosecutor's conclusion retained the old charges: "she was an agent of French intelligence and was present at anti-Soviet gatherings of a certain group. . . . This having been established, the case is forwarded to the Procurator of the USSR for trial." The date of the formal charge was 16 May 1940.

A Special Board (the triumvirate of the People's Commissariat of Internal Affairs that was used to try cases outside normal legal processes), before which the accused never appeared, decided Ariadna's fate on 2 July 1940: "A term of 8 years in a corrective labor camp for her espionage activities." But Ariadna was kept in the inner prison (for political prisoners) until the beginning of the following year. They let her know her sentence only on 24 December—half a year after its pronouncement. I don't know whether this was a widespread practice at the time.

8. We have gained important information about Ariadna Efron's life from reading her file. Thus, she recounted that she was initially an ordinary member of the Parisian Union for Repatriation and then organized a youth group. She worked for the journal *Our Union* as an editorial assistant and designer. In an application sent to Procurator Rudenko in 1954, she characterized the Union for Repatriation as an organization that constituted "one of the undercover anchors of our counterespionage in Paris."

9. Marina Tsvetaeva, *Pis'ma k Anne Teskovoi* (St. Petersburg: Vneshtorgizdat, 1991), p. 87.

Chapter 4. Yelabuga

1. The young Tatyana Kvanina was in Golitsyno with her husband, the writer Nikolai Moskvin. Kvanina's memoir about her friendship with Tsvetaeva was published in the journal *Oktiabr'* (Moscow, 1982, no. 9). (trans.)

2. Gordon, *Vospominaniia*, p. 447.

3. See Ida Shukst-Ignatova, "Vospominanniia", in I. V. Kudrova, *Gibel' Mariny Tsvetaevoi* (Moscow: Nezavisimaia gazeta, 1995), pp. 290-98.

4. Dimitry Sezeman, *Paris–Gulag–Paris.*

5. Gordon, *Vospominaniia,* p. 449.

6. Tsvetaeva's acquaintance with Flora Leites on the boat and the date of the telegram that was sent to Flora from Yelabuga come from M. Belkina's research; my part here lies only in the attempt to explain the inner logic of events.

7. Belkina, p. 320.

8. Kirill Khenkin, *Okhotnik vverkh nogami* (Moscow: Terra-Terra, 1991), pp. 49-50.

9. Belkina, p. 307.

10. A. I. Sizov's story was first published in Lilit Kozlova, *Voda rodnikova-ia k istokam lichnosti Mariny Tsvetaevoi* (Ul'ianovsk, 1992), p. 207.

11. V. V. Schweitzer, "Poezdka v Elabugu," *Marina Tsvetaeva. Neizdannye pis'ma* (Paris, 1972), p. 643.

12. *Bolshevo,* p. 211.

13. I am citing L. K. Chukovskaia's text. See *Vospominaniia,* p. 328.

14. *Vospominaniia,* p. 533.

15. Ibid., p. 536.

16. Ibid., p. 537.

17. Ibid., p. 538.

18. Letter of Tsvetaeva to Pasternak, February 11, 1923, in Marina Tsvetaeva, *Sochineniia v dvukh tomakh,* vol. 2 (Moscow, 1988), p. 481.

19. *Vospominaniia,* p. 543.

20. Ariadna Efron. *O Marine Tsvetaevoi. Vospominaniia docheri* (Moscow: Sovietskii pisatel', 1989), p. 455. D'Anthés killed the poet Pushkin in a duel.

21. Russian State Archives of Literature and Art (RGALI), f. 2833 (fond V. N. Orlova), ed. khr. 322.

22. *Novyi mir,* 1993, no. 3, pp. 189, 193.

23. Belkina, p. 326.

24. Letter of G. S. Efron to S. D. Gurevich, January 8, 1943 (*Russkaia mysl',* Paris, 9 June 1991).

25. Marina Tsvetaeva, *Gde otstupaetsia liubov?* . . . (Petrozavodsk: Kareliia, 1991).

26. Marina Tsvetaeva, *Pis'ma k Anne Teskovoi,* p. 115.

27. Entry in Tsvetaeva's notebook 1940-1941.

28. I. B. Shukst-Ignatova, "Vospominaniia," p. 297.

29. Belkina, p. 307.

30. N. N. Aseev.

31. Aseev's wife, Oksana Mikhailovna, was born Sinyakova. Her two sisters also lived in Chistopol then.

APPENDIX

PROTOCOLS OF THE QUESTIONING OF M. TSVETAEVA AT POLICE
HEADQUARTERS IN PARIS (1937)

Until recently little was known about the interrogation of Marina
Tsvetaeva in the fall of 1937 at the Paris police headquarters. Mark Slonim
wrote the most detailed account of it in his memoirs (*Vospominaniia*):
"During the interrogations by the French police (Sûreté) she insisted on
her husband's honesty, on the conflict between duty and love, and from
memory she cited Corneille or Racine (later she told first M. N. Lebedova
about this and then me). At first the officials thought that she was being
cunning and pretending, but when she started to quote French translations of Pushkin and of her own poetry, they began to doubt her emotional stability and presented her to the specialists in émigré affairs who
had come to help as 'this crazy Russian' (*cette folle Russe*)."

Tsvetaeva laconically reported the same thing in a letter to Ariadna
Berg, 26 October, two weeks after her husband's flight from France and
four days after the first interrogation in the Direction générale de la Sûreté
Nationale: "I cannot write more right now, because I am completely broken by events that are also *misfortune*, and not *fault*. I'll tell you what I said
during the interrogation: 'C'est le plus loyal, le plus noble et le plus

humain des hommes.—Mais sa bonne foi a pu être abusée.—La mienne en lui—jamais.'"

Further, in a letter to the same correspondent, 2 November 1937: "Whatever bad things you heard or read about my husband, don't believe them, just as they're not believed by *a single person* (even extreme rightists) who *knew* him or had met him. . . . As for me: you know that I didn't commit any kind of 'act' (by the way, they know this in the Sûreté, too, where they held me and Mur from morning till evening——and not only from total incapability, but from the deepest aversion to politics, *all* of which— with the rarest exceptions—I consider *dirt.*"

The talk about her husband's guilt and her unshakeable faith in his nobility that she reported to Berg are not to be found in the transcripts, which appear below. Marina Tsvetaeva's "poetry reading" before the Parisian investigators is also not recorded in these texts, of course. But that does not mean that either is the fruit of the poet's fantasy.

Tsvetaeva was apparently proud of the formula she had found to defend her husband's honor from accusations she felt were a monstrous misunderstanding and mistake. In her letter to Stalin she repeats her passionate claim in almost the same words: "I do not know what my husband has been accused of, but I know that he is not capable of any kind of treachery, double dealing, or perfidy. I know him: 1911–1939—a little less than 30 years, but what I know about him I knew from the first day: that he is a person of extreme purity, self-sacrifice, and responsibility. His friends and enemies would say the same thing about him."

Let us recall the conditions in Paris at the end of 1937. Tsvetaeva's interrogations were connected with the police investigation of a murder committed in the outskirts of Lausanne on 4 September of that year. The dead man was the Soviet citizen Ignace Reiss (Poretsky), who shortly before had decided not to return to the USSR as ordered by the foreign section of the NKVD. Poretsky reported his refusal in a denunciatory letter addressed to the Central Committee of the Bolshevik party in Moscow. When the letter was delivered to the Soviet embassy in Paris (through Walter Krivitsky), it was immediately opened there. At that time the deputy head of the foreign section was S. M. Shpigelglas.

Quickly an operative group was formed to search for the author of the letter, who had disappeared from Paris. The group included, in particular, François Rossi (also known as Viktor Pravdin), Charles Martignat, the Swiss citizen Renata Steiner, the Frenchman Jean-Pierre Ducomet, and also two Russian emigrants who lived in France, Dimitry Smirensky and Vadim Kondratiev. According to KGB general P. A. Sudoplatov, the group also included a Bulgarian "illegal," Boris Afanasiev, who went with Pravdin to Moscow immediately after the murder.

There is no doubt today that Efron was outside Switzerland during these days. But in the testimony Renata Steiner gave during her first interrogations the name Efron was mentioned repeatedly, not in connection with the "Lausanne action" but as a person who recruited her and later gave her occasional jobs.

The supposition that Efron was with those who took part in the Reiss murder became a certainty for almost all of Russian Paris when Sergei Yakovlevich suddenly disappeared. This occurred on 11-12 October 1937. Early in the morning of 22 October four inspectors from the French police appeared at the building where Tsvetaeva lived. They conducted an extensive search in the apartment and when they left they took S. Ya. Efron's personal papers and correspondence. On the same day the first interrogation of Marina Ivanovna took place in the Paris prefecture. Tsvetaeva reported that she spent the whole day there with her son. The record of the interrogation does not, of course, reflect even a small part of what was said that day within the walls of that respectable establishment. Yet the documents are of unquestionable interest to us.

The text of the interrogations is reprinted from an article by Peter Huber and Daniel Kunzi, "Paris dans les années 30: Sur Serge Efron et quelques agents du NKVD" (*Cahiers du Monde russe et soviétique* 32, no. 2, pp. 285-310). It is clear that the text cited contains Marina Tsvetaeva's response to different questions: the investigator's questions themselves are not reflected in Huber and Kunzi's publication.

1

MINISTÈRE DE L'INTÉRIEUR
DIRECTION GÉNÉRALE DE LA SÛRETÉ NATIONALE
CONTRÔLE GÉNÉRAL DES SERVICES DE POLICE CRIMINELLE

Case of Ducomet, Pierre[1] and others accused of murder and complicity.
Deposition of Mme. Efron, née Tsvetaeva, Marina, 43 years old, residing
at the address: 65, rue Jean-Baptiste Potin in Vanves (Seine).

22 October 1937

We, PAPIN Robert, Commissaire de Police mobile at the Contrôle
Général des Services de Police criminelle (Direction générale de la Sûreté
Nationale) in Paris, officer of the Criminal Investigation Department,
assistant to the Attorney General, hear Mme. EFRON, née TSVETAEVA,
born 31 July 1894 in Moscow of the now deceased Ivan and Maria BERN-
SKY,[2] a writer residing in Vanves at No. 65, rue J.-B. Potin, who after taking an oath, attested:

"I have supported myself all my life by my profession, I work for the
journals *Russkie zapiski* [*Les Annales Russes*] and *Sovremennye zapiski* [*Les
Annales Contemporaines*], I earn from six hundred to eight hundred francs
a month. My husband, a journalist, writes articles for the journal *Nash
Soiuz* [*Notre Patrie*], which is published by the Union for Repatriation[3]
whose residence is on rue de Buci in Paris.

As far as I know, my husband had gone to work there every day since
the Union was founded. My daughter, Ariadna, was born on 5 September
1913[4] in Moscow; she also worked there[5] as an artist. In April of this year

she left this job and returned to Russia. At the present time she is in Moscow where she works in the editorial office of a French weekly that is printed in this city—*Revue de Moscou.*

The Union for Repatriation, as the name itself indicates, has the goal of helping our compatriots, Russian emigrants who have found sanctuary in France, to return to Russia. I do not know any of the leaders of this organization, though a year or two ago I became acquainted with a M. AFANASOV,[6] a member of the organization who went to Russia a little more than a year ago. I knew him because he came to our home several times to see my husband. My husband was an officer in the White Army, but after we came to France in 1926 his views changed. He was the editor of the newspaper EURASIA,[7] which came out in Paris and was published, I think, in Clamart or its vicinity. I can tell you that this paper no longer appears. I personally do not take part in politics but it seems to me that my husband has been a supporter of the present Soviet regime for two or three years.

Since the start of the Spanish revolution my husband became an ardent champion of the republicans and this feeling became more intense in September of this year when we took a vacation in Lacanau-Océan in Gironde, where we witnessed a mass arrival of refugees from Santander.[8] From that time he began expressing the desire to go to Spain and fight on the side of the republicans. He left Vanves on 11-12 October of this year and from that time I have had no news of him. Thus, I cannot tell you where he is right now and I don't know whether he went by himself or with someone.

I don't know any male acquaintance named "BOB,"[9] I also don't know SMIRENSKY or ROLLIN Marcel.[10]

At the end of the summer of 1936, in August or September, I went for a rest with my son Georgy (who was born 1 February 1925 in Prague) to my compatriots, the STRANGUE [Shtrange] family, who lived in the Château d'Arçine in St.-Pierre-de-Rumilly (Upper Savoy/Hte-Savoie).

The STRANGUES had a family pension at the address indicated. They have a son Michel,[11] age 25 to 30, who is engaged in literary work. Michel STRANGUE usually does not live in Paris but at his parents' home. I don't know if he comes here often and I don't know if he continues to maintain relations with my husband.

My husband brought practically no one home and I do not know all his acquaintances.

Among the many photographs you have shown me, I know only KONDRATIEV,[12] whom I met at the home of common friends, the KLEPININS, who were living in Issy-les-Moulinaux, on rue Madeleine Moreau, no. 8 or 10. I met him about two years ago when KONDRATIEV planned to marry Anna SUVCHINSKAYA who worked as a governess for Mme. KLEPININ.[13]

My husband and I were astonished when we learned from the press about KONDRATIEV's flight in connection with the REISS affair.

On one of the photographs I also recognize M. POZNYAKOV.[14] This man, a photographer by profession, enlarged several photographs for me. He also knew my husband, but I do not know anything about his political convictions and what he is doing now.

My husband and I responded to the REISS affair with pure indignation. We both condemn all acts of violence no matter what side it comes from.

Thus, as I have told you, I know only those acquaintances of my husband who were in our home and I cannot tell you if Poznyakov was acquainted with Mlle. STEINER[15] or with some other person in the photographs that you showed me.

I cannot give any information about the people you are interested in.

On 17 July 1937, my son and I left Paris for Lacanau-Océan. We returned to the capital on 20 September. My husband came to us on 12 August and returned to Paris on 12 September 1937.[16]

In Lacanau we stayed in the villa "Coup de Roulis" on avenue des Frères Estrade à Lacanau. This building belonged to M. and Mme. COCHIN.

On vacation my husband was with me the whole time. He did not go off anywhere.

In general, my husband left at times for several days, but he never told me where he was going and what he was going to do. For my part, I never demanded an explanation from him, or when I did ask, he would simply answer that he was going on business. Therefore I cannot tell you where he was."

Lecture faite, persiste et signe
Le Commissaire de Police Mobile
R. Papin (signature)
M. Tsvetaeva-Efron (signature)

2

Transcript from 27 November 1937

The case of Steiner, Renée, Schildbach,[17] Rossi[18] and all others.
Deposition of Mme. Efron, née Tsvetaeva, Marina, 43 years old, residing at the address: 65, rue Jean-Baptiste Potin in Vanves.

We, BOREL Robert, Inspecteur Principal de Police mobile, at the Contrôle Général des Services de Police criminelle (Direction générale de la Sûreté Nationale) in Paris, officer of the Criminal Investigation Department, assistant to the Attorney General.

In view of the letters rogatory attached, dated 16 September 1937, from M. Subilla, examining magistrate of the Tribunal of Lausanne, transmitted to us for execution on the 6th of the same month by the senior examining magistrate of the Department of Seine and relating to the investigation of the case of STEINER Renée, ROSSI and all the authors accused of murder and complicity.

Having summoned before us for questioning the witness Mme. EFRON, née TSVETAEVA, Marina, 30 July 1894, in Moscow, a woman of Letters, who resides on 65, rue Jean-Baptiste Potin in Vanves (Seine).

Who, after having declared that she is not related or married to or an employee of the accused, and having sworn to tell the whole truth and nothing but the truth, testified as follows:

"I was already questioned on 22 October of this year in accordance with the letters rogatory, dated the 21st of the same month, by the examining magistrate in Paris, Mr. BETEILLE, concerning my husband's political activity. I have nothing to add to the first testimony.

My husband left for Spain in order to serve in the ranks of the Republicans,[19] on 11-12 October of this year. Since this time I have not received any news from him.

I know that before his departure for Spain he was helping to arrange a departure for those compatriots who had expressed a desire to serve in the ranks of the Spanish Republicans, I do not know how many there were. I can cite two names: Khenkin, Kirill[20] and [first name] Lyova (Lev).[21]

I maintain that I did not know that in 1936 and at the beginning of 1937 my husband was organizing a surveillance of Russians or other persons with the help of the woman STEINER Renée, SMIRENSKY Dimitri, CHISTOGANOV,[22] and DUCOMET Pierre. I also do not know if my husband was in correspondence with these individuals.

I shall not presume to verify my husband's handwriting on the telegram dated 22 January 1937, a copy of which you have shown me.

In response to your request I am handing over nine documents (letters in envelopes and one post card) written in my husband's hand.

LECTURE FAITE, PERSISTE ET SIGNE
L'INSPECTEUR PRINCIPAL DE POLICE MOBILE
OFFICIER DE POLICE JUDICIAIRE (SIGNATURE)
M. TSVETAEVA-EFRON (SIGNATURE)

NOTES

1. Ducomet, Jean-Pierre (1902-1961). French photographer. Recruited into the Soviet secret police by N. Poznyakov in 1936. A member of the task force created in the summer of 1937 in France for the purpose of following and killing the defector Ignace Reiss. He was arrested by the French police and spent 13 months in prison. He gave extensive testimony. He was released from prison when the main organizers of the murder were not arrested. His conspiratorial name was Bob.

2. Incorrect information. Tsvetaeva was born on 26 September (old style), 1892; her parents were I. V. and M. A. Tsvetaev.

3. The Union for Repatriation originated in Paris in 1925, but at the beginning of the thirties it was transformed radically and became completely dependent ideologically and materially on the Soviet embassy [polpredstvo] in France. In the first half of the thirties E. V. Larin was secretary of the Union, but starting in 1937 (in connection with Larin's transfer to work at the Soviet pavillion at the World Fair in Paris) he was replaced by A. A. Tveritinov. Both later returned to the USSR and were repressed.

4. Ariadna Efron was born 5 September (old style) 1912.

5. "She worked there"; that is, at the journal *Nash Soiuz*.

6. Afanasov, Nikolai Vanifatevich (1902-1941)—Russian émigré, a friend of S. Ya. Efron since 1918. At the time of the civil war he participated in the White movement. In Bulgaria he worked as a miner and woodcutter. After relocating in France, he lived for the most part in Grenoble, from time to time working as a taxi driver, but unemployed for long periods of time. He was recruited as a Soviet agent in 1934. In turn, he recruited Mark Zborovsky, who subsequently became the personal secretary of L. D. Trotsky's son, L. L. Sedov. Afanasov returned to the Soviet Union in the fall of 1936. He lived in Kaluga. He maintained contacts with V. A. Guchkova-Traill, E. E. Litauer, and S. Ya. Efron. Arrested at the beginning of 1940. Executed 28 July 1941 in Moscow.

7. The newspaper *Eurasia* was published in Paris by the "left" Eurasians from November 1928 through September 1929.

8. Concerning the episode of the refugees' arrival, Tsvetaeva recalled in a letter to Anna Tesková, "a Spanish republican boat that arrived here—refugees from Santander, and a day spent with a Spaniard who didn't know a word of French, just as I don't know Spanish, in a lively conversation which absolutely contained everything." Marina Tsvetaeva, *Pis'ma k Anne Teskovoi* (Saint Petersburg, 1991), p. 135.

9. Bob—see note 1.

10. Smirensky, Dimitry Mikhailovich (1897-?)—also Marcel Rollin. Russian émigré, participant in the White movement. In France from 1922, worked at the Renault factory, member of the French Communist Party, member of the Paris Union for Repatriation. Recruited by Efron as a Soviet agent. Joined

the group of agents that trailed Sedov and later was part of the group that pursued I. Reiss. He was arrested and spent a year in a Paris prison. He was released for insufficient evidence. Returned to the USSR in the spring of 1939. Arrested in 1940. His subsequent fate is unknown.

11. Strangue, Michel (*Shtrange* in Russian) (Mikhail Mikhailovich, 1907-1968)—son of Russian émigrés, proprietor of a Russian pension-sanitorium in Haute-Savoie. Efron and Tsvetaeva and their children spent the summers of 1930 and 1936 there. Efron also repeatedly came here by himself in the mid thirties. M. M. Strangue studied history and literature at the Sorbonne and was a writer himself. He was recruited as a Soviet agent by Efron. Some think that he "coordinated" the action of the group that pursued Reiss. During the Second World War he participated in the French resistance. A member of the Soviet military mission in France at the end of the war, he returned to the USSR in 1947. Author of the monographs *Russian Society and the French Revolution of 1789-1794* and *The Democratic Intelligentsia in Russia in the 18th Century*, published in Moscow. His name was often mentioned sympathetically by Tsvetaeva in her letters to the poet Shteiger (see Marina Tsvetaeva, *Pis'ma k Anatoliiu Shteigeru* [Kaliningrad, 1994], pp. 76, 88-89, 108-9).

12. Kondratiev, Vadim (1903-1939). During the civil war he fought in the White Army, then emigrated, worked in France as a taxi driver, was often out of work. Recruited as a Soviet agent by N. A. Klepinin in the mid thirties. A participant in the secret police group that pursued Reiss. After Reiss was murdered, he fled Paris before the others. Died of tuberculosis in Moscow.

13. Klepinins—Nikolai Andreevich (1897-1941) and Antonina Nikolaevna (1892-1941). See section 7, chap. 1 of this book.

14. Poznyakov, Nikolai Sergeevich. Studied with Efron in the gymnasium, during the First World War worked for the Red Cross. During the civil war he was in the White movement. In Paris he had a photography studio. Together with K. B. Rodzevich and V. V. Yanovsky he "worked with the Trotskyites of POUM" (Partido Obrero de Unificación Marxista) during the civil war in Spain, which allowed him also to take on some role in the reprisal against the leadership of POUM in 1936. K. Khenkin, who knew Poznyakov, speaks very negatively about him in his book *The Topsy-Turvy Hunter*. When he returned to Moscow (1939), Poznyakov was assigned to work with former Republican

soldiers from Spain, now in exile. He escaped arrest and died in the sixties in his homeland.

15. Steiner Rénée (Renata) (1908-1986)—Swiss teacher, recruited as a Soviet secret agent in the mid thirties. She executed a number of missions for Efron and after her arrest gave extensive testimony about it. In particular, on Efron's instructions she and Smirensky took part in trailing Sedov. In the fall of 1937 (on whose orders is not clear) from a firm in Geneva and in her own name she rented the car that was used by Reiss's murderers. She spent several months in prison. She was freed in connection with the disappearance of the main organizers of the murder. During her interrogations she insisted (as did Ducomet and Smirensky) that Efron had no relation to the Reiss "action."

16. The murder of Reiss took place on 4 September 1937; the kidnapping of General E. K. Miller on 22 September of that year.

17. Schildbach (née Neigebauer), Gertrude (1894-?)—an old friend of Reiss-Poretsky, a German Communist who collaborated with the special services and worked in Italy. She agreed to help in the secret police group that was following Reiss. She was in the car at the time of the murder. According to P. Huber and D. Kunzi, she later lived in the USSR. In 1938 she was arrested and sent to Kazakhstan.

18. Rossi, François (also known as Roland Abbiate, Viktor Pravdin, 1905–?). At the time he participated in the Lausanne affair he was a citizen of Monaco. He had worked in the NKVD since 1929. Became a member of the group of agents who pursued Reiss. He and his compatriot, Charles Martignat (1900–?), from the very beginning of the police investigation were named the direct killers of Reiss. During the Second World War Rossi was a correspondent of TASS in New York. Lived in India, Great Britain, Mexico, and the United States. The brother-in-law of B. E. Afanasiev, whom P. Sudoplatov names in his memoirs as still another believable participant in Reiss's murder. (It's possible that B. E. Afanasiev and Charles Martignat are the same person.)

19. The version of Efron's departure for Spain was firmly maintained in the Tsvetaeva-Efron family and was undoubtedly thought up by the Soviet secret police. It was they who organized the transfer of Kondratiev, Efron, the Klepinins, and others of their collaborators from France to the USSR in the fall of 1937.

20. Khenkin, Kirill Viktorovich (b. 1916)—emigrated from Russia with his

parents in 1923. Fought in the Spanish Civil War. He was recruited as a Soviet agent. Returned to his motherland in 1941. Served in a division of the NKVD, then worked for a Moscow radio program for foreign countries, and later in the editorial offices of the journal *Problems of Peace and Socialism (Problemy mira i sotsializm)*. Left the USSR in the early 1970s. Worked for Radio Liberty. Author of several books based on autobiographical material.

21. Lyova—Lev Borisovich Savinkov (1912-1987), son of B. B. Savinkov, a well-known Socialist Revolutionary activist and a writer. Lived in France. Fought in Spain on the side of the Republicans. Recruited by Efron in 1937. A friend of Ariadna Efron. After he left for the USSR, A. S. Efron corresponded with him for some time.

22. Chistoganov, Anatoly (1910-194?)—Russian émigré, participated in the White movement. Member of the Union for Repatriation. Recruited by the Soviet secret service. Participated in the shadowing of Trotsky's son, Sedov.

MARINA TSVETAEVA, NOTEBOOK ENTRY, 1940

I resume this notebook on 5 Sept. 1940 in Moscow.

June 18, arrival in Russia, the 19th to Bolshevo. To the dacha, meeting with S., who is sick. Discomfort. Go to get kerosene. S. buys apples. Gradually pain in my heart. Ordeal with the telephone.[1] The enigmatic Alya, her false gaiety. I live without documents,[2] no one comes by. Cats. My favorite nonaffectionate adolescent is a cat. (All this is for *my* memory and no one else: If he reads it, Mur won't understand. But he won't read it, he avoids *that sort of thing*.) Tortes and pineapples—that doesn't make it easier. Walks with Milya.[3] My *loneliness*. Dishwater and tears. The overtone—the undertone of everything—is terror. They promise a partition—days pass.[4] A school for Mur—days pass. An ordinary wooded landscape, no rocks: no foundation. S.'s illness. Fear of his bad heart. Fragments of his life without me—I don't have time to listen: my hands are busy with chores, I listen, but on edge. A hundred times a day to the cellar. When can I write?

The little girl Shura.[5] For the first time the feeling of *someone else's* kitchen. Insane heat that I don't notice: streams of sweat and tears into the pan for dishes. No one I can hold on to. I begin to understand that S. is helpless, completely helpless, in everything. (I, unpacking something: "You really didn't see? Such wonderful shirts!" "I was looking at you!")

(I'm exposing a wound, open flesh. In short:) during the night of the 27th Alya's departure.[6] Alya was cheerful, she behaved bravely. She laughed it off.

I forgot: The last happy sight of her—4 days ago—at the S. Kh. exhibit,[7] a "kolkhoznitsa" in a red Czech scarf—my gift. She was radiant.

She leaves without saying good-bye! I: "Alya, how can you go without having said good-bye to anyone?" She waves, in tears, over her shoulder! The commandant (an old man, kindly), "It's better that way. Long farewells mean extra tears . . ."

About myself. Everyone thinks that I'm courageous. I don't know anyone who is more timid than myself. I am afraid of everything. Eyes, darkness, footsteps, and most of all—of myself, my head, if it is this head that has served me so well in my writing and is killing me so in life. No one sees, no one knows, that for a year already (almost) I have been looking around for a hook, but there aren't any, because electricity is everywhere. There aren't any "chandeliers."

N. P. brought me some translated folk songs.[8] My very favorite thing. Oh, how I loved all that! For a year[9] I have been trying on death. Everything is ugly and terrifying. Swallowing is vile, jumping despicable, water by nature repulsive. I don't want to scare people (posthumously),[10] it seems to me that—posthumously—I am already afraid of myself. I do not want to die. I want not to be. Rubbish. As long as I am needed . . . but, Lord, how small I am, how little I can do! Dragging out life is like drinking the dregs. Bitter wormwood.

How many lines have got by me! I'm not writing anything down. That's over with now.

NOTES

1. There was no telephone in the Bolshevo house.

2. Without papers, meaning without documents. Tsvetaeva did not get a Soviet passport until the second half of August.

3. Milya—Emiliya Emmanuilovna Litauer.

4. Apparently, there was a proposal to divide the common living room in the Bolshevo house with a partition.

5. She is talking about the adolescent girl, a commandant's daughter, who came to help with cleaning and other household chores.

6. August 27, 1939.

7. The All-Union Agricultural Exhibit in Moscow.

8. N. P.—most likely, N. N. Vil'yam-Vil'mont, a literary critic and translator.

9. During the previous year both Tsvetaeva's daughter (27 August) and her
husband (10 October) were arrested.

10. "I don't want to scare"—a repeated motif in Tsvetaeva. She believed
that after death the dead "appeared" to those close to them.

MARINA TSVETAEVA
LETTER TO STALIN

AUTHOR'S PREFACE

Marina Tsvetaeva's letter to Stalin was published twice—in slightly different variants. The first was a publication by Lev Mnukhin in the Paris newspaper *Russkaia mysl'* (21 August 1992) under the heading "A Letter of Marina Tsvetaeva to I. V. Stalin." In the second publication (*Literaturnaia gazeta*), almost the same text was presented, but this one turned out to be addressed to Lavrenty Beria. M. Feinberg and Yu. Klyukin had obtained it from the archives of the Russian Ministry of Security. The disagreement between the two publications was soon explained. The first publication was flawed because in the text that Mnukhin had at his disposal (whose source was a private archive) the addressee's name was missing and had been reconstructed solely on the basis of Ariadna Efron's oral testimony.

The following text is the third publication of the "letter."

The source of our text is the archive of the secretary of the Writers Union of the USSR, K. V. Voronkov, where the letter of Ariadna Sergeevna Efron was discovered. The typewritten text of the present letter was attached. Its author was Marina Tsvetaeva. A. S. Efron named the addressee of her mother's letter with certainty: "I. V. Stalin."

The scholar Marina Katseva received the letter from a librarian in California.[1]

A comparison of the given text with the two published ones shows above all how painful it was and how long it took Tsvetaeva to write and rewrite her letter. Perhaps she asked someone for advice: who would be the best person to send it to? There is no addressee cited.

Two signatures of A. S. Efron appear on the typescript of her letter: a signature at the end of her letter to K. V. Voronkov and an inscription in her hand on the first page of the "Letter to Stalin." Thus, Tsvetaeva's daughter was certain about the addressee, although we do not know precisely on what she based her confidence. Mnukhin's conjecture is completely realistic: Tsvetaeva might have sent two identical letters to two addressees.

The most important thing about the publication of this text, in our view, however, is not the quarrel about the addressee. The opportunity to hear Marina Tsvetaeva's voice is extremely valuable to us—her vacillation and doubts, the tormented search for tone and arguments—at a tragic moment when she was searching for words able to affect an executioner, to stop the arm raised above the heads of her family.

Most likely, this is the first *variant* of a letter that Marina Tsvetaeva later rewrote, embellishing it significantly as well as making cuts. The additions are particularly revealing: they intensify such themes as the enumeration of the contributions of her father, Ivan Vladimirovich Tsvetaev, to Russian culture, and the description of Efron stresses his irreproachable honesty, unselfishness, and devotion to the idea of communism. Also noteworthy are certain sentences that Tsvetaeva rejected while rewriting.

Our publication of the letter notes the most significant corrections. The reader can evaluate the sense and intention of the reworking; we don't believe it requires special commentary.

NOTE

1. At the end of 1991 a stranger phoned me. During our conversation I learned his name and occupation: Viktor Kholodkov had lived, since 1989, in San Diego, California, where he headed an information center and reference library on Russian culture in the first half of the twentieth century. He called regarding an article I had written on Ariadna Efron. (M. Katseva, "Vse popravimo—krome smerti," *Novoe Russkoe Slovo*, 13-14,

September 1991.) After reading it, V. Kholodkov remembered that he had several documents relating to Tsvetaeva; in particular, a draft of her letter to Stalin. He said that all the papers came into his hands after the death of a prominent literary bureaucrat who worked in the archive where they were kept. Since Kholodkov was not a specialist in the field of literature, he wondered if Tsvetaeva scholars knew about this letter and if it might interest anyone today. If so, then he was ready to send me a free copy of the Tsvetaeva draft for publication.

Early in December 1991, I received a copy of the promised documents. It was clear from their contents how, when, and under what circumstances the Tsvetaeva *draft* turned up in the hands of a "prominent literary bureaucrat." It was not hard to "declassify" the name of this bureaucrat: Konstantin Vasilievich Voronkov, who by the will of fate had assumed the high post of Secretary of the Union of Writers, was the addressee and keeper of the most important literary documents for an entire literary epoch. Among them were the papers in question. (A. I. Solzhenitsyn wrote about this in an essay: "How did Voronkov get this easy chair? Why was he in charge of six thousand Soviet writers? Was he the best writer among them? I heard that Fadeev once took one of the Union secretaries as a lover, and consequently she would no longer do simple clerical work, and so they used the fawning Kostya Voronkov for small jobs. He learned the ropes and wormed his way up in the ranks. But what did he *write?* People joked that his most important works were the directories of the Writers' Union" [A. I. Solzhenitsyn, *Bodalsia telenok s dubom*. Paris: YMCA Press, 1975, p. 219]).

In April 1967 in the hope of a jubilee pardon (for the approaching 50th anniversary of Soviet rule), Ariadna Efron requested the Union of Writers "to submit a petition to the Government for a *real* (A. S. Efron's italics) rehabilitation" of her father. (This and further quotes are from A. S. Efron's letter to K. V. Voronkov, 17 April 1967.)

The cold official certificate of rehabilitation containing the conventional formula "for the absence of elements of a crime," which had been obtained with much trouble in 1956, was not enough for Ariadna. Filial duty demanded more: "so that he [S. Ya. Efron] would greet the 50th year of Soviet power in the ranks of its *eternally living* warriors." This was important, in Ariadna Efron's opinion, not only as an act of justice to her father, but for future biographers of Tsvetaeva. She wrote: "Everything in the biographies of Marina Tsvetaeva and her husband Sergei Efron must be set straight, so that he does not remain in the Soviet people's imagination as just some kind of White Guard makeweight in Tsvetaeva's biography, or simply a minor detail in it—for thirty years." Apparently counting precisely on the significance of Tsvetaeva, who by that time had been acknowledged by official literary circles, A. S. Efron appended to her own letter a copy of the draft of Tsvetaeva's letter to Stalin.

The upper right corner of the first page of Tsvetaeva's letter, which Ariadna Sergeevna also typed out, contains her handwritten notation: "A copy of the draft of M. I. Tsvetaeva's letter to Stalin. Sent in the winter of 1939-40. It remained unanswered. The real letter is in her working notebook of 1939-40." This notation, as several other of Ariadna's handwritten notes, is one of the most important proofs of the following text's authenticity.

I appeal to you on behalf of two arrested persons—my husband Sergei Yakovlevich *Efron* and my daughter—Ariadna Sergeevna *Efron*.

But before I talk about them, I should tell you a few words about myself.

I am a writer. In 1922 I went abroad on a Soviet passport and stayed abroad—in the Czech Republic and France—through June 1939, that is, for 17 years. I took absolutely no part in the political life of the emigration, I was occupied by my family and literary work. I worked for the most part for the journals *The Will of Russia* [*Volya Rossii*] and *Contemporary Notes* [*Sovremennye zapiski*], I once published in the newspaper *Latest News* [*Poslednie novosti*], but I was dismissed from there because I openly hailed Mayakovsky in the newspaper *Eurasia*. In general, I was a solitary figure in the emigration.[1]

The reasons for my return to the homeland: the passionate desire of my entire family to return there—my husband, Sergei Yakovlevich Efron, my daughter, Ariadna Sergeevna Efron (she was first to leave in March 1937), and my son, who was born abroad but had ardently dreamed about the Soviet Union since his early years. The desire to work in my own home. And my complete isolation in the emigration, to which I had no ties during the last years.

I was given verbal assurance that there were never any obstacles to my return.

In 1937 I renewed my Soviet citizenship, and in June 1939 I

received permission to return to the Soviet Union, which I did—together with my 14-year-old son Georgy—on 8 June 1939.

If I need to say something about my background—I am the daughter of Ivan Vladimirovich Tsvetaev, Professor Emeritus of Moscow University, a philologist well known in Europe, for many years director of the former Rumyantsev Museum, founder of and collector for the Museum of Fine Arts—now the Pushkin Museum of Fine Arts—14 years of an unpaid labor of love.[2]

My mother, Maria Alexandrovna Tsvetaeva, born Meyn, was an outstanding musician. A tireless assistant to my father in the affairs of the museum, she died young.

So much for me.

Now about my husband, Sergei Yakovlevich *Efron*.

Sergei Yakovlevich *Efron* is the son of the prominent revolutionary populist Elizaveta Petrovna *Durnovo* (*Liza Durnovo*) and the populist Yakov Konstantinovich *Efron*. Liza Durnovo was lovingly described to me in 1917 by P. A. Kropotkin, after he had returned from abroad, and she is still remembered by N. Morozov. Stepnyak also writes about her in his book *Underground Russia*. There is a portrait of her in the Kropotkin Museum.

My husband's childhood was spent in a revolutionary home, amidst searches and arrests. *All* members of the family were jailed: his mother in Schlüsselburg Fortress, his father in Vilnius, the older children—Pyotr, Anna, Elizaveta, and Vera Efron—in different prisons. In 1905, his mother entrusted Sergei Efron, my future husband, who was 12 at the time, with responsible revolutionary tasks. In 1908, Elizaveta Petrovna Durnovo emigrated.[3] In 1909 she committed suicide in Paris, shaken by the death of her 14-year-old son.

In 1911, I met Sergei Efron. We were 17 and 18. He had tuberculosis. He was crushed by the tragic deaths of his mother and brother. Serious beyond his years. I immediately decided that I would *never, no matter what*, part with him and in January 1912 we were married.

In 1913, Sergei Efron became a student at Moscow University, specializing in philology. But the war began and he went to the front as an orderly [*brat miloserdiia*]. In October 1917, soon after finishing the Peterhof School for ensigns, he was wounded in the ranks of the Whites. The whole time he was in the Volunteer Army he was continuously in the fighting ranks, *never* on the staff. He was wounded twice—in the shoulder and in the knee.

I believe all of this is known from the forms he filled out earlier.[4]

The turning point in his convictions was the execution of a commissar—before his eyes: the face with which this commissar met his death. "At that moment I understood that our cause was not the *people's*."

But how did the son of the populist Liza Durnovo turn up in the ranks of the White Army and not the Red? Sergei Yakovlevich Efron considered this a fatal mistake in his life. I will add that he—a very young man at the time—was not the only one to make this mistake; a great many people fell into this category. He saw the Volunteer movement as the salvation of Russia and truth; when he lost faith in it, he left, completely—and never looked back in that direction.

After the end of the Volunteer movement he starved in Gallipoli and Constantinople, then in 1922 moved to the Czech Republic, to Prague, where he enrolled in the university in order to finish his historical and philological studies.

In 1923-1924 he started a student journal *By Our Own Paths* [*Svoimi putiami*], the first in the entire emigration to print Soviet prose, and he founded the Student Democratic Union—in contrast to the monarchist ones that were present.[5] After moving to Paris in 1925, he joined a group of "Eurasians" and became one of the editors of the journal *Mileposts* [*Versty*], from which the entire emigration recoiled. After *Mileposts*, the newspaper *Eurasia* (there I also hailed Mayakovsky, who was then in Paris), which the emigration called open Bolshevik propaganda. The Eurasians broke up. Into right and left. The left group soon ceased to exist, since it merged into the Union for Repatriation. (I was never a Eurasian, as I have never been anything, but I witnessed both its beginning and breakup.)[6]

I do not know precisely when Sergei Efron finally went over to the Soviet side and began to work for the Soviet state, but this must be known from his earlier records. I believe it was around 1930.

He did not let me into his political life. I only knew that he was connected to the Union for Repatriation, and then with Spain.[7]

But what I knew and know with certainty is his passionate and steadfast commitment to the Soviet Union. Without knowing the details of his work, I knew the life of his soul day after day—that all took place before my eyes. I swear as a witness: this man *loved* the Soviet Union and the idea of communism *more than life.*

(Concerning the quality and number of his activities I can cite the exclamation of the French investigator who questioned me after Efron's departure for the Soviet Union: "M. Efron menait une activité soviétique foudroyante!")[8]

On 10 October 1937, Sergei Efron left in haste for the Soviet Union. And on the 22nd they [the police] appeared at my home with a search warrant and took me and my 12-year-old son to the prefecture where we were kept a whole day. I told the investigators everything I knew—namely that this was the most unselfish and noble person in the world, that he passionately loved his homeland, that it was not a crime to work for a republican Spain, that I knew him—1911-1937—for twenty-six years, and that that was all I knew.

The newspapers (the Russian émigré papers) began an attack. They wrote that he was a Chekist, that he was involved in the Reiss affair, his departure was an escape, and so forth. After a while I was summoned to the prefecture a second time. I was presented with copies of telegrams on which I did *not* recognize his handwriting. "Don't be afraid," the investigator said, "this is not about the Reiss affair at all, it concerns the S. case"—and he actually showed me a file with a signature. I said again that I did not know either Reiss or any "S."—and they let me go and didn't trouble me again.[9]

From October 1937 to June 1939 I corresponded with Sergei Efron through diplomatic channels. His letters from the Soviet Union were completely happy. It's a pity they were not preserved, but I had to destroy them as soon as I read them; he only missed me and his son.

On 19 June 1939, after almost two years of separation, when I walked into the dacha in Bolshevo and saw him—I saw a gravely ill man.

A serious heart disease, discovered half a year before my arrival, and an automatic nervous system disorder. I learned that for these two years he was almost always ill—bed-ridden. But with our arrival he revived, his attacks came less frequently, he began to dream about work, without which he *languished*. He began making arrangements for work with one of his superiors, started traveling to the city.

Then on 27 August—the arrest of my daughter.

Now about my daughter. My daughter Ariadna Sergeevna Efron was the first one of us to travel to the Soviet Union, on 15 March 1937, to be precise. Before this she spent a year in the Union for Repatriation. She is a *very* talented artist and writer. And an absolutely loyal person. (*All of us are loyal*, this is a distinctive family trait in both our families—the Tsvetaevs and the Efrons.)[10] In Moscow she worked for the French journal *Revue de Moscou*, they were *very* satisfied with her work. She wrote and illustrated. She loved the Soviet Union with her whole soul and never complained about any kind of everyday adversity.

And after my daughter—on 10 October 1939, they arrested my husband too; a completely ill man, consumed by her misfortune.

On 7 November the Lvov family, our housemates, were arrested at the same dacha, and my son and I found ourselves completely alone, in a sealed dacha, without wood, in terrible anguish.

They accepted the first parcel from me: for my daughter on 7 December, that is, a little over 3 months after her arrest; for my husband on 8 December, 2 months later.

I do not know what my husband has been accused of, but I know that he is not capable of any kind of treachery, double dealing, or perfidy. I know him: 1911-1939—a little less than 30 years, but what I know about him I knew from the first day: he is a person of extreme purity, self-sacrifice, and responsibility. His friends and enemies would say the same thing about him. Even in emigration no one accused him of taking bribes.[11]

I end with an appeal for fairness. Selflessly, a man served his homeland and the idea of communism. His closest helper—his daughter—was arrested, then he. They were arrested—though innocent.[12]

He is gravely ill, I don't know how much time is left him. It will be terrible if he dies *without* vindication.[13]

NOTES

1. In the variant of the present letter, now known as "Letter to L. P. Beria" (hereafter cited as PB), a long insertion follows: "For the entire winter of 1936, working for the French revolutionary chorus (*Chorale Révolutionnaire*), I translated Russian revolutionary songs, old and new, among them the Funeral March (*Pokhoronnyi marsh*) and, from Soviet songs, a song from 'Merry Children' (*Veselye rebiata*) and many others. My songs were being sung."

2. Insertion in PB: "The idea for the Museum was his idea, and all the work of creating the Museum—the search for financial resources, the assembling of an original collection (by the way my father acquired one of the best collections in the world of Egyptian painting from the collector Mosolov), the selection and ordering of copies and all the equipment for the museum was the work of my father, an unpaid work of love for the last fourteen years of his life. One of my early memories: my father and mother are going to the Urals to pick out marble for the Museum. I remember the sample of marble they brought back. After the opening of the Museum, my father declined the official quarters due him as director and had four apartments made out of it for subordinates. All Moscow was at his funeral—his innumerable male and female students at the University, students from the Higher Courses for Women and the Conservatory, and employees from both of his museums (for 25 years he was the director of the Rumyantsev Museum)."

3. In PB there is an insertion here: "who was threatened with life imprisonment."

4. In PB there is an addition. "And here is something perhaps *not* known: not only did he not shoot a single captive, he saved all those he could from execution by placing them in the machine-gun unit he commanded."

5. Insertion in PB: "He was the first in the entire emigration to reprint Soviet prose in his journal (1924). From that time his 'movement to the left' proceeded steadily."

6. Tsvetaeva removed the last sentence in PB.

7. This paragraph was removed from PB. The following paragraph was completely rewritten. The new redaction is very informative: "But what I truly knew and know is his passionate and steadfast dream of the Soviet Union and his passionate service to it. How happy he was, reading in the papers about the latest Soviet accomplishment, how he shone from the smallest economic success! ("Now *we* have that . . . Soon *we* will have this or that.") I have an important witness— our son, who grew up with such exclamations and from the age of five heard nothing else.

A sick man (tuberculosis, liver disease), he left early in the morning and returned late at night. The man—before your eyes—was on fire. Everyday conditions—the cold, mess in the apartment—didn't exist for him. There were no topics except the Soviet Union. Without knowing the details of his work, I knew the life of his soul day after day, it all took place before my eyes—the total regeneration of a man."

8. Further in PB: "The investigator spoke about his case file and knew these matters better than I did (I only knew about the Union for Repatriation and about Spain). But what I knew and know is the selflessness of his devotion. This person by nature could not but give himself completely."

9. Tsvetaeva omitted this entire paragraph in PB. We can surmise that the "S. case," the folder with that title that was shown to Tsvetaeva during her interrogation, was the case being prepared against Mikhail Shtrange, whose last name was transcribed into French as "Strangue."

10. Tsvetaeva eliminated this sentence from PB.

11. In PB this sentence is extended: "and his communism was explained as 'blind enthusiasm.' Even the detectives who carried out the search at our home, who were astonished by the poverty of our dwelling and the hardness of his bed ('What, M. Efron slept on this bed?'), spoke of him with such respect, and the investigator—how simply he told me, 'M. Efron was a zealot, but zealots can also make mistakes.'"

12. The last two sentences were omitted in PB.

13. In PB another ending is added: "If this is a denunciation, that is, material selected unscrupulously and maliciously—then investigate the informer. If this is a mistake—*I beg of you*, correct it before it's too late."

INDEX